What People Are Saying About
Chicken Soup for the Father's Soul . . .

"*Chicken Soup for the Father's Soul* reminds us all there is no more special or sacred role than that of being a father."

—Merlin Olsen
NFL Hall-of-Famer, actor

"*Chicken Soup for the Father's Soul* highlights the limitless love a father can have for his child."

—Robert Dedman
chairman, Clubcorp

"The stories in this wonderful collection show that the love of a father can be one of the greatest gifts we can ever know."

—Barbara De Angelis, Ph.D.
author, *What Women Want Men to Know*

"The wonderful stories in *Chicken Soup for the Father's Soul* remind me that being a father is the greatest gift I could ever receive, and being a great dad is the best gift I could ever give my children."

—Matt Markstaller
father

"*Chicken Soup for the Father's Soul* is a fun read for those who wish to recall the best decision they ever made: becoming a dad."

—Clyde Drexler
former NBA player

"A loving father is a blessing to his children, and these touching stories illustrate the complex emotions and countless joys of parenthood, setting a spiritual example for dedicated, caring fathers everywhere."

—Sara O'Meara and Yvonne Fedderson
founders of Childhelp

CHICKEN SOUP
FOR THE
FATHER'S SOUL

Chicken Soup for the Father's Soul
Stories to Open the Hearts and Rekindle the Spirits of Fathers
Jack Canfield, Mark Victor Hansen, Jeff Aubery, Mark Donnelly, Chrissy Donnelly

Published by Backlist, LLC,
a unit of Chicken Soup for the Soul Publishing, LLC. www.chickensoup.com

Front cover design by Lisa Camp
Originally published in 2001 by Health Communications, Inc.

Back cover and spine redesign by Pneuma Books, LLC

Distributed to the booktrade by Simon & Schuster. SAN: 200-2442

Publisher's Cataloging-in-Publication Data
(Prepared by The Donohue Group)

Chicken soup for the father's soul : stories to open the hearts and rekindle the spirits of fathers / [compiled by] Jack Canfield ... [et al.].

   p. : ill. ; cm.

   Originally published: Deerfield Beach, FL : Health Communications, c2001.
   ISBN: 978-1-62361-099-9

   1. Fathers--Literary collections. 2. Fathers--Anecdotes. 3. Fatherhood--Literary collections. 4. Fatherhood--Anecdotes. 5. Anecdotes. I. Canfield, Jack, 1944-

PN6071.F3 C48 2012
810.8/0352/51   2012944876

PRINTED IN THE UNITED STATES OF AMERICA
on acid free paper

25 24 23   09 10 11

CHICKEN SOUP
FOR THE
FATHER'S SOUL

Stories to Open
the Hearts and Rekindle
the Spirits of Fathers

Jack Canfield
Mark Victor Hansen
Jeff Aubery
Mark Donnelly
Chrissy Donnelly

Backlist, LLC, a unit of
Chicken Soup for the Soul Publishing, LLC
Cos Cob, CT
www.chickensoup.com

Contents

5. SPECIAL MOMENTS

6. OVERCOMING OBSTACLES

7. A FATHER'S WISDOM

Introduction

Motherhood. The word evokes warm images of comforter, nurturer, healer and giver of unconditional love. *Fatherhood,* on the other hand, summons more stalwart visions of protector, provider and purveyor of wisdom. A father's love, though just as strong and reliable, is not always wholly captured or conveyed with quite as much emotion.

We embarked on this project three years ago because we wanted to try and capture the elusive essence of fatherhood in all its myriad forms. Often misunderstood, the relationships between fathers and their children are many times more difficult to define than the bond mothers form with their offspring. In the course of this journey, we found that fathers, too, can be comforters, nurturers and healers. They can be comedians, coaches, leaders and teachers of life's greatest lessons.

Each contributor to this book writes of someone touched and transformed by fatherhood. Many of the stories were written by fathers, but you'll also find insights from sons, daughters and grandchildren who have felt, understood, and have been changed for the better because of the love of a father.

Perhaps some of the stories will help you to better

appreciate the vital role you play as father; others may give you new ideas on how to express love to your family. Yet others may touch a place in your heart and awaken a truth hidden about the depth of love your own father harbors for you.

We were enchanted and enlightened by these stories, and we hope that you will be, too. We discovered that even though some fathers don't express their feelings verbally, they experience just as much emotion, and at times even more deeply, than mothers. Fatherhood is filled with incidences of pain and healing, confusion and insight, tears and laughter. It is indeed unconditional love, but in a different flavor than motherhood. It is this quiet celebration of the father's soul that we have sought to bring you.

Jack Canfield, Mark Victor Hansen, Jeff Aubery,
and Mark and Chrissy Donnelly

1

FATHERHOOD

*F*atherhood is the greatest opportunity in the
world—to have children and watch them grow
at various stages of life. I stop and look at these
pictures three or four times a day, remembering
what a wonderful time that was in my life.
Children are the greatest gift that God can
give you.

Bill Bell

A Moment Can Last Forever

Loading the car with the paraphernalia of our youngsters, ages three to nine, was hardly my idea of fun. But precisely on schedule—and at a very early hour—I had performed that miracle. With our vacation stay on Lake Michigan now over, I hurried back into the cottage to find my wife Evie sweeping the last of the sand from the floor.

"It's six-thirty—time to leave," I said. "Where are the kids?"

Evie put away the broom. "I let them run down to the beach for one last look."

I shook my head, annoyed by this encroachment on my carefully planned schedule. Why had we bothered to rise at dawn if we weren't to get rolling before the worst of the traffic hit? After all, the children had already spent two carefree weeks building sand castles and ambling for miles along the lakeside in search of magic rocks. And today they had only to relax in the car—sleep if they liked—while I alone fought the long road home.

I strode across the porch and out the screen door. There, down past the rolling dunes, I spotted my four youngsters on the beach. They had discarded their shoes and were tiptoeing into the water, laughing and leaping each time a wave broke over their legs, the point obviously being to see how far into the lake they could wade without drenching their clothes. It only riled me more to realize that all their dry garments were locked, heaven knew where, in the overstuffed car trunk.

With the firmness of a master sergeant, I cupped my hands to my mouth to order my children up to the car at once. But somehow the scolding words stopped short of my lips. The sun, still low in the morning sky, etched a gold silhouette around each of the four young figures at play. For them there was left only this tiny fragment of time for draining the last drop of joy from the sun and the water and the sky.

The longer I watched, the more the scene before me assumed a magic aura, for it would never be duplicated again. What changes might we expect in our lives after the passing of another year, another ten years? The only reality was this moment, this glistening beach and these children—*my* children—with the sunlight trapped in their hair and the sound of their laughter mixing with the wind and the waves.

Why, I asked myself, *had I been so intent on leaving at six-thirty that I had rushed from the cottage to scold them?* Did I have constructive discipline in mind, or was I simply in the mood to nag because a long day's drive lay ahead? After all, no prizes were to be won by leaving precisely on the dot. If we arrived at our motel an hour later than planned, no forty-piece band was going to be kept waiting. And how could I hope to maintain communication with my children, now and in later years, if I failed to keep my own youthful memory alive?

At the water's edge far below, my oldest daughter was motioning for me to join them. Then the others began waving, too, calling for Evie and me to share their fun. I hesitated for only a moment, then ran to the cottage to

grab my wife's hand. Half running, half sliding down the
dunes, we were soon at the beach, kicking off our shoes.
With gleeful bravado, we waded far out past our youngsters, Evie holding up her skirt and I my trouser cuffs,
until Evie's foot slipped and she plunged squealing into
the water, purposely dragging me with her.

Today, years later, my heart still warms to recall our
young children's laughter that day—how full-bellied and
gloriously companionable it was. And not infrequently,
when they air their fondest memories, those few long-ago
moments—all but denied them—are among their most
precious.

Graham Porter

Wake-Up Call

I was sitting in a bathtub full of moldy sheetrock when my thirteen-year-old son asked the question. "Can you take me golfing sometime?" he said.

I had a bathroom to remodel. It was fall, and the forecast for the next week was for a 100 percent chance of Oregon's liquid sunshine. I wanted to say no. "Sure," I said, "what did you have in mind?"

"Well, maybe you could, like, pick up Jared and me after school on Friday and take us out to Oakway."

"Sounds good."

Friday came. The showers continued. Looking out the window, moldy sheetrock seemed the saner choice. But at the appointed hour, I changed from home-improvement garb to rain-protection garb and loaded the boys' clubs and mine in the back of the car. In front of the school, Ryan and Jared piled in. Ryan looked at me with a perplexed expression.

"What's with the golf hat, Dad?" he said.

It was, I thought, a silly question, like asking a scuba diver what's with the swim fins.

"Well, I thought we were going to play some golf."

A peculiar pause ensued, like a phone line temporarily gone dead.

"Uh, you're going, *too*?" he asked.

Suddenly, it struck me like a three-iron to my gut: I hadn't been invited.

Thirteen years of parenting flashed before my eyes. The birth. The diapers. The late-night feedings. Helping with homework. Building forts. Fixing bikes. Going to games. Going camping. Going everywhere together—my son and I.

Now I hadn't been invited. This was it. This was the end of our relationship as I had always known it. This was "Adios, Old Man, thanks for the memories but I'm old enough to swing my own clubs now, so go back to your rocking chair and crossword puzzles and—oh yeah—here's a half-off coupon for your next bottle of Geritol."

All these memories sped by in about two seconds, leaving me about three seconds to respond before Ryan would get suspicious and think I had actually expected to be playing golf with him and his friend.

I had to say something. I wanted to say this: *How could you do this to me? Throw me overboard like unused crab bait?* We had always been a team. But this was abandonment. Adult abuse.

This was Lewis turning to Clark in 1805 and saying: "Later, Bill. I can make it the rest of the way to Oregon without you." John Glenn radioing Mission Control to say thanks, but he could take it from here. Simon bailing out on Garfunkel during "Bridge over Troubled Water."

Why did it all have to change?

Enough of this mind-wandering. I needed to level with him. I needed to express how hurt I was. Share my gut-level feelings. Muster all the courage I could find, bite the bullet and spill my soul.

So I said, "Me? Play? Naw. You know I'm up to my ears in the remodel project."

We drove on in silence for a few moments. "So, how are you planning to pay for this?" I asked, my wounded ego reaching for the dagger.

"Uh, could you loan me seven dollars?"

Oh, I get it. He doesn't want *me*, but he'll gladly take my *money*.

"No problem," I said.

I dropped Ryan and Jared off, wished them luck and headed for home. My son was on his own now. Nobody there to tell him how to fade a five-iron, how to play that tricky downhiller, how to hit the sand shot. And what if there's lightning? What about hypothermia? A runaway golf cart? A band of militant gophers? He's so small. Who would take care of him?

There I was, alone, driving away from him. Not just for now. Forever. This was it. The bond was broken. Life would never be the same.

I walked in the door. "What are you doing home?" my wife asked.

I knew it would sound like some thirteen-year-old who was the only one in the gang not invited to the slumber party, but maintaining my immature demur, I said it anyway.

"I wasn't *invited*," I replied, with a trace of snottiness.

Another one of those peculiar pauses ensued. Then my wife laughed. Out loud. At first I was hurt. Then I, too, laughed, the situation suddenly becoming much clearer.

I went back to the bathroom remodel and began realizing that this is what life is all about: Fathers and sons must ultimately change. I've been preparing him for this moment since he first looked at me and screamed in terror: not to play golf without me, but to take on the world without me. With his own set of clubs. His own game plan. His own faith.

God was remodeling my son. Adding some space here.

Putting in a new feature there. In short, allowing him to become more than he could ever be if I continued to hover over him. Just like when I was a kid and, at Ryan's age, I would sling my plaid golf bag over my shoulder and ride my bike five miles across town to play golf at a small public course called Marysville that I imagined as Augusta National.

I remember how grown-up I felt, walking into that dark clubhouse, the smoke rising from the poker game off to the left, and proudly plunking down my two dollars for nine holes. Would I have wanted my father there with me that day? Naw. A boy's gotta do what a boy's gotta do: Grow up.

I went back to the bathroom remodel project. A few hours later, I heard Ryan walk in the front door. I heard him complain to his mother that his putts wouldn't drop, that his drives were slicing and that the course was like a lake. He sounded like someone I knew. His tennis shoes squeaked with water as I heard him walk back to where I was working on the bathroom.

"Dad," he said, dripping on the floor, "my game stinks. Can you take me golfing sometime? I need some help."

I wanted to hug him, rev my radial-arm saw in celebration and shout, "I'm still needed!" I wanted to tell God, "Thanks for letting me be part of this kid's remodel job."

Instead, I plastered one of those serious-Dad looks on my face and stoically said, "Sure, Ry, anytime."

Bob Welch

Warning: An American Teenager Is Loose in Europe

The last thing I said to my teenaged son as I put him on the plane for Europe was: "Don't lose your passport!"

The second-to-the-last thing I said was: "Don't lose your passport!"

In fact, if you were to analyze all the statements I made to my son in the week before his departure, they'd boil down to: "Don't lose your passport!"

The message I was trying to convey was that he should not lose his passport. Of course he did not need to be told this. He is a teenaged boy, and teenaged boys already know everything. When a boy reaches thirteen years of age, the Knowledge Fairy comes around and inserts into his brain all the information in the entire universe. From that point on, he no longer needs any parental guidance. All he needs is parental money.

This is why a teenaged boy who has had a driver's license for a total of two hours knows that he can drive 367 miles per hour in heavy traffic while devoting 2 percent of his attention to the actual road and 98 percent to the critical task of adjusting the radio to exactly the right volume setting ("Death Star"). If you criticize him, he'll give you a look of contempt mixed with pity, because you are a clueless old dork who was last visited by the Knowledge Fairy in 1873, and your brain has been leaking information ever since.

And so, when I told my son, as he got onto the plane, not to lose his passport, he rolled his eyes in the way that knowledgeable teenagers have rolled their eyes at their parents dating back to when Romeo and Juliet rolled THEIR eyes at THEIR parents for opposing a relationship that turned out really swell except that they wound up fatally stabbing and poisoning themselves.

At this point, you veteran parents are asking: "So, when did your son lose his passport?" The answer is: Before he legally got into Europe. He may have set an Olympic record for passport-losing, because apparently his was stolen, along with all his traveler's checks, while he was on the plane.

Don't ask me how this could happen. My son has tried to explain it to me, but I still don't understand, because I have a leaky old brain.

All I know is that when the plane landed, my son had no passport and almost no money. Fortunately, the plane landed in Germany, a carefree, laid-back nation that is not a big stickler for paperwork.

Ha ha! I am of course kidding. The national sport of Germany is stickling.

So my son spent a number of hours trying to convince various authorities that he was a legal human. Mean - while, back in the United States, unaware of what had happened, I was exchanging increasingly frantic telephone calls with the mother of the boy my son was supposed to meet in the Frankfurt airport, who had reported back to her that my son had not arrived. The mother had suggested several things that her son could do, such as have my son paged or ask an authority, but of course, her son scoffed at these ideas, because he is also a teenaged boy, and thus did not need to be told how to find somebody in a large, unfamiliar foreign airport. He preferred the time-tested technique of wandering around aimlessly. His mother, who also has a daughter, assured me that girls do not act this way.

Eight fun-filled and relaxing hours after his plane landed, my son finally called me, and I nearly bit my tongue off not telling him I Told You So. He told me that the Germans had graciously agreed not to send him back to Miami, which is good, because he would probably have ended up in Kuala Lumpur.

He got a new passport the next day, but replacing the traveler's checks was not so simple. I will not name the brand of traveler's checks involved, except to say that it rhymes with "Wisa." As I write these words, my son and I have both been calling the Wisa people for a week, and they still haven't given us a Final Answer on whether they'll replace the checks. It says on the Wisa Web site that you can "easily get a refund if your cheques are lost or stolen," but in my son's case it apparently is going to require a vote of the full United Nations. For security and convenience, my son would have been better off carrying his money in the form of live cattle.

But never mind that. The main thing is, he's safely and legally in Europe, where he and his friend will be backpacking around for a month, relying on their common sense. So if there's a war, you'll know why.

Dave Barry

How I Got into the Movies

When I was eighteen years old, I came to America from Tel Aviv to break into the movies. It was a secret I kept from my parents, whom I had sold on the idea that I was leaving home to study journalism.

Forty-five years later, I finally lived my fantasy—a gift from my eldest son.

He is Peter David, *New York Times* bestselling author of science-fiction novels, *(Star Trek: The Next Generation, Deep Space Nine, The Hulk)*, comic books, television scripts *(Babylon 5, Space Cases)* and movies.

His script, *Backlash: Oblivion II*, was being filmed in Romania. Peter wrote a cameo for me. I would have words to speak and even a close-up.

I gave up my dreams of Hollywood while in my early twenties, for a career in journalism on major city newspapers and radio. As a youngster, Peter was my faithful companion in the newsroom, pounding away on the typewriter with his little fingers, just like Dad. "Are you cloning this kid?" an editor asked one day. I thought I was.

Yet the invitation to join Peter in Romania was totally unexpected. My son and I had grown apart emotionally by geographic distance and the demands of his busy career and family life. He was a husband and father of three. My wife Dalia and I saw Peter perhaps three times a year, since we live in different states. We briefly talked on the phone now and then. I knew little about his life, nor did he know much about mine. I had feelings of loss, an awareness of my own mortality, and the sense that time was running out for my firstborn and me. But I could never express any of it to Peter. He is not one for sentimentality.

Our trip to Romania began on a clear, crisp fall day at Kennedy Airport in New York. "We're going to spend so much time together, you'll be sick of me," Peter said. I assured him this would never happen. Of course, I didn't know how he would come to feel about me.

But then, above the clouds, a few hours into the trip, Peter began to open up to me. My son, outwardly so self-confident, said he felt that nothing he was writing was ever good enough. He always thought he could have done better. He also said that he had a great need for the approval of others. And sometimes he feared that his flow of ideas would suddenly dry up.

I felt badly for him, and yet I was joyous. My son was sharing himself with me as he used to when he was at home, growing up. I never shared myself with my own father. As my son and I became distant, I knew how shut out my father must have felt. Now I was exhilarated; my son was coming back to me.

The morning after arriving in Bucharest we drove to the set. In the heart of plowed Romanian fields and small farm houses, there emerged a town from another time and place—the old American West: The General Store, Miss Kitty's saloon, the town bank, horses at the post.

Since Peter's films were a blend of westerns and science fiction, a space ship was parked at the train station. The Wild West bank was equipped with an automated teller machine.

"Incredible," I exclaimed. "This is wonderful, Peter. You have such great imagination."

He smiled. "You know how when children play, they want their parents to see them?" he said. "They want to say to their parents, 'Look at me, Mom, look at me, Dad.'"

I put my hands on his shoulders. "And you brought me here, all the way to Romania, to say, 'Look at me Dad, look at what I've accomplished'?"

Peter nodded.

At that moment, layer upon layer of emotional distance, of defenses built against disappointment and hurt, began to peel off. I felt a wonderful sense of relief, as if a physical burden had been lifted off my chest. I realized how much he loved me, as I loved him, and how he needed my acknowledgment and approval. I told him then how impressed I was with all he had accomplished, and how proud I was of him.

In the days that followed, Peter and I talked a great deal, about his life, his hopes and dreams. And I told him about mine. There, in Romania, it was as if we were back home again and he was my kid once more.

My big day came about halfway through our eleven-day stay. Peter gave me tips on how to act in front of the camera. Clad in western garb, complete with a cowboy hat, leather gloves and boots, I was installed in the General Store to do some shopping.

"Action!" yelled the director. It was a magic word.

A seven-foot actor dressed in black, wearing a tall black hat, entered. He played a funeral director with psychic powers, and his appearance often meant death would soon follow.

Upon seeing him, I stammered to the shopkeeper, "I . . . I think I'll come back later." With a great deal of noise, I dropped the canned goods I had selected on the wooden floor as I dashed out, slamming the door shut behind me.

Next came the close-up. "That's a take," the director shouted. Then he, cast and crew applauded. Leading the applause was my son.

Peter thoughtfully obtained the Western hat and gloves of my costume as mementos for me. On our last evening, as cast members were writing kind words on the title page of my script, I asked Peter to do the same.

"I can't put my feelings into just a few words," he said.

But he would put some of them into the diary he kept during the trip. He was making his final entry on his laptop computer an hour before we were to land at Kennedy.

"When I started the diary, I referred to you as my father," Peter turned to me and said. "As time went on, I began referring to you as Dad. Why do you think that is?"

Tears filled my eyes. I wanted to reach over and hug him, right there, on the plane. But I was afraid to embarrass him, and perhaps myself. So instead, I took his hand in mine and squeezed it. Tight. Real tight.

My son squeezed my hand in return.

Gunter David

The Smell of Grass

*It doesn't matter who my father was; it matters
who I remember he was.*

Anne Sexton

Oh, how cool and tranquil it was, lying in the freshly
cut jade grass. The aroma of wet grass was enough to take
Amber back to when she was four. Spread out in that
grass, she gazed into the soft, blue heavens. She and her
father would make clouds into animals, and her father
would always say they looked like elephants. The cicadas
would buzz, a sound of summer. Even though the heat
was sweltering, the cool backyard grass was just the trick
to refresh Amber and her father.

Every time she thinks of her early childhood summers,
she remembers grass, melon, Popsicles, plastic pools,
sprinklers, blue skies, clear water and green, green grass.
Amber snapped out of her memory and unlocked the
front door. Lately, she had been thinking a lot about her
backyard and those summers she spent with her dad.

Amber's father had died August 24, 1990, when she was
five years old. He'd been diagnosed with cancer that

summer but kept it a secret from Amber, not wanting to ruin their last few weeks together. She'd missed him a lot lately; last Tuesday he would have been forty-five years old. Even though she was so young when he died, she remembered everything about him. His big smile, tan complexion, his comforting laugh. She loved every second of the day she spent with him; she was definitely her father's daughter.

Amber plopped her stuff down on her mother's desk and started her history work. After twenty minutes had passed, she stretched and looked around. She needed a pencil sharpener. She fumbled through every drawer of the old oak desk. She came across a ragged blue book in a pile of others. Her hand trembled as she felt the leather cover. She took a deep breath. She opened it up and began to read the black scribbly writing:

July 26, 1990

I still haven't broken the news to my little angel. Every time I look into her sweet eyes, I can't find the words to put it lightly. I know I will miss her the most. If only I could stay to see her grow; we are so much alike. I pray to the Lord every day to keep her strong and beautiful, and I know I will watch over her, when I no longer exist in this world. I will desperately miss all of our fun times playing in the grass in our yard. I will be waiting for the day she comes to play with me up in heaven.

Amber put the book down. She did not need to read any more. She was already sobbing quietly—partly out of sadness, partly out of happiness, but mostly because four small blades of dried grass fell out of the book and into her hands.

Adelaide Isaac

Rapid Rites of Passage

When you're pretty sure that an adventure is going to happen, brush the honey off your nose and spruce yourself up as best as you can, so as to look ready for anything.

Winnie the Pooh (from A. A. Milne)

I'd come up to the Canadian wilderness with the idea of initiating my just-turned-thirteen-year-old son, Adam, into manhood, and I was ready for something wild. If I'd wanted to play it safe, I'd have stayed home. A mother's role is to teach a boy to keep out of harm's way, I reasoned; a father's job is to show him how you play the game a little closer to the edge.

So at an outfitter in Ely, Minnesota, we'd loaded up with maps, tents, fishing gear and food for five days in the wild. Then we took a float plane to Quetico Provincial Park, Ontario—seventeen hundred square miles of blue-black lakes and woods haunted by wolves, loons and moose, just over the Minnesota border from the Boundary Waters wilderness.

At the Hilly Island ranger station, where the plane

landed in a wooded cove, we loaded our gear into an aluminum canoe and pushed off. As soon as we rounded the first rocky point, we were completely alone. The afternoon was overcast, and slate-colored light shimmered off the tilting panes of the waves. Around us the rocky shoreline held back a dark line of woods that stretched into wilderness.

We came to our first portage after a few hours of paddling—a short hike around Brewer Rapids, a churning chute of whitewater that dropped perhaps twenty feet over a distance of two hundred yards. We carried our gear from the bottom to the top of the rapids in two trips, then the canoe.

"Why don't we run it?" Adam asked suddenly, as we stood there at the top of the rapids with the now-empty boat. Momentarily suspending my better judgment in the interests of initiation, I responded, "Sure, why not?"

After all, it really didn't look all that bad—we'd recently been whitewater rafting on the New River, in West Virginia, and compared with the New River, it looked tame. Adam reminded me to put on my life jacket, and then I climbed into the stern, he in the bow, and we went for it. The tea-colored water sucked our boat into the surge.

"Keep to the left!" I shouted, trying to guide us out of the foaming tumult in the center of the rapids.

"Naw, let's go straight for it!" he shouted back.

So we did.

And that's when a three-foot dropoff that hadn't been visible from the shore appeared directly ahead of us. In a flash the boat caught on the lip of the precipice, swung around broadside and capsized. I saw Adam go flying over the gunwale, and then I did, too. I went under and came up choking, raking the water for a handhold. Then I went under again, dragged beneath the surface and tumbled

over submerged boulders by the sheer tonnage of the
torrent. My hiking boots, filled with water, instantly
turned to lead weights. I glimpsed Adam's purple life
jacket being swept away from me.

"Adam!" I shouted, but I couldn't hear his voice.

When I originally began planning this trip, death by
drowning had not been my greatest fear. My greatest fear
was that we'd have nothing to say to each other . . . that
Adam would quickly tire of my company and begin longing for a pal or (worse) his Game Boy.

When I talked to him about taking some kind of
thirteenth-birthday adventure trip, he told me that what
he really wanted was to walk to the bottom of the Grand
Canyon and back. He basically wanted bragging rights to
a good story. But I really preferred something slower and
quieter; I wanted to show him the wilderness without
having to prove anything to anybody. But most of all I
wanted to reacquaint myself with my son, whom—in the
bustle of boyhood, Smashing Pumpkins, Nintendo, backward ball caps and all the rest of it—I seemed to have lost.
He was passing from the sweet vulnerability of childhood
to the hulking sullenness of adolescence so fast, I sometimes imagined I'd wake up to discover he'd grown a full
beard overnight.

Like many fathers of my generation and my culture, I
also longed for some sort of celebration, some rite of passage that would clearly delineate my son's child-self from
his impending man-self—preferably an event more spiritual than getting a driver's license and less painful than
circumcision.

We settled on a canoe trip. To my relief, my worries
about having nothing to say to each other proved absurd.
In fact, he seemed almost as famished for my company as
I was for his. I rediscovered the delightfully daft and inge-
nious mind I remembered from his childhood. A steady

machine-gunfire of questions came back at me from the front of the boat: "What's a hide-a-bed?" "What's an epiphany?" Then suddenly, his voice filled with dismay:

"Dad, I forgot the words to 'Frosty the Snowman'!"

Paddling through those lovely, glimmering lakes, the two of us riding a slender vessel across the dark water, I was startled to discover how much the kid weighed—since in order to keep the boat from tipping over I was forever trying to strike a balance between the ballast of our two bodies. With a surge of sympathy I realized that his skinny, little-kid's body was shuddering under the onslaught of testosterone, and he'd been packing on muscle mass by the hour. I also became acutely aware that his movements were like a series of kinetic explosions—he'd abruptly rock from side to side, bang on the side of the boat, not paddle at all and then suddenly start paddling like fury. My job, I reckoned, was not to squelch that riotous energy, but to teach him how to steady it.

In the back of my mind, I think I'd also intended to use this trip to have serious fatherly talks about Growing Up, Taking Personal Responsibility and all that. My prepared text was boring and pretentious. When my own father took me aside and furrowed his brow like that, I didn't listen, either.

All these thoughts swept over me in a rush of panic and longing as the two of us tumbled helplessly down through the rapids. I glimpsed again the purple flash of Adam's life jacket and spotted him frantically dog-paddling toward me. Then, abruptly, we were both swept out of the main channel into a deep, still eddy. To my amazement, I could hear him laughing and shouting: "Awesome, dude!" I was scared to death, but he was having a ball.

Finally my feet made contact with the bottom and I was able to stand. When Adam gained a footing, I looked over at him, still wearing a sopping Redskins cap, and then we both started laughing and shouting deliriously. The

canoe, upright but so full of water that only the tips of the
bow and stern were showing, had drifted out into the
cove and was now perhaps two hundred yards away.
We'd have to swim across the channel, floating a log
ahead of us for safety, then hike through the woods to
fetch the badly banged-up boat.

Only later did it occur to me that during the whole mis-
adventure, we'd been swapping roles of boy and man. My
son made the suggestion that we take a wild chance and
ride the rapids in the first place, and he reminded me to
put on my life jacket. I agreed to his ill-considered plan
and then tried to play it safe like a grown-up. My boy
laughed all the way downstream while I—like my own
father—wound up desperate with worry.

I was teaching Adam to be a man, but at the same time,
he was reminding me not to forget my own boyishness.
He was also demonstrating something else: that he could
occasionally be more sensible and grown-up than I am;
that he could sometimes be right when I am wrong; that
some small part of him already is an adult. I found this revelation both comforting and unsettling. After all, inherent
in the notion of initiating my son into manhood is the idea
of my own demise. I was training my own replacement. In
the end, my original highfalutin' notion that I was going to
take my son into the woods to be initiated proved to be a
bit too prideful, and a bit too simple. In truth, I seemed to
have almost as much to learn as to teach.

We waded up out of the water onto the rocky shore,
and for a few moments we just felt exhilarated and
supremely alive—soaked, baptized, awakened. We'd had
an adventure together. We'd actually done something,
been somewhere. Something had happened to us, and
we'd survived.

The journey had just begun.

Stefan Bechtel

Mollie's Moment

For years I worked in politics, a career choice that required long hours and a lot of travelling. When Senator Bob Kerrey ran for the U.S. presidency in 1992, for example, I helped on his campaign and ended up spending a great deal of time away from my wife, Bonnie, and our two young children, Zach and Mollie.

After the campaign, I came home to learn an important lesson about balancing career and family, about what kids really need from a dad—and about the building and dismantling of walls.

Shortly before Mollie's third birthday, I had just returned from a series of long trips with the senator, some of which had lasted six or seven days, with only a quick stop at home to change laundry.

Mollie and I were driving through our Silver Spring, Maryland, neighborhood on the way back from the grocery store when, from her car seat in the back, she said, "Dad, what street is your house on?"

"What?" I thought I hadn't heard correctly.

"What street is your house on?"

It was a telling moment. Although she knew I was her dad and she knew her mom and I were married, she did not know I lived in the same house that she did.

Though I was able to convince her that we resided at the same address, her uncertainty about my place in her life continued and manifested itself in many ways. A skinned knee sent her toppling towards Mom, not me. A question raised by something overheard at school would be saved for hours until Mom was around to ask.

I realized that not only did I have to spend more time with Mollie, I also had to spend it differently. The more I sensed her distance from me, the more goal-oriented things I tried to do with her—like going to the swimming pool or to the movies.

If Mollie and I didn't have some specifically scheduled activity, I would typically go and work on chores. For maximizing time and being productive, it made perfect sense.

When it was time to read a bedtime story, Bonnie would call me after the rest of the presleep routine had been completed, and I would walk into Mollie's room like a dentist who waited until the patient was prepped so he wouldn't have to waste a minute's time. It was the way I felt, and I'm sure now it was the way it made Mollie feel, too.

A turning point came one summer evening. Mollie was growing increasingly frustrated trying to build a secret hideout in the backyard. The sun was setting, and Mollie should have been winding down before bed, except that the thin slate tiles she tried to prop against one another kept falling over. She'd been at it for days, sometimes with a neighboring friend, sometimes on her own. When the walls fell over for the last time, cracking as they did, she burst into tears.

"You know what you need to make this work, Molls?" I said.

"What?"

"You need about sixty bricks."

"Yeah, but we don't have sixty bricks."

"But we could get them."

"Where?"

"The hardware store. Get your shoes on and hop in the car."

We drove the five or so miles to the hardware store and found the bricks. I started to load them, a few at a time, onto a big, flat cart. They were rough and heavy, and I realized that I had my work cut out for me. After being loaded onto the cart, they would need to be unloaded into the Jeep, and then unloaded yet again at the house.

"Oh, please, let me do that, Dad. Please!" Mollie begged.

If I let her, we'd be there forever. She would have to use two hands just to pick up one of them. I glanced at my watch and tried to keep my impatience in check.

"But sweetie, they're very heavy."

"Please, Dad, I really want to," she begged, moving quickly to the pile of bricks and hoisting one with both hands. She lugged it over to the cart and laid it next to the handful I'd placed there.

This was going to take all night.

Mollie walked back to the pile and carefully selected another brick. She took her time choosing.

Then I realized she wanted it to take all night.

It was rare for the two of us to have time like this alone together. This was the kind of impulsive thing her older brother Zach would usually get to do, past bedtime, just the two of us. Only with Zach, in maybe typically male fashion, I would see this as a task to finish quickly, so that we could go build the wall. Mollie wanted this moment to last.

I leaned back against one of the wood pallets and took a deep breath. Mollie, working steadily at the bricks, relaxed and became chatty, talking to me about what she'd build, and about school and her girlfriends and her upcoming horseback-riding lesson. And it dawned on me: Here we were buying bricks to make a wall, but in truth we were actually dismantling a wall, brick by brick—the wall that had threatened to divide me from my daughter.

Since then I've learned what her mother already knew: how to watch a TV show with Mollie even if it isn't a show I wanted to see; how to be with her without also reading a newspaper or magazine, to be fully present. Mollie doesn't want me for what I can give her, for where I can take her, or even for what we can do together. She wants me for me.

Bill Shore

The Tooth

As far as rearing children goes, the basic idea I try to keep in mind is that a child is a person. Just because they happen to be a little shorter than you doesn't mean they are dumber than you.

Frank Zappa

My seven-year-old son had lost his second tooth sometime during the night. My wife and I woke up early Saturday morning to his devastating news that it was nowhere to be found and a visit from the Tooth Fairy was in jeopardy. Between the sobs, we managed to obtain a rather lengthy explanation of his misfortune and the endless theories as to the whereabouts of the lost front tooth.

"Well, Jason," my wife explained, winking to me on the sly, "surely the Tooth Fairy would understand if you wrote her a note explaining what happened."

The tears were dried, and he wandered off to compose his letter. At two o'clock the following morning, as I tip-toed into his room with the expected two dollars, I found a small three-by-five-inch piece of paper pierced by the end of a coat hook beside his bed. It read simply:

"Tooth lost. Please pay."

David R. Wilkins

The Red Chevy

My father loved cars. He tuned them up, rubbed them down, and knew every sound and smell and idiosyncrasy of every car he owned. He was also very picky about who drove his cars. So when I got my driver's license at sixteen, I was a little worried about the responsibility of leaving home in one of his beloved vehicles. He had a beautiful red Chevy pickup, a big white Suburban and a Mustang convertible with a hot V-8 engine. Every one of them was in prime condition. He also had a short temper and very little patience with carelessness, especially if his kids happened to be the careless ones.

One afternoon, he sent me to town in the Chevy truck with the assignment of bringing back a list of things he needed for some odd jobs around the house. It hadn't been long since I'd gotten my license, so it was still a novelty to be seen driving around, and Dad's red pickup was a good truck to be seen in. I carefully maneuvered my way toward downtown, watching carefully at each light, trying to drive as defensively as he'd always told me to do. The thought of a collision in one of Dad's cars was enough to make me the safest driver in town. I didn't even want to think about it.

I was heading through a green light and was in the middle of a main downtown intersection when an elderly man, who somehow hadn't seen the red light, plowed into the passenger side of the Chevy. I slammed on the brakes, hit a slick spot in the road and spun into a curb; the pickup rolled over onto its side.

I was dazed at first, and my face was bleeding from a couple of glass cuts, but the seat belt had kept me from serious injury. I was vaguely concerned about the danger of fire, but the engine had died, and before long, I heard the sound of sirens. I had just begun to wonder how much longer I'd be trapped inside when a couple of firemen helped me get out, and soon I was sitting on the curb, my aching head in my hands, my face and shirt dripping with blood.

That's when I got a good look at Dad's red pickup. It was scraped and dented and crushed, and I was surprised that I had walked away from it in one piece. And by then I was sort of wishing I hadn't, because it suddenly dawned on me that I would soon have to face Dad with some very bad news about one of his pride-and-joy cars.

We lived in a small town, and several people who saw the accident knew me. Someone must have called Dad right away, because it wasn't long after I was rescued from the wreck that he came running up to me. I closed my eyes, not wanting to see his face.

"Dad, I'm so sorry—"

"Son, are you all right?" Dad's voice didn't sound at all like I thought it would. When I looked up, he was on his knees next to me on the curb, his hands gently lifting my cut face and studying my wounds. "Are you in a lot of pain?"

"I'm okay. I'm really sorry about your truck."

"Forget the truck, Son. The truck's a piece of machinery. I'm concerned about you, not the truck. Can you get up?

Can you walk? I'll drive you to the hospital unless you think you need an ambulance."

I shook my head. "I don't need an ambulance. I'm fine."

Dad carefully put his hands under my arms and lifted me to my feet.

I looked up at him uncertainly and was amazed to see that his face was a study in compassion and concern. "Can you make it?" he asked, and his voice sounded scared.

"I'm fine, Dad. Really. Why don't we just go home? I don't need to go the hospital."   .

We compromised and went to the family doctor, who cleaned up my wounds, bandaged me and sent me on my way. I don't recall when the truck got towed, what I did for the rest of that night, or how long I was laid up. All I know is that for the first time in my life, I understood that my father loved me. I hadn't realized it before, but Dad loved me more than his truck, more than any of his cars, more than I could have possibly imagined.

Since that day we've had our ups and downs, and I've disappointed him enough to make him mad, but one thing remains unchanging. Dad loved me then, he loves me now and he'll love me for the rest of my life.

Bob Carlisle

CLOSE TO HOME   JOHN McPHERSON

"Now's the part where you're supposed to say,
'The important thing is that you're okay, Son.'
Give it a try, Dad. Eight simple words."

My First Fish Story

Positive lessons are not always taught in positive ways.

Anonymous

My father always tried to get me to do outdoorsy things. He'd say, "Why don't you go fishing?" Fishing, to me, was like a nap with a stick.

"Just go," my mother told me. "If you catch one fish, you can at least show your father that you tried."

One day at school I heard they were draining a lake near our house and there were all these fish flopping around. So I rode my bike over and scooped up about twenty-five.

I walked in the house and said, "Hey, Pop! Look what I caught!"

My father just beamed with pride. "Hey! Look at my boy! Look at all the fish he got there!"

Mom cut them open and started gagging. "These fish stink!" she said. "We can't eat them!"

"Oh, I'm sure they're fine!" Dad said. "What a little fisherman!"

My mother finally took me aside, and I confessed under threat of frying pan: "Okay, okay—I found 'em! They were all dead!" Mom was exasperated, but so as not to disappoint my dad, she ran out to the store and bought fresh fish, which she served that night. Dad never found out.

Jay Leno

CLOSE TO HOME JOHN McPHERSON

8-29

"Check it out. I've been cutting a half-inch off Dad's chair legs every day for the last two weeks."

2

SPORTS, VACATIONS AND OTHER ADVENTURES

You don't raise heroes, you raise sons. And if you treat them like sons, they'll turn out to be heroes, even if it's just in your own eyes.

Walter Schirra Sr.

Finding My Way with Jesse

On a June morning high in the Rocky Mountains, snowy peaks rose before me. A creek brimful of meltwater roiled along to my left, and to my right an aspen grove shimmered with freshly minted leaves.

With all of that to look at, I gazed instead at my son's broad back as he stalked up the trail. Anger had made him quicken his stride until I could no longer keep up. I had forty-nine years on my legs, heart and lungs, while Jesse had only seventeen on his.

My left foot ached from old bone breaks, and my right knee creaked from recent surgery. Jesse would not slow down unless I asked, and I was in no mood to ask.

The day, our first full one in Rocky Mountain National Park, had started out well. Jesse slept while I sipped coffee and soaked in the early light. We made plans over breakfast without squabbling: walk to Bridal Veil Falls in the morning, raft on the Cache la Poudre River in the afternoon, return to camp and get ready for backpacking the next day.

For the previous year or so, no matter how long our spells of serenity, Jesse and I had kept falling into quarrels. We might be talking about soccer or supper, about car keys or the news, and suddenly our voices would clash like swords.

I had proposed this trip in hopes of discovering the source of that strife. Of course I knew that teenage sons and their fathers always fight, yet I sensed that Jesse was troubled by more than a desire to run his own life, and I was troubled by more than the pain of letting him go.

The peace between us held till we turned back from the waterfall and began discussing where to camp the following night. Jesse wanted to continue up the mountain and pitch our tent on snow. I wanted to stop a thousand feet lower and sleep on dry dirt.

"We're not equipped for snow," I told him.

He loosed a snort of disgust. "I can't believe you're wimping out, Dad."

"I'm just being sensible."

"You're wimping out. I came here to see the back country, and all you want to do is poke around the foothills."

"This isn't wild enough for you?" I waved my arms at the view. "What do you need, avalanches and grizzlies?"

"You always ruin everything." With that, he lengthened his stride and rushed on ahead.

I was still simmering when I caught up with him at the trailhead, where he was leaning against our rented car. Having to wait for me to unlock the car no doubt reminded him of another gripe: I had the only set of keys.

The arguments all ran together, playing over and over in my head as we jounced along a rutted gravel road toward the highway. I glanced over at Jesse from time to time, looking for any sign of détente. His eyes were glass.

"So how do I ruin everything?" I asked when I could no longer bear the silence.

He cut me a look, shrugged, then stared back through the windshield. "You're just so out of touch."

"With what?"

"With my whole world. You hate everything that's fun. You hate movies and video games, Jet Skis and malls. You complain that fast food's poisoning our bodies, TV's poisoning our minds and we're all poisoning the Earth."

"None of that concerns you? "

"Of course it does. But you make me feel the planet's dying and nothing can be done." Jesse rubbed his eyes. "Maybe you can get along without hope. I can't. I have to believe there's a way we can get out of this mess. Otherwise, what's the point?"

That sounded unfair to me, a caricature of my views, and I thought of many sharp replies. Yet there was truth in what he said. Had I really deprived my son of hope? Was this the source of our strife?

"You're right," I finally told him. "But I don't think we're doomed. It's just that nearly everything I care about is under assault."

"See, that's what I mean. You're so worried about the future you can't enjoy anything. We come to these mountains, and you bring the shadows with you. You've got me seeing nothing but darkness."

Stunned by the force of his words, I could not speak.

When we arrived at the rendezvous point for river rafting, Jesse and I turned out to be the only customers for the wild twelve-mile canyon run. All the others—the reedy kids and puffing parents—were going on the tamer trip.

The water in the Poudre River looked murderous, all spume and suck holes and rips. Every cascade, every jumble of boulders reminded the guides of some disaster, which they rehashed with gusto.

At the launching spot Jesse and I wriggled into our black wet suits, cinched tight the orange flotation vests, buckled on white helmets. The sight of my son in that armor sent a blade of anxiety through me. What if he got hurt? Lord, God, what if he were killed?

We clambered into the raft. Before we hit the first rapids, our guide made us practice synchronizing our strokes as he hollered: "Back paddle! Forward paddle! Stop! Left turn! Right turn!"

The only other command, he explained, was "Jump!" Hearing that, the paddlers on the side away from some looming boulder or snag were to heave themselves *toward* the obstruction, in order to keep the raft from flipping. "I know it sounds crazy," he said, "but it works. And remember: from now on, if you hear fear in my voice, it's real."

Fear was all I felt, a bit for myself and a lot for Jesse, as we struck white water and the raft began to buck. Waves slammed against the bow, spray flew, stones whizzed by. A bridge swelled ahead of us. The guide shouted, "Duck!" and steered us between the pilings and out the other side into more rapids. The raft spun and dipped and leapt with ungainly grace, sliding through narrow flumes, kissing cliffs and bouncing away.

"Forward paddle!" the guide shouted. "Give me all you've got! We're coming to the Widowmaker! Let's hope we come out alive!"

In a lull between rapids, I glanced over at Jesse, and he was beaming. I laughed aloud to see him. When he was little, I could summon that look of delight merely by coming home and calling, "Where's my boy?" In his teenage years the look had become rare, and it hardly ever had anything to do with me.

"Jump!" the guide shouted.

Before I could react, Jesse lunged at me and landed heavily. The raft bulged over a boulder, nearly tipping, then righted itself and plunged on downstream. "Good job!" the guide crowed. "That was a close one."

Jesse scrambled back to his post. "You okay?" he asked.

"Sure, how about you?"

"Great," he said. "Fantastic!"

For the remaining two hours of our romp down the Poudre, I kept stealing glances at Jesse, who paddled as though his life truly depended on how hard he pulled. His face shone with joy, and my own joy was kindled from seeing it.

Tired and throbbing, we scarcely spoke during the long drive back to our campground. This time the silence felt easy, like a fullness rather than a void.

That night we left the flap of our tent open so we could lie on our backs and watch the stars. Our heads were so close that I could hear Jesse's breath, even above the shoosh of the river, and I could tell that he was nowhere near sleep. "I feel like I'm still on the water," he said after a spell, "and the raft's bobbing under me and the waves are crashing all around."

"I feel it, too."

A great horned owl called. Another answered, setting up a duet across our valley. We listened until they quit.

"You know," said Jesse, "maybe we don't need to sleep on snow. We can pitch camp in the morning on bare ground, then snowshoe up the mountain in the afternoon."

"You wouldn't feel we'd wimped out?"

"Naw," he said. "That's cool."

The stars burned on. The moon climbed. Just when I thought he was asleep, Jesse murmured, "How's that knee?"

"Holding up so far," I told him, surprised by the question.

"Glad to hear it. I don't want to be lugging you out of the mountains."

I lay quietly, following the twin currents of the river and my son's breath. Here were two reasons for rejoicing, two sources of hope. For Jesse's sake, and mine, I would get up the next morning and hunt for more.

Scott Russell Sanders

He's Your Fish, Son

The swells of the Straits of Juan de Fuca seemed to toy with Dad's fourteen-foot Lund as we searched for Kings in front of what locals called "the cave" near Sekiu, Washington. *This isn't all that bad,* I thought as I reached into Dad's green tackle box for another peanut-butter cracker. The sloshing in my ten-year-old belly was finally giving way to the crackers and the excitement brought on by the brightening yellow glow in the east.

"Make sure you hold your mouth right, Son. The bite's comin'." Dad put his coffee cup back into the holder he had bolted to the wood seat that summer.

I studied his mouth, looking for the secret grownups never reveal to each other but pass down to their sons, like the Old Timer knife Dad gave me for my tenth birthday. Although I couldn't tell exactly how Dad was holding his mouth, I was convinced this was the secret to Dad's success with salmon.

I stuck my tongue in the corner of my cheek and waited, staring at the eye staring back at me on the end of my six-foot salmon rod. Suddenly my face felt hot and the boat seemed to exaggerate its motion with every swell. Up, down, up, down. The green and white pole in my hand became two poles, then three. Dad eyed my changing appearance cautiously.

"Oh, oh, looks like it's time to feed the fish," Dad's voice sounded muffled, so far away.

"Feed the fish?" I puzzled, looking down at the frozen herring in the package at my feet. That was all it took. Seconds later, pieces of cracker and peanut butter floated behind the eighteen-horse Johnson.

"You'll feel better when it quits hurtin'," Dad assured me, his cheeks vibrating with the throttle in his left hand. Before I could even think through the significance of Dad's comment, something tried to rip the Fiberglas pole out of my frozen fingers.

"Fish on!" Dad's yell echoed from the boat to the shore and back.

"What do I do?" I pleaded.

"Just keep your tip up and don't stop reeling."

I reeled as fast as I could while Dad swung the Lund around in the direction of my rapidly descending line.

"I can't do it, Dad. It's too strong." My arms ached after only seconds of trying to hold the tip of the pole above my head. Exhausted, I succumbed and the rod crashed against the edge of the oar lock.

"Keep your tip up, Son, you don't want to lose him." Dad's face was bright and glowing.

"I can't, Dad. My arms hurt. You reel for me!" My forearms and wrists begged with me, as the salmon continued to dive.

"He's your fish, Son."

"But I can't keep my tip up, Dad. I can't reel. You gotta help me."

"You can do it. Put your leg over the end of the rod. It'll help you keep your tip out of the water." I saw my dad reach for the pole and then quickly pull his hand away. "He's your fish, Son. We're gonna get him. You wait and see."

Somewhere from deep inside me new strength surfaced, and fifteen minutes later so did the twenty-pound King.

"There he is!" Dad let go of the throttle and grabbed for the net. The little Lund rocked sideways, slamming my knees into the aluminum rivets that held the boat together. Dad grabbed the belt loop on my Levis and yanked me back into my seat. I stuck the end of the pole under my leg again and repeated the circular reeling motion.

One turn. The muscle-rending strain of the fish made the small distance my wrist had to turn seem like a mile.

Two turns. The line edged one inch, two inches—dragging the salmon closer.

Three turns. I felt the fish give up.

"Hold on, Son, just a few more minutes." Dad seemed to talk more to the fish than to me.

A few more minutes? I thought. *Isn't he going to net the fish?* My questions were drowned by the singing of my reel as the salmon powered his way downward, rubbing his victory in my face with each yard of line he tore from my spool.

"Not again!" I sobbed. "I'll never get him!" The aches doubled instantly. I was beat.

"Dad, I'm gonna lose him. You've gotta reel him in! Please, Dad." I tried to move my wrists around and around, but the salmon's dive was stronger. The leg I had put over the end of the pole lifted off the wood seat, and I slid toward the ocean. Dad grabbed for me again and pulled me back.

"You almost have him now. He's your fish, Son. Don't give up." I saw him reach for the pole again. This time his hand moved back more slowly. I searched for strength within, but nothing came.

I prayed, "Please God, just this one fish. I promise I'll go to church for the rest of my life and be nice to my sister." I felt sure God liked fishing since he'd given Jonah quite a story. I wasn't sure what he thought about my sister.

Suddenly, the line went limp. It was the most horrible feeling I had ever felt. The fish was gone. All that work. All that aching. For what?

"Son, keep reeling! He's comin' straight toward the boat!" Dad's voice shattered my sobs, and I reeled faster than I knew possible. The empty spool began to fill with line. Dad grabbed the net with one hand, scooted me to the opposite side of the boat with the other and lunged toward the line. His knees slammed against the aluminum frame as he buried his arms and the net beneath the boat.

For what seemed longer than a math class, Dad stayed there. Bent over. Silent. Then with a sudden surge, his shoulders shot backward, his back straightened and the net and the biggest fish I'd ever seen came flying straight over Dad's head into the boat.

That was the first and only time I stood up in that fourteen-foot Lund.

Neighboring fishermen cheered as I held the fish up, my fingers through his right gills and I am sure, now, my dad's through his left. I looked up into Dad's face and saw the widest smile and the first tears I had ever seen.

It proved the biggest salmon on Olson's dock that day. At least, it was the biggest one I saw. All the way back to Tretevick's campground, I stared back through the window of Dad's 1970 Chevy at the long silver body draped across a dull-red fish box. The pain in my arms and back, although numbed by the sight of the salmon, reminded me what I had done. I had reeled in a fish when all my strength was gone. I had done something I felt I couldn't do. And now the best fish I had ever seen had my name written all over him.

My family gathered around for the picture. Mom

focused the camera and counted, "One, two," as a smile stretched over my face and I struggled to keep the fish's tail out of the dirt. My dad put his arm on my shoulder, and I heard him whisper again, "He's your fish, Son!"

Marty Trammell

Father at Sea

Everybody knows about the physical demands of motherhood. But with all due respect, once the baby's a year old, fatherhood is the Ironman Triathlon. It's Dad who carries kids to the car, Dad who rides the roller coaster, Dad who does piggyback. Sure, pregnancy is no picnic, but try having twenty-eight to sixty-six pounds hanging around your neck for seven or eight years. Worse, the trials of fatherhood usually come out of nowhere.

One vacation day after we visited the Baltimore aquarium, Josh and Rebecca hit me with, "Daddy, can we ride the paddle boats? Please? Please?"

Dozens of families flecked the harbor on those pontoons with pedals. Alas, there was nowhere to hide.

"That'll be eight dollars, plus a five-dollar deposit on the boat," said a sailor-capped teenage girl. "Be back by 5:22 or we charge for another half hour."

"Aye, aye," I said. "Back by 5:22." My nautical spit and polish went unnoticed.

We walked down the gangplank, where a seventeen-year-old harbor master tossed us life jackets. "Your time's up at 5:22," he repeated, shoving us away from the dock.

For the first few minutes our voyage was smooth. The

kids loved being on the water, and my wife Jody looked at me as though this was the life she'd imagined.

But I knew something the others didn't: To move through perfectly placid water demanded the energy output to power an entire town. Although pedaling furiously, I had absolutely no sensation from my hips to my toes.

Jody caught my expression. "Are you all right, Hugh?" she called.

I tried a carefree "I'm cool" wave.

"Hugh, I'd feel better if you'd say something."

I waved again. Josh said, "Daddy, why can't we go out as far as everybody else?" he pointed to a paddle-boat speck out in the shipping lanes.

Suddenly, the sky grew dark. The water began to chop. I looked around and saw an armada of red-faced fathers madly pedaling into the wind, racing both the coming squall and the clock.

I didn't make it. At 5:23, Rebecca said, "Uh-oh, Daddy."

When I finally climbed off the boat, I nearly fell into the harbor. My left leg got soaked up to my thigh. One of my deck shoes sank full fathom five. Pulling myself up, I stumbled and took a splinter in my knee. All around me men were wobbling out of boats and collapsing.

The teenage harbor master looked as though he was about to mention the additional charge. "Don't even think about it," I snarled.

I took off my soaked pants and slipped behind the wheel. I was wearing boxer shorts and one shoe when we pulled into a tollbooth. Jody hastily covered me with a blanket.

"Everything all right, ma'am?" the tollbooth guy asked, peering past me to Jody.

"Daddy took off his pants," Becky answered helpfully.

"You shouldn't drive without shoes, sir," he said, peeking inside the car. I floored it and fishtailed out of there.

"Is Daddy going to prison, Mommy?" Becky asked.

"I get the front seat if he does," Josh chimed in.

"Nobody's going to jail," Jody said through her laughter.

Oh, sure, I thought, *easy for you—with your clothes dry and childbirth but a faint memory—to enjoy the humor in all this.*

But hearing the children reliving our desperate race against the clock was balm for my beleaguered soul. While they turned the day into legend—The Day Daddy Drove with No Pants—my heart and lungs and quadriceps began to mend, preparing themselves for tomorrow.

Hugh O'Neill

Becoming a Jock Dad

Participate with your child in sports. Go to his games and help develop his skills. Showing him that you think what he's doing is important will build his confidence.

Lou Patton

Being a man, there is always that dreaded macho stigma hanging over you that a real man never shows his true emotions. Being a father pretty much puts an end to such a silly notion. I have accepted the fact that I have never been, nor will I ever be, a real man.

I am a fraud of manhood. I should be banned from the brotherhood of male ego. I'm nothing but a softy. A disgrace to everything that manhood stands for.

Actually, I'm just a father. When it comes to my girls, a long time ago I gave up holding in my emotions like a true man. Be it a banquet, recital, athletic competition or cheerleading, I have long established myself as a blubbering father who is quite generous in shedding a few tears of pride on my girls' behalf.

I remember my oldest daughter's last high school

cross-country meet, when she broke the school record. She had a room full of trophies, plaques, medals and certificates for her achievements over the past four years, but the one thing she didn't have, that she really wanted the most, was the school record. She wanted to leave her high school with her name up on the gym wall proclaiming her the best distance runner in her school's long history.

Last week, she had a great run, but came up four seconds shy of the school record. Today would be her last chance. There would be no more tomorrows.

I positioned myself away from the crowd, on the final bend where the runners come into view and head for the home stretch. If she wasn't going to break the record, it would break my heart. She had worked so hard and wanted it so bad. It was now or never, and a parent hates the emotional volcano rumbling inside, as you stand on the sidelines, unable to do anything but watch. Especially in a race that covers a little over three miles, lasts some nineteen minutes or more, and is run out of view of neurotic parents.

As the race began, things were looking fairly good for my daughter. She looked fresh and focused. Conditions were perfect for her. It was cloudy, cold, with snow flurries fluttering about. She always loved running when conditions were bad. She was my mudder.

The toughest part of the race for the parents was when the runners disappeared from our view for about a quarter of a mile, until they rounded the bend on the hill where I stood and headed for home. It was in this quarter mile where those who had it made their move, while those who didn't simply faded off.

As I anxiously waited at the bend, a few of the girls made the turn and headed for the finish line. These were the girls who always won, and today would be no different for them.

I continued to pace. I was a nervous wreck. I kept watching my time clock, then the corner. She still had plenty of time. She looked good throughout the race, but I didn't know if she had run out of gas while out of view or if she was making her move.

Then it happened.

Around the bend came the familiar green and white that I had been following for the past four years. It was her! I frantically looked at my clock and absolutely fell apart. She could pretty much walk the rest of the way and still beat the school record!

I started jumping and running alongside of her, screaming and yelling with excitement, as she tried to remain focused on her race and ignoring the fool running next to her. I'm sure that she told everyone at the finish line that she had no idea who that lunatic was up at the bend, but I'm sure they all knew. Only a father would behave like that in public, and only a father like me would do so without any apologies.

You hope in a race like this that you might be able to beat the record by one or two seconds. Today, my daughter beat the school record by a whopping twelve seconds! Of course, unofficially, I smashed the world's record for the high jump of fatherhood.

As her coach, teammates and friends all celebrated with her down at the finish line, I laid on the ground alone, up by the bend, crying buckets of tears of joy for what my daughter had accomplished. She had worked so hard for this moment, and there was no one more thrilled than her father.

So, maybe I'm not a macho, cool and collected kind of real man. Fatherhood has always taken a priority in my heart. If that makes me more a lunatic than a man, so be it. My daughter had just presented her high school with an impressive new record in cross-country for young ladies to strive for in years to come. In a few months, she would graduate from her school as the greatest distance runner the school has ever had.

My daughter had become a champion because she applied her God-given talents to a sport that she really enjoyed.

I had become a champion jock dad because I set aside the macho images of manhood that a boy always has to grow up with, and simply learned to enjoy watching my daughter do what she loves to do. My only concern was not in what people were thinking about me, but thinking that the temperature might be cold enough to freeze my proud tears to the ground below me.

Andy Smith

That's My Boy!

It's late October, and I'm watching my son play football. Well, okay, he's not technically playing. He's on the sidelines, No. 85, standing near the coach, looking alert, hoping the coach will notice him and send him in. I'm not so sure this is a good idea, because the other team's players are extremely large. They're supposed to be junior high students, but if they are, they apparently started junior high later in life, after having played a number of years for the Chicago Bears. They look EXTREMELY mature. You can actually see their beards growing. They probably have to shave in the huddle.

In stark contrast, my son's team, the Raiders, consists of normal-sized seventh- and eighth-grade boys, except for player No. 9, Nicole, who is a girl. From a distance, with their helmets and shoulder pads on, the Raiders look big enough, but this illusion is shattered when you see them up close, or when one of their moms walks past, towering over them.

For some reason the Raiders' opponents are always larger. Also they seem more aggressive. They punch each other a lot and spit and sneer and probably eat live chickens on the team bus. Also, they're always gathering together and emitting loud, menacing, unintelligible football roars whereas the Raiders tend to chat. The Raiders are a more laid-back group. Sometimes they try to make a menacing football roar, but it comes out sounding halfhearted, like a group throat-clearing.

This is the Raiders' sixth game. So far they've won one; that victory was sealed when the opposing team, in what has proved to be the Raiders' season highlight so far, failed to show up. The Raiders lost all the other games, in large part because—at least this is how I analyze the situation, from a strictly technical standpoint—they have not scored any points. None.

Usually, when the Raiders have the ball, giant live-chicken-eating Chicago Bears knock them down and take it away. Whereas when the opponents have the ball, they give it to some enormous player who cannot possibly be in junior high school because any given one of his calves is larger than a junior high school. This player lumbers toward the plucky Raider defenders, who leap up and latch on to him, one after the other, until the runner is lumbering down the field with what appears to be the entire Raider defensive unit clinging desperately to his body, the whole group looking like some bizarre alien space creature with many extra heads and arms and legs and two really huge calves.

On the sidelines we grown-ups yell helpful advice.

"Tackle him!" shouts a Raiders coach.

"Somebody tackle him, okay? Okay?"

"Bite his ankles!" shouts a mom.

Inevitably the Chicago Bears score a touchdown, causing us Raider parents to groan. The Raider cheerleaders, however, remain undaunted. They have a cheer for just this situation. It goes (I am not making this cheer up):

"They made a touchdown!

"But it's all right!"

The Raider cheerleaders remain perky and upbeat no

matter what happens in the game. This may be because they wisely refuse to look at the game. They face us parents, going through their routines, happy in their own totally separate cheerleading world. A plane could crash on the field and they might not notice, and even if they did, I bet it wouldn't seriously impact their perkiness ("A plane crashed on the field! But it's all right!").

Of course, they have good reason to be cheerful. They're in no danger of being converted into gridiron roadkill by the Chicago Bears. My son, on the other hand, is. . . .

My son is going into the game.

The coach is telling him something; I hope it's good advice (such as "Tennis is a much safer sport"). And now No. 85 is trotting onto the field; and now he's taking his position on the Raider defensive line; and now both teams are lined up; and now my son is crouching down in his stance, ready to spring forward, and. . . .

THERE HE GOES! GET 'EM, ROB! STICK YOUR HELMET COMPLETELY THROUGH SOME BIG FAT CHICAGO BEAR'S BODY AND OUT THE OTHER SIDE! YES! WAY TO GO! WAY TO POUNCE! WAY TO BE . . . Offsides. Whoops.

Okay, so he was a little overeager. But he did fine after that, as far as I could tell, lunging around out there just like everybody else and managing to go four full plays without once losing an important limb or organ.

Another positive note was that Nicole got into the game and was actually sort of involved in a tackle, a feat that earned her some major high-fives when she returned to the bench.

But that was pretty much the highlight for the Raiders, who became increasingly resigned and philosophical as it became clear that they were going to lose yet again. Meanwhile, the Chicago Bears, feeling smug, were punching each other and emitting fierce victory grunts.

"I bet our SAT scores are higher," I wanted to yell, but of

course, I did not, as I generally prefer not to have my head stomped into pudding.

Finally the game ended, and even though the Raiders again failed to score any points, we parents were tremendously proud of their efforts. We clapped and cheered with pride as they trotted off the field.

They think we're crazy.

Dave Barry

Softball People

When you're the only pea in the pod, your parents are likely to get you confused with the Hope diamond.

Russell Baker

First grade was more than just learning to read and write; it brought me other lifelong joys. That year I learned to play softball, and I got to know my father. On game days I went to school wearing a bright green uniform. I loved waiting at the office early in the morning to get an early dismissal for games. I loved walking through the hallways and seeing other teammates in matching attire. I loved carrying my glove with me, nodding matter-of-factly when the cute boys asked, "Are you a lefty?"

Toward the end of the school day, my teacher Ms. Capinagro always said, "Softball people, it's time." With that signal, seven of my classmates shut their books, shoved them into their small wooden desks and grabbed their bags. For the next ten minutes, the lesson was suspended while we noisily put on cleats, stirrups and caps. We left the room slowly, but once we hit the corner, the race was on. When we reached a doorway, we'd stop and walk softly, glancing at the students inside. Then we'd start up again. By the time we reached the main entrance of New City Elementary School, we were all pretty much out of breath. Yet at the sight of the maroon Chevy station wagon at the curb, we resumed our race.

"Okay, two in front, four in the back, and one on the roof," my father said, trying to guide us into his car. We all piled in, rejoicing. Once again, we had gotten dismissed thirty minutes early! Coach Howie liked having a pre-game practice and we weren't about to argue with that.

At the field, everybody had to help carry equipment: balls, bases, bats, helmets, rope (to measure the distance from the pitcher's mound to home plate), ice packs and water coolers. The first order of business was batting order. Coach Howie used a void, blank check on which he wrote the numbers one through twelve. He ripped up the check, and placed the numbers in a hat. He always did the batting order like that, and somehow I always wound up last. As a six-year-old, it wasn't easy to take.

Once after Coach Howie had read the lineup, I marched up, pouting. "Dad, why am I always last?" I watched the arc of his bushy eyebrows tense up and form wrinkles of mild concern across his forehead. He looked so tall then, even though he wasn't more than five-six.

After a few seconds of silence, he crouched down on his knees with the smile I knew so well and he whispered into my ear, "We can't reveal our secret weapon too early in the lineup, can we?"

I nodded, and the game was underway. Our secret weapon? I would bat last any day to remain the secret weapon.

After the game, it was ice cream for everyone. Coach Howie congratulated each player on her performance while each player blushed and wiped a chocolate mustache from her tiny face. As we headed home, my father always went on about how great I had played. "And the way you fielded that misthrow at first base was incredible. You can't teach that, you know."

It was in this way that I learned to love softball. Our green "Bears" uniforms worn when the parents pitched to the players changed to blue "Angels" apparel once we reached second grade and a member of the team could handle pitching, but Coach Howie was still our leader. First grade through sixth, he didn't miss a single game. Players came and went, but everybody loved to play for Howie. Everybody fielded, and everybody batted. At the end of each season, he organized a parent-versus-child softball game. He would always get up to the plate, with ten bats in his arms, and pretend he forgot that first base and not third is where the runner had to go.

It was at the last one of these particular games, the spring of sixth grade, when I realized that my softball days under Coach Howie would soon be over. The players' parents had gotten together and collected money for a gift.

Nobody said anything, but we all knew that this was the last game that my father would ever coach. He unwrapped the gift, a plaque inscribed with all of our names and a huge, "Angels 1989." He read the top aloud: "To Coach Howie, a Little Guy with a Big Heart, We Thank You." With tears forming in his eyes, he could only say repeatedly, "This is so nice, thanks." Sitting on a checkered blanket, eating a hot dog and munching on some chips, a lump formed in the pit of my stomach. Little League had ended, and with it the days of playing for Coach Howie.

In ninth grade, when most people took the bus, I convinced my father that if he drove me, I could sleep a whole forty-five minutes later and therefore do better in school. When he'd pull up to school, some of his former softball players and some other friends would see my father and wave.

In high school, my interest in friends and boyfriends sometimes took priority over my family. My father always tried to include himself. It was amazing how much gossip he could pick up by reading *The New York Times* on the steps outside of my room. My telephone rang nonstop and when I shut my door for privacy, he wouldn't leave me alone until I told him who it was.

"You're so nosy," I said. "Don't you have anything better to do?"

"No," he said. "Anyways, you're going to miss me when you go off to college. I've got to annoy you now as much as I can."

In senior year, major decisions had to be made. Where would I be going to college? The day I got accepted to the University of Pennsylvania, my father brought flowers to my softball game. I had never seen him speechless since the day he had accepted that plaque from our old team's parents. My heart pounded with joy at how proud he was of me. He drove me to meet the softball coach after I learned that they were recruiting me for softball. As we walked around the campus that day, I felt that something very secure and supporting was slipping away and an entirely new world was waiting for me to enter.

After weeks of debate I chose to go to Emory, a smaller school with a more comfortable environment. My father had a difficult time understanding why I chose a school so far away.

"But Emory doesn't have a softball team," he pleaded one day. Once I had made my decision to go there, he said, "Maybe you can start one."

As a junior in college, I did manage to start a softball club after showing the administration that there was a high interest in fast-pitch softball.

Laws like Title IX, demanding equal numbers of varsity sports between men and women's teams, carved a path for me to push for an Emory team. I found many students who, like myself, craved to play.

With two practices a week and over twenty girls showing up each time, we competed in scrimmages. Then the campus sports office found a softball team from a neighboring college who was looking for an opponent. In the spring, the softball club played in the first-ever women's fast-pitch softball game at Emory. Packing up equipment in the dugout, I realized that out of the fifteen years I had been playing softball, that game was the first one my father had ever missed.

During my senior year at Emory University, I became captain of the first-ever women's Varsity Softball team. With a brand-new field, uniforms and seventeen teammates, it has been an exciting experience. There is nobody happier than my father.

"Just think, Stacey," he said. "You will be part of history."

Although I love softball, what I want more than anything is to have my father back.

"But Dad, it doesn't mean a thing to me if you can't be there," I said. I want to get picked up from school early and go run towards his car. I want to hear him outside of my door asking me who is on the phone. I want to look over into the bleachers during a game and see his reassuring smile.

As for life after college, my father has informed me that whatever I do, I must do it closer to home. "Your mother won't be able to handle it if you're not around here," he said. "Maybe you can move back into your old room."

"Don't worry about it, Coach," I said. "I'll still call you all the time from wherever I am."

I hung up the phone and stared at a recent picture of my parents. My father looked older and a bit tired. His bushy eyebrows showed hints of gray and white. What stood out the most was his navy-blue sweatshirt with the letters EMORY, across his chest. I put on my socks and metal-spiked cleats and got ready for practice. I have to work hard. After all, I'm not guaranteed even the last spot in the lineup anymore. I've come a long way since first grade, and I owe much of my success to Coach Howie. It's an extra blessing to know that although he's no longer my softball coach, he'll always be my dad.

Stacey Becker

Hunters' Bond

Often the deepest relationships can be developed during the simplest activities.

Gary Smalley

Fortunately for me, the war in Vietnam ended before I received my draft notice. This was good for world peace, and especially for my own inner peace. Guns, senseless bloodshed, fear—I couldn't understand any of it. I was lucky not to have to face the killing in Vietnam, and I managed to successfully avoid any involvement with firearms for many years thereafter—that is, until about middle age when my only son reached adolescence.

My son's childhood preoccupation with weapons gave me little concern at first, since it did not seem an unusual fascination among young boys. However, just when I thought that his interest in guns would begin to fade, it escalated instead. He began to openly express his desire to take up deer hunting. In fact, on several occasions, he proposed this to me as a good idea for a father-and-son activity. Now, this was not what came to my mind when I thought about ways in which my son and I could find common ground. I hoped that I could placate him with "maybes" or "we'll sees," and that his idea would eventually fade away like earth shoes did in the seventies. After all, I had watched him go through phases when his life focused on Tonka toys and Legos, and they passed. But his preoccupation with firearms was tough. His interest only intensified and so, too, his incessant hounding of me to go hunting with him. So I began to give the matter my serious attention, trying to figure out ways to dissuade him from living out his fantasies.

This was a difficult one, and I decided to call in reinforcements. I consulted several of my friends, one of whom was an FBI agent, a man I always found to be levelheaded and a source of good advice. I thought that he could especially appreciate my concern about firearms. But much to my surprise, he was all for it.

"Let him learn the right way," he said. "Better under your supervision than with anyone else. Besides, hunting is probably the most appropriate use for a gun anyway." My friend's words hit home. If my son was eventually going to do it with or without my consent, it was better if we learned together.

Reluctantly, I entered into the wide world of sports, a world that was essentially foreign to me. Eventually, I went shopping for a rifle. I started by trying to persuade my son that a light .22 was the way to go. However, I was repeatedly informed by the experts that you couldn't hunt deer with a .22, and I was forced to purchase higher-powered equipment.

After buying our rifles, we joined a rod-and-gun club, which had a rifle range and provided us with paper targets for practice. Even at this stage, I held out the hope that it would go no further than the rifle range and that somehow my son would be satisfied with shooting cardboard figures. I was wrong again, and his interests continued to grow, particularly after talking to several hunters we met there.

One older fellow, who actually belonged to a hunting club and owned land in the mountains, invited us to come up for the first day of deer season. I thought of every possible excuse to get out of it, but found myself once again purchasing hunters' gear—boots, camouflage clothing and all the accessories that went along with joining the brotherhood of hunters. This was a paradoxical experience for me, since I had such an aversion to the entire concept of hunting animals for sport. At the same time, I was intrigued and most inspired by my son's obvious sense of excitement in preparing for our expedition. But I found myself wondering how he would actually react upon coming face-to-face with the game that he was supposed to shoot. It all looked so easy in the hunting films that we viewed during the hunters' safety course and, on some level, I was thrilled by the chance to bond with my son who, up until this point, had not been motivated by very much in life. After months of practicing at the rifle range and conversations about the ideal hunting situation, deer season finally arrived. It was time to become bona fide hunters.

On the day of the big hunt, I was as nervous as a kid on a first date. The prior night's sleep was interrupted by nightmares and harrowing screams in the night—most of which were mine. We rose at three in the morning in order to arrive at the mountains before dawn, so that we could set up our stakeout post. We laid out all of our clothing and paraphernalia the night before, including thermal underwear, backpacks, boots, gloves with the fingers cut out, 150 square inches of orange cover material (so that we wouldn't be mistaken for deer), a knife, toilet paper, a Thermos with coffee and, of course, our weapons of destruction.

As we climbed toward our mountain destination, snow flurries became a steady snowfall, which I was told is ideal for hunting. While my son slept in the seat next to me, I drove like a white-knuckle flyer through a squall of snow in the early morning darkness, asking myself repeatedly why in God's name I was doing this. Of course, glancing to my right—where the great white hunter was sleeping like a baby—somehow helped me to reconcile my avoidance and his enthusiasm.

On the mountainside, the newly fallen snow sparkled a fresh and clean scene in the first rays of sunlight. What a beautiful and serene setting—the stillness and silence of this enchanted forest. How could such a murderous act, tracking down innocent prey in their own domicile, take place here? I felt like a ruthless assassin. We pulled off of the main road and onto an abandoned dirt path. The ground was littered with Styrofoam cups and fast-food wrappers—all of the evidence of salivating predators out for the kill. We unloaded our equipment and made our way through the thick brush, hauling our gear into the dense, dark woods. I trudged along like a schoolboy on his way to the principal's office, all the while attempting to hide my anxiety behind a bravado and a false display of enthusiasm for my son's sake. *So this was the hour of reckoning,* I mused. Facing our foe. All those months of target shooting have led to this day, when a father has to challenge his long-held beliefs and a son has to follow his own distinct dream. I wondered who was the more anxious, me or the deer, which no doubt had already sensed our presence.

Now, the hunters' task is different, depending on what is being hunted. With fowl such as pheasants, it's the hunter's chore to walk through wilted cornstalks, usually with a trained hunting dog, and roust the pheasants from their hiding place. But with deer, as with many other large game, the hunt consists of waiting quietly in one spot—sometimes for hours—until your prey crosses through the line of fire. As fate would have it, my son and I share one trait that would have a powerful effect on our success as hunters; we have no patience. We sat back-to-back, my son and I, camouflaged against a mound of brush, shivering in the cold morning air. My son anxiously prayed that he would soon see a deer in his sights. I anxiously prayed that the deer would have the good sense to go in the other direction. It didn't take long before these brave hunters broke the golden rule of silence. We began to chat.

"Dad, what if we get a deer, what will we do with it?" he asked me innocently. Yipes! Now there's something that we hadn't thought about. What *would* we do with it? Part of the art of hunting is also knowing how to gut the animal and field dress it and prepare it for the trip to the butcher.

I had forgotten about those horrible parts of the training film that showed the gruesome technique of eviscerating your catch and hanging it upside down to drain.

"Well," I said, "you remember what we saw in the films about cleaning the deer and preparing the carcass for butchering."

"Yeah," he muttered with the same enthusiasm he responds with when asked to clean his room. "That's the part that I don't want to do. I'll let you do it, Dad."

"Oh no," I snapped, "the hunter who bags the trophy does it. That's part of the experience."

"I don't know if I can," he sighed. "I feel like I am kind of hurting the deer."

"Well, what do you think you're doing when you shoot it?" I asked. The look on his ashen face told me that it had really never sunk in until now.

This was my opportunity to make my move. I leaned into him gently and whispered, "Are you trying to tell me that you have second thoughts about killing these animals?" He tried to speak, but couldn't. As a knowing smile slowly crossed his face, I realized that he was just like me, except that he had become caught up in the whirlwind and excitement of being a hunter with all of the gadgets and glory. I inched over to him and put my arm around him.

"Listen," I said, "there is nothing wrong with having those feelings. Lots of people have them." I winked at him and smiled. "How many guys do you think froze out there when it was time to pull the trigger?" My mind shot back in time to the popular movie of the 1970s, *The Deer Hunter*, in which Robert DeNiro—sighting a buck in the scope of his rifle—suddenly let it get away, shouting, "Alright, we're even." *We are even,* I thought to myself.

From that day on that time spent "hunting" with my son became an intimate and precious activity. We would talk about all kinds of things, from cars to girls—just plain guy talk. We would always quit by 9 A.M. and stop for breakfast at a bleak little diner that we had found on that first ride up, one with lousy pancakes.

In all of our years of hunting, we have never even seen a deer, except the one that happened to leap through the parking lot of the diner while we were eating breakfast one morning. Very cunning of that animal to jump through enemy lines while our guard was down.

Perhaps the best was when my son and I were so anxious to get up to the mountains that we actually forgot to pack our guns. Clearly, hunting had never been the point anyway. We never did bag a deer, but we did manage to bag a trophy far more valuable to both of us—a hunters' bond!

Frank M. Dattilio

The Family Ski Trip

Maybe I've been spending too much time watching television shows like *The X-Files* or something, but I'm trying to think how I would describe skiing to extraterrestrials.

Aliens: Take us to your leader.

Me: Can't right now, we're going skiing.

Aliens: What is skiing?

Me: Well, first you go to the top of this really, really high mountain that's covered with this cold, slippery stuff called snow. Then you strap these skinny little sticks on your feet, and try to go straight down the steep mountain in a standing position without killing yourself. And if you survive, you stand in a long line for the opportunity to do it again.

Aliens: Good-bye.

Me: Where are you going?

Aliens: In search of intelligent life.

It was crowded at the rental shop. Plus, with the temperature only twenty degrees outside, everyone was dressed like the Pillsbury Dough Boy—only in shades of mauve and lime green.

"Maybe we should have rented equipment back in town," my wife suggested.

"No way," I said. "Remember last time? They gave me two left skis and two right boots. All day long I kept running into myself. Besides, now that I'm more experienced, I need more sophisticated stuff."

"You and I never got off the bunny slope," she said. "The kids are the only ones who advanced."

"Well sure, but with better equipment I'll be skiing circles around everyone out there."

"That's what I'm afraid of," she said.

A young man approached us, wearing a ski hat pulled down to his eyebrows and a T-shirt that read "Ski Naked."

"Are you like into radical carving or do you get off by just dropping in and tucking?"

I hesitated.

"He kinda skis all over the place," my wife told him.

"Oh, right, vary the terrain, challenge the brain. Cool. Got just the set-up for you." He handed me a set of skis that looked like they might have been made by NASA. "Progressive force bindings with environmental friction control, and ultrafast racing skis with deep side cuts and a beta torsion core. You'll fly with these babies."

He turned to my wife. She glanced at me and my new racing outfit.

"I just want something for the other parent who can't afford to be out of work on crutches for six weeks," she told him.

To me, the worst part of skiing is getting from the ski lodge to the chairs. There's always a slope, and it's always slippery. Usually, after thirty minutes or so, I find I have actually lost ground and am now standing in the parking lot.

Apparently, the twelve-hundred-dollar skis helped, because in just minutes, we safely made it to the bunny slope and got into line with all the other five-year-olds.

That's when the rest of the family came barreling up, skidding to a stop right in front of us. I watched them for a second, smiled, then immediately fell down, taking the entire waiting line with me.

"Wow. Cool skis," Jon said. "But this is the wrong lift. You want that lift over there."

I followed the path of the chair lift up the mountain until it became a tiny speck that disappeared into the thick clouds.

"You're not . . . scared, are you?" asked Patrick.

"Of course not. It's just that these skis may not be fast enough to ski up there on. . . ."

"Black Death Run . . ."

"Right. Black Death Run."

My wife opted for coffee instead of sheer terror, leaving me as parent-in-charge. Next thing I knew, we were standing somewhere that even mountain goats wouldn't go. I immediately issued a warning to the others.

"Don't get too close to the edge of that cliff," I shouted. "Follow me."

"This isn't a cliff," Christy said. "This is the trail. The cliff is over there somewhere . . . Dude?"

I've often wondered what my last words would be. I figured maybe something like "I did it for God and country," or "I'm sorry that I have but one life to give." As it turns out my last words contain only vowels, as in,

"Yiiiieeeeeooooooooo . . ."

I'm not exactly sure what happened over the next few minutes. I remember a lot of white, some muted voices, and being poked by a number of sharp objects all over my body. Fox Mulder of *The X-Files* would have called it an alien abduction. Maybe it was. Of course, why the aliens rolled me up like a giant snowball and dropped me off at the foot of the mountain I'll never know.

But everyone seemed glad to see me, including the rental-shop guy, who quickly removed my progressive force bindings and ultrafast racing skis, and returned to his shop muttering something about hot-shot adults and why couldn't they be more sensible—like teenagers.

The rest of the family arrived just as my wife handed me a cup of something that looked like coffee, but tasted like brandy.

"Thanks, dear," I said. "And you'll be happy to know, I'm giving up skiing."

"We are, too," said Stacey.

"Really?" my wife asked.

"Yup," added Shane. "Tomorrow, we're all going snowboarding."

I sighed, pulled a pinecone out of my ear and then immediately downed the entire contents of the cup.

Ernie Witham

CLOSE TO HOME   JOHN McPHERSON

12-5

"I thought the family rental rate
was too good to be true."

The Last Rainbow

This is for every boy who learned to hunt and fish at his father's elbow. It's for all those boys who then became men, and sadly saw their dads grow too old or too sick to hike the fields and wade the streams anymore. But especially, it's for all those hunting and fishing fathers who are no longer with us. And who, with their passing, left an emptiness we never feel quite so keenly as when we put a hand to rod and gun.

On the day of this story, the day of the last rainbow, the old man was still getting around pretty well; in slow motion, to be sure, with a plodding delicacy that bespoke the pain of terminal cancer—but getting around nevertheless. I'd taken a few days off from my job as a cop in Phoenix to join him at the cabin in northern Michigan, the one he'd built with his own hands from the foundation up when my brother Jack and I were barely tall enough to reach his waist.

The cabin. Those two words will evoke a warm montage of memories for as long as I live. Goldeneyes whistling down the lake, seining minnows in the morning chill, the rowboat, perch in the pan, baby loons riding their mother's back, and trout—certainly the trout.

And this day was superb for chasing trout. I glanced at the rods in the corner of the cabin, wondering if I should suggest it, wondering if the old man still had the strength.

"Might be a good day," he said slowly, grinning slightly, "to try the old bridge at Silver Creek."

We were there in minutes, at a spot to which he'd first brought me thirty years before. In those days it was a rickety, dangerous-looking crossing fashioned from old timbers. You could look down at the creek between each plank. A rusty sign peppered with birdshot said "Cross at your own risk."

I'm sure you remember a sign like that somewhere.

But the bridge was sadly different this day. The timber planks had been replaced with concrete, the single wooden railing with an orange-painted pipe. The sign was gone. But Silver Creek was everything it had ever been. Cool and clear and rushing, choked with overhanging branches and moss-covered logs, a stream that sang "Trout!" to anyone with a lick of sense to listen.

We would fish from the bridge today as usual, but unlike years gone by we would not hike downstream afterward in our hip boots, slipping up on a dozen beautiful holes that always seemed to yield a creel full of trout.

Today, because the old man was already tired from the short ride, we would begin and end at the bridge.

And it began just as we hoped. Dad had no sooner begun stripping out line when a good 10-incher darted from beneath the bank and nailed his night crawler. He played the trout as he had always played them. A slight, patient smile on his face, the rod held gently at a sixty-degree angle. No horsing. He just smoothly tired the fish as it flashed back and forth, then swept it with one easy motion up and into the weeds.

That was number one.

I unhooked the rainbow, placed it in the creel with a bit

of grass, and baited his hook again. Not thirty seconds later, he'd enticed another trout from the same dark patch of water.

That one refused to run and wrapped itself around a log. I slipped off my shoes, waded into the creek, and followed the line down to shoulder depth before I felt its snout wiggling against my fingers.

That was number two.

He offered me the rod then, but I declined. Dad had always said he enjoyed watching my brother or me catch a fish as much as he enjoyed catching one himself. That day, for the first time, I understood what he meant.

The old man had exhausted the downstream hole, but we both knew the best had been saved for last. Under the bridge—that was where the biggest rainbows always waited. It was right there, in fact, three decades before, that I had caught my very first trout: a fat 12-incher that had forgiven all my childhood clumsiness, graciously remaining on the hook as I jerked it unmercifully straight up and out instead of swinging it to the bank.

But this was now, and I watched the tip of the old man's rod as he floated a fresh crawler toward the hole neither of us had ever really seen, but had fished a hundred times. He stopped feeding line just when I thought he should. Instinctively, we both knew the bait was precisely where it ought to be. We waited. Five seconds, maybe ten. Then it happened.

The tip of the rod twitched, twitched again, and then bent double like a divining rod as the trout bit down and held on, and the old man began easing that fighting fish out of the hole.

"It's a good one," he said. And as he said it, I knew for that moment at least, he had forgotten he was dying. Forgotten that this stream and all the streams he loved so deeply would soon be flowing past without him.

"It's a good one," he said again, and my eyes traveled up the rod to his face. That slight, patient smile was a little wider than usual.

It *was* a good one. Before it was over the old man was breathing heavily and tiring as fast as the fish. But he worked it out of there, out of the bridge's shadow and into the upstream light.

That was number three. The last rainbow.

It wasn't any record. Maybe 15 inches, but fat and thick and feisty all the way. As good as any we'd ever taken from under the bridge at old Silver Creek.

"It was a great fishing trip," I said, putting my arm around him as we walked slowly to the car.

"Yes," he replied. "We'll do it again sometime. Sometime again soon."

Several months later, I traveled to Michigan once more, this time for his funeral. And I remember walking into his bedroom and finding his fishing rod, rigged with a brand-new Eagle Claw and two tiny split shot.

My mother came in and saw me holding it.

"He had it all ready for another trip," she said. "He thought maybe the two of you could go fishing together one more time."

We will, old man. We will.

Jim (Fieberg) Berlin

Final Season

There's a time—all too brief as it too soon becomes apparent to parents—to be little; a time to be in between; and a time to be old. Let each have its season. Let little be little.

Malcolm Forbes

The other night, after the parents had all come to pick up their sons and I was picking up catcher's equipment, bats and, of course, one forgotten mitt, it dawned on me that this was it: the last season I would coach one of my sons' baseball teams.

Two sons. Twelve seasons. Hundreds of games. Maybe three decent umps. And thousands of memories, hidden in my mind like all those foul balls lost in the creek behind the Ascot Park backstop.

Sitting in the rickety bleachers that spring evening after everyone had gone, I found myself lost in thought, mentally walking along the creek, finding those long-forgotten foul balls and listening to the stories they had to tell.

The time our left fielder got locked in a Dairy Queen bathroom during a postgame celebration. The time I handed a protective cup to our new catcher and he thought it was an oxygen mask. The time a tee-baller cleanly fielded a grounder, picked it up and tossed it to his mom, who was sitting behind third base reading Gone With the Wind.

For something that became more than a decade-long family affair, it had begun casually enough. While watching one of my five-year-old son's tee-ball games in 1985, a manager asked if I would coach second base.

"Uh, second base?"

"Yeah. At this level you need coaches at second base or the kids will forget to take a left and wind up at Safeway."

So I coached second base. And before long, our family's summers revolved around a diamond: me coaching, my wife Sally keeping score and the boys playing. Like the Israelites trudging out of Egypt, we hauled our equipment—lawn chairs, video cameras and sixty-four-ounce drinks—from ballfield to ballfield, week after week, summer after summer.

The time our right fielder turned up missing during a championship game, only to be found at the snack bar eating licorice and flirting with girls. The time we showed up at an empty field, only to discover that I'd read the schedule wrong and our game was actually ten miles away.

The time I explained to my fifth-grade team that, because we'd given up eighty-nine runs in the last four games, we needed to set a defensive goal.

"It's a six-inning game," I explained. "Let's just try to hold them to twelve runs per game. Two per inning. Can you do that?"

Silence. Then my philosophical right fielder spoke up.

"Coach," he said, "do we have to give up the runs even like that, or could we like give up all twelve in the last inning?"

Our teams were more than a collection of kids. They were extended family, some of whom would end up sleeping overnight and going to church with us. And some of the boys desperately needed that. One year, of fifteen players, only five had a mother and father living together under the same roof. Once, a boy missed practice because his aunt had been murdered. And I can't count the number of times I took kids home, because nobody came to pick them up.

But I've always remembered the advice I heard at a coaching clinic: "Who knows? The six hours a week you spend with a kid might be the only six hours that he actually feels loved."

The out-of-control coach who pushed me off the field. The kid who didn't get picked for my team firing a splat gun at our left fielder. The father who dropped off his son, Willie, and told him to get his own ride home; he and his girlfriend were going to a tavern to throw darts. We went into extra innings that afternoon, and the man's son played the game of his life, going all nine innings at catcher and making the game-winning hit.

We tried to make it more than just baseball. With help from our sons, we established a team newspaper. A few times, I'd put candy in the sack at second base and let players dig in every time they threw out a runner. (Best defensive practice we ever had.)

Sally was our DH—designated healer—with her ever-present cooler of pop and packages of frozen corn for sprained ankles and bruised arms. Once, we had pizza delivered to the ballfield just after we'd lost to a team with one of those scream-and-yell coaches. I think we had more fun that night than the team that won.

The time we won with only eight players. The time Michael, a friend of my youngest son, spent the night at our house and played hours of backyard baseball, the rules stipulating that you must run the bases backward. The next morning, in a regulation game, Michael hit a hot grounder and promptly took off—for third base.

Over the years we won games, we lost games and we lost baseballs—zillions of them. But for every ball we lost, we gained a memory. As a family, we laughed together, cried together, got dusty together—as if each of those hundreds of games was a microcosm of real life, which it was.

A weak-hitting kid named Cody stroking a three-run double and later telling his mom, "I'm trying to stop smiling, but I just can't."

My oldest son becoming my assistant coach and reaching a few kids in a way that I could not.

Kids I coached as third-graders, now taller than I am. And, of course, the night we were going to win the city championship. But for the first time in two months, it rained. Instead of playing on a field of dreams with perfectly straight white lines and a public address system, some official handed us a bunch of medals and called us co-champs.

Later that night, after the post-season pizza banquet, the restaurant manager approached me, broom in hand. "Excuse me, but are you the coach of the Washington Braves?"

"I sure am," I said, figuring he was going to pull me out of my doldrums by congratulating me on the co-championship.

"Coach," he said, handing me the broom, "your team trashed the indoor playroom. Wanna help sweep?"

Two sons. Twelve seasons. Hundreds of games. As a family, we had shared them all. *But what*, I wondered, *had we missed in the process?* What had we given up in order to pursue what some might see as trivial?

Nothing. Because whether your family is together at baseball games or camping trips or rodeos or dog shows or soccer tournaments or swim meets, the common denominator is this: families together—a rarity in our busy times—making memories. Learning lessons. Sowing seeds that can be nourished only by time.

Regrets? Only one. I wish Willie's father had considered his son more important than a game of darts. He missed seeing his teammates mob him after making the game-winning hit.

The time a tall third baseman was making fun of my

four-foot-nine son at the plate—until my son nearly took off his head with a line-drive double.

My oldest son proudly posing for pictures with his grand-parents after the team won a city championship.

The time he played his final game, and walking to the car afterward it hit me like a line drive in the side of the head. This was it. I'd never coach him in baseball again.

Dusk was descending. It was time to head for home where my family—the boys were now seventeen and fifteen—would be. As I slung the equipment bag over my shoulder and walked down from the stands, I noticed a young father and his son playing catch between short and third.

I smiled slightly and headed for the car, leaving behind plenty of lost balls for others to find.

Bob Welch

3

RITES OF PASSAGE

There are only two lasting bequests we can hope to give our children. One of these is roots; the other, wings.

Hodding Carter

No More Sunday Matinees

I have loved movies since I was a child. I attended Sunday matinees at the Monroe Theater, seeing films like *The Love Bug, Charlie the Lonesome Cougar* and *The Reluctant Astronaut.* Then in 1970 I turned ten, and my hormones kicked in big-time. I got into trouble (at that time, "getting into trouble" meant lighting gasoline in the street and stealing comic books) and my tastes turned from Disney movies to more mature fare. Still, I was precluded from seeing R-rated movies.

All at once, commercials appeared on TV for *The French Connection.* They looked exciting, streetwise, powerful and testosterone-driven. This was going to be a man's movie. And I was going to miss out, because I wasn't old enough. I can remember when my dad and older brother went to see it, stepping into the freezing night calling, "We'll be back later," Peter running ahead of my father in anticipation.

The French Connection broke new ground. The car chase was daring, edgy and thrilling, like nothing ever seen before (the commercial focused on this now-famous scene and made me long to see the movie). Gene Hackman's portrayal of Popeye Doyle was far from the clean-cut cop audiences were used to seeing. Instead, he played this New York City detective as a trash-mouthed, racist and angry antihero (the film would later snag Academy Awards for best film, director, actor, screenplay and editing). I was a movie fanatic, and I felt I was missing out on something historical, daring and new. Peter was thrilled to be seeing it. I, however, was relegated to another dreary night at home with my mom and younger brother, Steven.

When Peter and my dad got home, they expressed what I already knew. The movie was great. They talked about the car chase. "Unbelievable!" Hackman was "fantastic!" Oh, how I wished I were older and could. . . .

"You want to go see it, Leonard?"

Was that my father who just said that? Did I hear right? Confirmation came in a second, from my mother.

"Ed, do you really think he should see it?" *Oh Mom, don't kill my chances. Don't plant the seed of doubt. Be quiet for just a little longer until I can extract a promise.* Then the sweet words came, and the foot gently came down with them.

"I don't see why not. I think he's old enough to handle it. We can go tomorrow night."

"But you just went with Peter tonight. You're going to go *again* tomorrow?"

My dad looked over at me. He must have seen my eyes, filled with excitement and anticipation.

"Sure, why not?" he said.

"Yeah!" I cried and leapt into the air.

The next night I could hardly eat my dinner. I couldn't wait to get out of the house and see something that I thought only my older brother would be allowed to see.

"Leonard, if you don't eat something you're going to be hungry at the movies," he said smiling to himself.

There it was again—confirmation of the event. Yes, we were actually going to go see this R-rated movie together. It would be my first one, my initiation. At last, dinner was over. We donned our winter coats and stepped to the front door. My dad grinned, tossed his head back and called out, "We'll be back later."

"Okay," said my mom, "have fun." I was so thrilled. Now it was Peter's turn to stay home with Mom and Steven.

We got into the car. It was freezing. My dad's Old Spice cologne gently enveloped me, and the car warmed as the heater kicked in. I could feel his love for me. This was a time for just he and I to be together. Even though he had just seen the movie the night before, he was going to take me tonight. He didn't even wait a few weeks. I was impressed and felt special.

The Monroe Theater was big (none of those shoebox multiplex theaters back then) and smelled of heat, popcorn and seat cloth. Back then, anyone under age twelve couldn't get into an R-rated movie. I looked older than I was, and my dad paid the extra money so we wouldn't have any trouble from the ticket lady. I was thrilled that my father thought I was mature enough to see an R-rated movie and that he had no problem saying, "Two adults, please," when buying our tickets.

The French Connection was better than I had anticipated. It was the most exciting movie I'd ever seen. And the most adult.

Hackman cursed like a sailor, beat suspects, crashed his car through New York City in pursuit of a sniper and shot him on the stairs of a train stop. For weeks afterward, I would stand at the bottom of my basement stairs, feign exhaustion, point my imaginary gun upward and yell, "Hold it!" just as Hackman did before he shot the bad guy.

As we walked up the steps at home after the movie, I turned to my dad and really looked at him. I wanted him to know how happy he'd made me, how wonderful it was to believe he thought of me as an adult (at least in some way), but all I could come up with was, "Thanks for taking me, Dad."

He hugged me, his big arms wrapping me tightly, and held me for just a little longer than usual. Old Spice never smelled so sweet.

"Oh, my pleasure," he said, "my pleasure!"

And it was.

After that, we went to the movies alone together all the time. The R-rating lost its importance and was no longer considered a sticking point. I had seen one and could now see all of them. My rite of passage was over. But when I was fifteen, things changed a bit and I went to the movies with my friends more than my dad.

In 1975, Peter and I, and my friends Glen Belfer and Cliff Konnerth, waited in line for two hours (this was very unusual back then!) to see *Jaws*. I went home raving about it. What a fantastic movie! I could see my father wishing he had been allowed to go with the teenagers to see this "event," because there was no way my mother was going to go with him and he certainly wouldn't see it by himself. But he was the parent now. Teenagers don't really want their parents around when going to the movies as a group.

"Hey, Dad," I said. "Ya wanna go see it?"

He seemed a little surprised. He hesitated, knowing how his place had changed, but said, "Well, yes, I'd love to."

"Okay, we'll go. Tomorrow night. Just you and me."

"Terrific," he said, turning away so I couldn't see him smiling from ear to ear.

The next night we waited in line for two hours to see *Jaws*. And this time, it was my pleasure to "take" my father to the movies. My pleasure.

Lenny Grossman

The Important Test

A tree cannot stand without its roots.

Zairian Proverb

I always thought Pinewood Derby cars defined your worth as a father, but my perspective may have been flawed. My father died when I was twelve, so the Pinewood Derby was one of the largest and last exams he faced. I remember with fondness how Dad passed his Pinewood Derby exam, and I knew that one day I'd have to take that same test.

When it came to woodworking, my father had a knack. I did not inherit that knack, which makes his test all the more impressive. One time, Dad gave me a pocket knife for my birthday. I'd seen him whittle, and it looked like fun. He warned me of the dangers and told me to wait until he could show me the proper and safe techniques. I couldn't wait. Almost before he had backed from our driveway, I sliced off a chunk of my thumb and had my knife confiscated.

Despite my woodworking deficiencies, Dad seemed to have confidence in our ability to make a functioning

Pinewood Derby car. Perhaps the confidence came from his own abilities—knowing there wasn't any mistake I could make with a block of wood that he couldn't fix.

We sat down at the kitchen table and made our plans for our car. "Our" car. Somehow "our" plans seemed to match my limited capacity for fancy craftsmanship. The car called for two simple cuts and a whole lot of sanding. Dad knew I could sand. So he supervised my two simple cuts and turned me loose on my sanding. Each day I sanded, and every night he'd inspect my progress and we'd talk about our project. Finally, we agreed to paint it red. He helped with the delicate wheel work, but I watched and learned. Our car won a couple of consolation speed prizes, and I thought he was just about the greatest father in the world.

The following year, we took our car-building a little more seriously.

We designed a car with wind resistance in mind and "our" design involved more complicated cuts. Our painting also addressed aerodynamic concerns. We won major speed and design prizes, and I thought Dad was the greatest father in the world.

By the third year, Dad pretty much turned it over to me. I ran some ideas by him, but he just supported them. We talked a lot about more complex woodworking techniques. We won more major awards, but more importantly, he had helped me overcome my woodworking deficiencies. We built a display case capable of housing all three cars and several of the trophies. Dad was the greatest man in the world.

Dad died before the next Pinewood Derby, and my woodworking skills seemed to always remain along the level of a twelve-year-old. Building those cars together created certain expectations—not only about woodworking and cars, but about parenting as well.

When my son brought home his Pinewood Derby kit, I remained afraid to open it—afraid I wouldn't understand the instructions, afraid I couldn't pass my fatherhood exam.

My son had no margin of error. If he made a mistake on his block of wood, I could not fix it. For that reason, I left the cursed thing inside the package for three weeks. My eight-year-old son, whom I'd lectured about procrastination, finally lost patience with me. That frightened me. If he lost patience, then I'd flunk my exam.

We sat down at the kitchen table and opened the package. We read the instructions together. They didn't make sense. So we read them again and discussed our interpretation of the instructions.

Soon we began to map out a design. He wanted a car shaped like a penguin, with wings and everything. That would have required whittling.

"No animals and no whittling."

"But a penguin is a bird."

"No birds and no whittling."

Most of my limited tool collection contained no tools suitable for an eight-year-old to operate, so we went and picked out a new coping saw together. At home we measured and talked and came up with a modified penguin design, in which most of the penguin part of the car would be represented in an elaborate painting scheme.

"But will it look like a penguin?"

"There's lots of black-and-white critters it could look like. A killer whale, a zebra, a duck, a skunk . . ."

"But will it look like a penguin?"

"If that's what you want it to look like, then we'll just have to find a way to make it look like a penguin."

Find a way? That sounded like something my father would say. Worse yet, the more we worked on the car, the more and more I could see the possibilities of making a penguin sliding down the track on his belly.

"Will it be a fast penguin car?"

My son had seen my Pinewood trophies and began to talk about his expectation to build a fast penguin car so he could fill a trophy case of his own. We talked about realistic expectations. I suggested for the first year, we build a car that would make it down the track without falling apart. He wanted more. He could see the penguin, too, and if we could see a black-and-white penguin in a block of brown wood, then speed could be obtained, too. Then I remembered Dad.

"You know, the second year when we started winning our races, Dad and I worked graphite into the wheels."

"Then let's go buy some graphite," he insisted.

We did. He made the small cuts needed to outline a belly-sliding penguin. He must have inherited my father's knack. He sanded each day, and we discussed the progress each night.

The penguin-mobile did make it all the way down the track. It even won every race. In my son's smile, I saw my father's pride.

Then I realized that all along, I had been wrong. I hadn't passed my fatherhood exam. Those awards my son held were the results of my father's final exam.

My own exam would come in twenty-five years, when my son sits down with his son and the two of them plan and talk and sand.

Brent L. Cobb

Daddy Loves His Car

Scholars have built careers exploring the importance of cars to the American male. The conventional wisdom is that our car stands for our freedom, the way a cowboy's horse stood for his. Whatever the explanation, there is no question: Cars are close to our hearts.

Fatherhood wreaks havoc with our car mythology. The dreams on which we came of age—swanky images of Italian sport cars, reconditioned 'Vettes—are replaced by station-wagon realities. Once he's a father, the same guy who imagined himself hairpinning through the Alps in a Lamborghini is driving a minivan very carefully. With fatherhood, a car devolves from a symbol of freedom into the exact opposite, a symbol of the ties that bind.

My Daddy Car Troubles began early.

We had just driven our brand-new Volvo family wagon (Atlantic blue, vinyl interior) off the lot. The kids were euphoric, bouncing around in the back seat, enthusing about everything.

"Dad, is this car really from Sweden?" Josh asked, as though that was just a little too good to be true.

"Yahvolg," I replied in sitcom Swedish.

"Sweden! Yes!" Rebecca said, as though Sweden was as good as it gets.

"Beck," Josh went on, "try the armrest."

In the rearview mirror, I saw them doing just that, leaning on their elbows, heads together. In one of the high moments of family life, Rebecca christened the car "Bluebell." Everybody knew instantly the name was a keeper.

As we pulled into the driveway, Josh asked if we could take the kids down the street for a ride.

Then it happened.

As Josh bolted off down the street to get his friends, Rebecca clambered up between the front seats to explore the cockpit. As she did, I leaned to my right and bumped into her. On contact, she dropped a bag of M&Ms. Little candy bullets went flying all over my brand-new car. Reader, what happened next actually occurred in slow motion.

The green M&M hit the back of my seat and then flipped end-over-end through the air. I reached out, hoping to grab it, but muffed the play. It hit the stick shift and ricocheted toward the parking brake, where it slipped with an eerie precision down into a crack that was exactly the width of an M&M.

I peered down into the crack, saw the Day-Glo green pellet sitting jauntily on top of the Swedish parking brake machinery, and fought back tears. Within twenty-two minutes of taking ownership of the car, it had chocolate in the works.

Over the next few weeks, I tried everything conceivable to retrieve that M&M. I went to a hospital supply store and bought some extra-long surgical tweezers. I tried a macho vacuum. I even considered disassembling the emergency brake unit. The Volvo rep just said that would void the warranty.

For weeks, the M&M just sat down there, taunting me.

I couldn't stop looking at it. At every stoplight, I'd take a peek. Once in a dream, the candy spoke. "I'm still down here, pally boy," it said. Then the candy laughed.

Jody wasn't very understanding. She kept minimizing what had happened, as though it was no big deal that there was snack food in the emergency brake. She didn't understand. To her, a car was just transportation. To me, and every other self-respecting man in America, a car was something more.

Then one day when I peeked down, the candy was gone. It had vanished. But not, I knew, to some distant place. No, it could only have migrated, or even melted, down deeper into the car. I feared that it could find its way into the carburetor. I wondered if there was a fuel additive that would break down the cocoa bean.

As bad as it was, the M&M was just the opening salvo in the kids' assault on me and my car. Consider the following entries from my diary of car destruction:

June 7: Josh kicked in rear stereo speaker. Opened door with a heel—first move made popular by federal narcotics agents entering premises uninvited.

July 24: Kids from down the street crouching behind Bluebell. Fusillade of small-arms fire whapping into the car. Josh and Rebecca firing chestnuts at their friends. Sixty-eight chestnut impact craters on the driver's side. Resale value of two-month-old car (original price $17,853.87), now somewhere between $150 and $200.

August 6: Crayons left on dashboard in ninety-eight-degree Fahrenheit conditions. Lime green. I am despairing. Lowest day of my life.

Perhaps no other crime against my car and my car mythology is more revealing than the story of what the kids did to the back seat.

It was the first day of spring.

All the neighbors were clattering around outside,

clearing away fallen winter branches, sweeping off their porches. The air was full of promise, and I was fully equipped—for the annual spring-cleaning of my car, that is. Rags, bucket, sponge, whisk broom and Dustbuster, furniture polish to make the dashboard gleam.

I waved howdy to Larry and Paula across the street, crossed to the car, opened the back door, leaned in and pressed the lever that released the bottom of the back seat. But when I lifted it clear and peered under the seat, I gagged, then staggered backward, whacking my head on the door frame as I drew clear of the car.

Plain decency forbids a detailed description of what I saw under there. But let's just say that apparently, on all those trips when Jody had so lovingly passed food over her shoulders to the kids—to calm their little carsick tummies—they hadn't been eating it at all. They had been making a compost heap under the seat.

Well, this was the last straw. I had had it with the way the kids treated Bluebell. I sat on the blacktop, stunned by what I had seen, and I swore that the kids would never ride in the car again. Next time we went to visit Aunt Eileen and Uncle Greg, they could arrange their own transportation.

Let's just say that lots of stuff congeals around old half-sucked Lifesavers. And that taco chips, pretzel nuggets and a melted red crayon ferment into a frightening mass—at least when they are honey-glazed with dried grape soda.

I stood up, took a deep breath and set to work reclaiming my car. As I worked angrily away, scraping, clawing at glutinous congealed masses of gum and apple cores and Popsicle sticks, I wondered what that green stuff was. And for what possible reason the kids had torn a coloring book into three million pieces. I also worked on my lecture, practicing the peroration the kids were going to get.

That night, I sat down at dinner, all set to deliver my lecture/ultimatum. As Jody brought in our plates, I launched into a good old-fashioned rant-and-rave.

"Kids, there are going to be some changes made about eating in the car," I said. But no sooner did I start to describe the grotesquerie under the seat, than Josh and Rebecca looked at me, stricken, as though falsely accused.

"We didn't do it, Dad," they said. "We're always careful about crumbs. We would never drop Jujubes. We always keep our wrappers in our pockets until we get home." They loved Bluebell, they assured me, and would never treat her so disrespectfully.

"Then who did it?" I countered, caught off-guard, I admit, by their brazenness. "You're the only people who sit back there."

"No, Dad," Josh said seriously, as though determined to ply his way to the bottom of this mystery. "When you and your brother went to play golf, Uncle Kevin sat in the back."

"Yeah," Rebecca added. "And remember when Dr. Turoff's car broke and we gave him a ride to the train station? He sat back there, too."

I was in awe. These two were cool customers. They looked me right in the eye and denied the whole thing. And not only that. They fingered their uncle and the dentist from across the street who had taken them to three Mets games last summer.

"So you think Uncle Kevin chewed a Mallomar, spit it out and then wedged it under the seat?" I said.

"He must have," Josh said.

"Or Dr. Turoff," Rebecca added, Sherlock on the case.

I took my plate and ate in my room.

Hugh O'Neill

CLOSE TO HOME JOHN McPHERSON

The Wormsleys had one too many milkshakes
spilled on their new cloth seats.

Fathers Are Good at Telling Tall Tales

Laughter is the sensation of feeling good all over, but showing it primarily in one spot.

Josh Billings

I thought I would share with you a father's greatest fear: answering a five-year-old child's question of "Where do babies come from?"

Even though I've reached an age at which I could be a grandpa (a young and virile one, I might add), it doesn't seem that it's been more than twenty years since I gave the "birds and bees" speech.

Because I did such a magnificent job of bungling my first attempt, my wife didn't entrust me with that chore a second time.

Although time has a way of mercifully erasing embarrassing moments from memory, I can recall, with depressing clarity, the circumstances of my father-son talk.

One night while Nancy and I were watching "All in the Family," she said calmly, "Jim, I think you should find time to tell Shawn about the facts of life. Soon."

"Aw, Honey," I whined, "the little guy is too young for that sort of thing."

"I don't know about that." She smiled and raised an eyebrow. "Yesterday, Shawn wanted to know if he could trade his G.I. Joe for a Raquel Welch."

"They don't make Raquel Welch dolls, do they?" I asked.

"No," she said, "but he didn't want a doll, he wanted Raquel Welch. THE Raquel Welch!"

I cleared my throat several times, fidgeted quite a bit and finally said, "Wellll . . . well, Honey, I guess you're right, but he's so young."

"Kids mature faster nowadays," she said comfortingly. "The curse of television and movie previews, I suppose."

"I better do it now and get it over with," I said.

If I remember correctly, our little talk ended with ". . . and so you see, an Indian shoots an arrow into the sky. If it lands in an oyster bed, the mommy will have a boy. If it lands in a strawberry patch, she'll have a girl."

"Then does the mommy have to eat the oyster?" asked Shawn.

"Ummm . . . ahhh . . . yeah, sure. And that's probably why there are more girls than boys," I said.

Suddenly, the bedroom door swung open. "Jim, JIM HORNBECK! How could you tell a story like THAT?" shouted Nancy. "Why, that's the most ridiculous thing I've ever heard."

"Mommy," said Shawn, "don't be mad. I knew it was just one of Daddy's stories."

"You did?" I said, overcome with relief.

"Sure," said Shawn, "Mikey already told me where babies come from."

"He did?" we chorused.

"What really happens," he continued, "is a man and a woman go to Hollywood and get married. After they do a bunch of kissing and hugging, they have a party and get lots of presents."

"Oh, good grief," sighed Nancy.

"And two of the presents are catalogs."

"What?" we chorused again.

"Then they choose a boy baby from Sears," said Shawn, "or a girl baby from JC Penney. That's what Mikey said."

"Who told him that?" I asked.

"His dad," said Shawn.

Nancy frowned. "Oyster beds and catalogs. Now, where would you men ever learn stories like that!"

I smiled sheepishly and said, "From our fathers, of course."

Jim Hornbeck

Nerd Day

You know it's going to be a bad day when your teenager knocks on your bedroom door first thing in the morning and says, "Today is Nerd Day at school, Pop. Can I borrow some of your clothes?"

Ron Chapman

Another Milestone

Several years ago my parents, my wife, my son and I ate at one of those restaurants where the menu is scrawled on a blackboard. After a wonderful dinner, the waiter set the check in the middle of the table. That's when it happened: My father did not reach for the bill.

Conversation continued. Finally it dawned on me. *I* was supposed to pick up the check. After hundreds of restaurant meals with my parents, after a lifetime of thinking of my father as the one with the bucks, it had all changed. I reached for the check, and my view of myself was suddenly altered. I was an adult.

Some people mark off their lives in years; I measure mine in small events—in rites of passage. I did not become a young man at a particular age, like thirteen, but rather when a kid strolled into the store where I worked and called me "Mister." He repeated it several times, looking straight at me. The realization hit like a punch: *Me!* I was suddenly a mister.

There have been other milestones. The cops of my youth always seemed big, even huge, and, of course, they were older than I was. Then one day they were suddenly neither. In fact, some were kids—short kids at that. The day came when I suddenly realized that all the football players in the game I was watching were younger than I was. They were just big kids. With that milestone went the fantasy that someday, maybe, I, too, could be a football player. Without ever having reached the hill, I was over it.

I never thought that I would fall asleep in front of the television set as my father did. Now, it's what I do best. I never thought that I would go to the beach and not swim. Yet, I spent all of August at the shore and never once went into the ocean. I never thought that I would appreciate opera, but now the pathos and combination of voice and orchestra appeal to me. I never thought that I would prefer to stay home evenings, but now I find myself passing up parties. I used to think that people who watched birds were weird, but this summer I found myself watching them, and maybe I'll get a book on the subject. I yearn for a religious conviction that I never thought I'd want, feel close to ancestors long gone and echo my father in arguments with my son that I still lose.

One day, I bought a house. One day—what a day!—I became a father, and not too long after that, I picked up the check for my own father. I thought then it was a rite of passage for me. But one day, when I was a little older, I realized it was one for him, too. Another milestone.

Richard Cohen

The Bank of Dad

You need a lot of money to raise a modern child. Hair gel alone will run you thousands of dollars.

Dave Barry

My roommate, Tom, who had never dated much, finally had a chance to take out one of the school's prettiest young women. However, the event caught him by surprise, and he had no money. He quickly sent off a telegram to his recently separated father: "Have date. Send money." Back came the answer: "Have money. Send date."

Mark Treyz

"My dad sent me a new bankcard. . . . He says if I get an A in chemistry, he'll send me the PIN number."

Last Words

*There is no friendship, no love like that of the
parent for the child.*

Henry Ward Beecher

I had been home from work for about fifteen or twenty
minutes, when my older son David came in from playing—looking very serious. He was only six years old at the
time. Our younger son Mark, who is two and a half years
younger, was right behind him.

I was watching the evening news on television when
David came in and stood right in front of me. I have to
admit that my thoughts were rambling between the news
and David. I knew he had something on his mind, and he
knew he could talk to me about anything. He also thought
I had the answers to everything.

As he stood there, I could sense that he was nervous
and wondered if there was something wrong, or if he was
just going to ask one of his very serious questions about
the rules of the game they were playing. But he was much
too serious for that. Now he had my full attention.

He spoke rather quietly when he said, "Daddy, I need to talk to you."

"Okay, Davie, what's on your mind?"

"I'm a big boy now, right?"

"You sure are. Tell me what you're thinking."

He said, "I don't want you to call me 'Davie' anymore, I want you to call me 'Dave,' and I don't want to call you 'Daddy,' I want to call you 'Dad.'"

With this out, he seemed even more serious or nervous. I smiled at him with the proudest smile I think I ever had.

I said, "That will be okay, Dave. I would like to call you 'Dave' or 'David' and look forward to you calling me 'Dad.' But, don't ever call me 'Father,' okay?"

He relaxed and said in a very strong voice, "Can I go back out and play now, Dad?" As I said yes, my younger son came over close to me and said, "I still want to call you 'Daddy.'"

I said, "I'm so glad you do!"

For the next few days, every time David had anything to say to me, he would begin it with "Dad." Even if he wanted to know what we were having for supper, he would ask, "Dad, what are we having for dinner?"

It didn't take Mark long to follow suit. I could barely keep the smile off my face! My wife would turn her head to smile.

My son David died July 1, 1993. The night before he died, he and I were talking on the telephone about how he was feeling. About six weeks before, he had surgery for removal of a testicular cancer. Then they did exploratory surgery to verify that his lymph system was clear of cancer. It was, thank God.

In this telephone conversation, David told me that he was experiencing blurred vision and numbness in his fingers, as well as slurred speech. I told him that he would be alright. He had just gone back to work too soon after the surgery. He agreed and said he would slow down a bit. We both laughed, because we both knew he wouldn't slow down.

I said, "I love you, Davie," to which he responded with loving laughter, "I love you, too, Daddy."

I laughed and said, "Goodnight, Davie."

"Goodnight, Daddy," he said, and we both hung up our telephones. These were the last words we ever spoke to each other.

The next day at about noon, I was notified that David had been taken by ambulance to the local hospital. His wife was with him during the trip. When I arrived at the hospital, he was in a coma. As the afternoon wore on, the doctor informed us that David had a ruptured aneurysm in his brain. He lived until 7:06 P.M.

As I prayed for his life, many things went through my mind. Mainly, I will forever be grateful to God for his last words. We had no fences to mend. We enjoyed a good relationship. Although David's passing was obviously painful—for him physically and for me emotionally—the innocence and sweetness of that shared childhood memory offered a poignant note on which a father can remember a son taken too early.

H. L. "Bud" Tenney

Taking Care of Things

"You're going to be alone on the place this weekend," my father said as though that was no big deal. "I expect you to handle it." We were walking back toward the barn from the fenced pasture where we kept our best brood cows. The ladies—as my dad called them—turned their white faces toward us, then went back to grazing the sweet short grass of their pasture.

"For how long?" I said, trying to control my uncertain voice that now and then still turned squeaky.

"Two days. I have to go to a medical conference in Chicago. There're a couple of presentations I need to hear. You'll be okay."

I had never been left alone on our farm, and the only thing I was ever in charge of was the dogs. My father always found time for the cattle, even if he'd had one of those days when everyone in town seemed to get sick. It didn't matter if he was tired to the bone when he came home, he still made the rounds of the place, looking after his herd of Herefords. My mother had gone to Canton, Ohio, to visit her sister for a few days, and now my father had to go away, too. I thought they could have planned things better, but it gave me a chance to show my stuff. I knew I could take care of just about anything that might come up, and I was ready to prove that to my dad.

I finished my chores at the barn and went to wash up for supper. The kid I saw in the mudroom mirror looked confident, even sort of smug. I gave him a thumbs up and went into the kitchen.

I had, in my fifteenth year, got the idea that I knew more than most people. Certainly more than my parents. And I did not hesitate to demonstrate how smart I was. If my father, for instance, started holding forth at dinner on baseball—a sport he cherished—and got a fact wrong or quoted a player's stats incorrectly, I would point out his error, whenever I could. My father wasn't always happy that I knew so much.

One summer night a while back, as he pushed some green beans around on his plate with his fork, he got to talking about responsibility and quoted a remark of Connie Mack's. Then my dad rested his chin on his hands thoughtfully and began by saying what a great baseball manager he thought Connie Mack was. "He knew what really matters. Once he told a reporter, 'I guess more players beat themselves than are ever beat by an opposing team. The first thing any man has to know is how to handle himself.'"

"He said 'licked,'" I said, correcting my father. "It's 'licked themselves' and 'licked by an opposing team.'"

He folded his napkin, laid it carefully on the table, leaned forward on his elbows, stared me in the face and said, "So what?"

"So you got it wrong," I said, emboldened by the plain fact that I was correct.

"I got the spirit right," he said. "You missed the point. The point is you got to know yourself. Know what you can do and what you can't. So why don't you just let up on the rest of us a little instead of missing the gist of what I'm saying to you?"

"Try not to be so annoying," my mother said. I thought for an instant she was talking to my father, but she was not.

My dad was often put out with me, and so I was a little surprised—a few weeks later—that he would go to Chicago and trust me with the cattle.

Our farm wasn't as large as most, but there was a lot to be responsible for, and I was determined to handle whatever came up, to show my dad I wasn't just all talk.

As soon as he left on his trip, I headed out to the barn lot to see that everything was okay when I noticed the water in the cattle trough was low. I didn't understand how that could be since a float and lever maintained the level.

When I investigated, I saw the float hanging in mid-air and not a drop of water came from the filler pipe.

I checked the pump. The casing was hot. I checked the fuses in the barn, and one was blown. So I disconnected the pump, took it into the workroom and in a half-hour had replaced the carbon brushes and repaired the short— the source of the problem.

When I turned the system back on, the sweet purr of the pump engine as it kicked made me feel like an old hand. But the problem with the pump turned out to be a breeze compared to the disaster that confronted me the very next day.

I mucked out one of the stalls in the barn where my father kept cows that were close to calving. Only Low Loretta was close to her time. She got her name because her unusually short legs kept her pretty low to the ground. She was not much to look at, but she threw some fine calves and was my dad's favorite.

She liked the orchard pasture especially because of her fondness for apples. She was allowed in that pasture during the day, as long as someone was working around the barn to keep an eye on her. And my dad always put her up at night when she was close to her time so she could be checked on easily. She often had trouble at calving. On Saturday afternoon, I went down to the pond in the afternoon to fish a little and take a swim. I left Loretta in the orchard lot. She was basking in a spot of sun under a tree and looked too content to move. I wasn't planning to be gone for very long.

As I lay on the raft I'd built a summer ago, I thought of how the first words out of my dad's mouth would be, "Everything okay?" I'd be able tell him that everything went fine. Nothing I couldn't handle.

My daydream ended abruptly, however. On my way back to the barn, I heard a sound I'd never heard before. There were two distinct and terrible noises. The first was like water gurgling through mud that was followed by a gut-wrenching cough.

I ran toward the orchard and found, about twenty feet from the barn, Loretta down on her front knees, throat stretched skyward, eyes rolled back in her head, looking as though she were about to die.

I knelt beside her and began to stroke and soothe her. She made a gasping sound and her sides heaved as though she was having a hard time breathing. I felt under her jaw and down along her throat. About a third of the way from her breastbone there was a hard place in her neck. I knew right away that she'd got a green apple stuck in there. Even though she was about to choke to death, I was determined to handle the problem myself.

I massaged her throat to try to force the apple loose, but I couldn't budge it in either direction. The apple was lodged too far down to pull out. I told her I was going to get someone who could fix her up and ran to the tack room to call our vet, Dr. Carrico.

When I told him what was the matter he said, "Stay with the stupid critter, keep her head up and I'll get there as quick as I can."

Doctor Carrico was an outspoken man of strong opinions and plain language. When he arrived and saw Loretta near death, he gave her a cussing like I'd never heard. "When's her calf due?"

"Week, maybe."

"I sure hope we don't lose it."

He felt around her neck studying the situation. Dr. Carrico moved deliberately. I never saw him hurry even in an emergency. Finally, he told me to go to the barn and get him a couple of short boards. When I found what he wanted, he pushed Loretta over on her side, placed one board under her neck where the apple was and another one on top. My dad's favorite cow was very near her last breath and suffering badly. I could not imagine what he was thinking of doing. Then, as I watched in horror, Doctor Carrico put his foot on the uppermost board and stomped hard on it. Twice.

There was a squishy sound, Loretta gave a great wheezing cough and swallowed the now-crushed apple. I sat back on my heels staring at the vet in amazement. I would never have thought of doing what he did. Never. If Loretta had to depend on me to save her, she'd be dead. I felt inadequate and ashamed. I even thought about not telling my dad, but dropped that stupid idea in a hurry. He was not a man you kept things from. Loretta, now free to breathe, struggled to her feet, regarded us both with a baleful eye as though we were the cause of her problem, and then walked off toward her stall in the barn. I guess she felt safe there.

"It'll be awhile before she eats another green apple," Doc said.

"I bet you're right about that."

"Where's your dad?"

"In Chicago."

"And he left you to see about things?"

"Yes, sir, he did."

"Well, he's lucky you know when to holler for help. Good thing you didn't wait one more second."

Late Sunday afternoon, I began watching for my dad's car to turn in our road from the highway just below the south pasture. I rehearsed telling him what had happened, hoping I could find a way to hide how much of a failure I felt. But when he finally got home, there was nothing to do but tell it straight.

My dad didn't say anything much when I told him what had happened to Loretta. I said that I went off to fish and left her in the orchard. I even admitted I tried to treat her myself instead of calling the vet right away.

He didn't seem to react much, just kept saying, "Hmm, I see," a lot. I guessed he was very disappointed in me.

Almost two weeks to the day after her terrible ordeal, Loretta had her calf. We were in the barn with her when she delivered. My dad wiped the newborn off with a burlap feed bag, and Loretta waited patiently while it stood for its first nursing. The calf was a pretty little heifer, wonderfully proportioned and strong boned. After a while my father said, "What are you gonna name it?"

That surprised me because he always named the cattle. Then he said, "She's yours. You earned her." I looked at him in wonder. He smiled at me and slapped me on the shoulder as he left the stall. "Take good care of her," he said as though he trusted I could do that. That evening, I went down to the pond to be by myself for awhile. The sun had set, but the sky still glowed. I looked up the gentle hill toward the house. Lights were now on in the living room, and I could see the shadow of my father as he got up from his chair and crossed the room to get something or other.

On that evening, in the fading light, I decided a few things: to stop tormenting my dad all the time, to give up being such a wise guy and to name my little Hereford calf after a legendary baseball manager. I called her Connie Mack.

W. W. Meade

You Can Share My Daddy

When we bury someone we love, we must also bury a part of our heart. But we should not bemoan this loss. Our hearts, perhaps, are all they can take with them.

David Parkin

As I sat in the garden weeding, my four-year-old neighbor came over to the fence and settled down to supervise my activities. Since her mother had just had a baby the previous week, she was allowed more freedom to entertain herself and explore her world. She asked endless questions about what this was and why that was, and she finally asked about a metal object that had been fastened on the fence. I told her that I didn't know exactly what it was, but I thought it was something that my father had put there for some reason or another.

She looked around the yard carefully and said, "Where is your daddy? Is he at work?"

I explained to her that he had died several years ago, and that was how I came to live in the house.

She thought about this for a minute and then asked, "Well, then did you get a new daddy?"

I was not sure how to answer her, so I just went with the simple truth and said, "No, I didn't."

She thought about that for a moment, as if the prospect of not having a daddy was just too complex to embrace, and then she suddenly offered a solution that made sense to her. "You can share my daddy, if you want to. He is a very good daddy, and I don't think he would mind."

Linda L. Kerby

Little Boxes of Chocolates

They are not gone who live in the hearts of those they leave behind.

Native American Saying

There they were in the store window. Even now, tears stung my eyes. How many years had it been? I made a quick calculation and realized that thirteen years had passed. It seemed like only yesterday when Dad was handing out those little boxes of chocolates to each of his sweethearts.

Valentine's Day was my father's holiday. He was in complete charge of all festivities for as far back as I could remember. On that day, he gave each child a small, heart-shaped box of chocolates, holding about eight candies. Mom always received a huge box decorated with plastic flowers.

At the age of four, I had asked my mother why Dad would bring home a box of candy to my baby sister. After all, she couldn't eat them. Mom told me that all of Dad's sweethearts received a box of candy on Valentine's Day no matter what age. It never mattered to him that she was too young to eat them.

We learned early to be extra good on Valentine's Day. We patiently waited for Dad to get home and then promptly lined up like good little soldiers, as he gave each child her box of goodies.

That little box of chocolates caused different reactions as we went through life's stages. In the elementary school years, we would rush home and wait for Dad. In junior high, my sisters and I felt a little embarrassed by this ritual, but we still accepted his gift with enthusiasm.

The high school years came, and we thought we were too cool to be rushing home to wait for Dad. Add a boyfriend to the picture, and we would do anything not to let him find out about our father's tradition. But during those years when we may not have had a boyfriend, we were comforted knowing that Dad was home waiting for us with his special treat.

My sisters and I thought the only way we would ever get out of this ritual was to move out of the house. We were wrong. My older sister was the first to leave when she married. But come Valentine's Day there was a little box of chocolates waiting for her, and so she made the trip over to collect it. One by one, all of Dad's children moved out of the house, but we all made it back on that special day to pick up his gift.

When Mom died, we thought this whole routine would fade away. Wrong again. We approached that first Valentine's Day without Mom carefully. We all gathered for dinner, and sure enough, those heart-shaped boxes were doled out the same as they had been for the past twenty-five years.

Grandchildren entered the picture and were also included in this ritual from the day they were born, even the two boys that Grandpa was so proud of.

The years rolled on, as did the tradition. When one sister moved out West, Dad was not deterred. The boxes of chocolates were bundled up and sent out to arrive on the holiday.

As adults, we had finally accepted and welcomed Dad's tradition. We always knew we could count on him.

Suddenly, everything changed forever. Dad's first grandchild would become a teenager on February 13. My sister decided to have a family dinner that night. Since Valentine's Day fell on Dad's bowling night, Dad went ahead and handed out the valentines a day early, stating it would be all right this one time.

Valentine's Day arrived with the threat of a blizzard. I had an early dinner with my boyfriend, alone for the first time that I could remember on the holiday reserved for sweethearts. Snow was falling when we left the restaurant, so we decided to get home rather than stop to see Dad, who was bowling a block away.

I was dozing in front of the television when the phone rang. It was the hospital. Dad had been brought in by ambulance after having an apparent heart attack at the bowling lanes.

Fighting blinding snow all the way, I silently prayed that he wouldn't die. We weren't in the waiting room long when a doctor emerged through the swinging emergency room doors. His face said it all. Dad didn't make it.

Weeks after the funeral, my sister called with tears in her voice. She had just realized that Dad had died on Valentine's Day. We decided it was just like him, dying on his favorite holiday, with an attack of the heart, no less.

For the first few years after his death, none of us could bring ourselves to observe Dad's holiday. But as our hearts healed, we began celebrating again. And come February, when those little heart-shaped boxes of chocolates appear in store windows, Dad's tradition lives on in my heart.

Barbara A. Crowley

Don't Let Go, Dad!

It's been more than a dozen years. Sometimes it seems like yesterday; sometimes it seems like a lifetime ago. My little girl finally had her own bicycle. Not a trike, but a real two-wheeler. The bike was the product of a successful visit to a nearby garage sale. It was the perfect pink, little-girl bicycle. My daughter loved it at once. I struck a bargain, stored our new treasure in the trunk and drove home. I couldn't unload the new prize fast enough. My little girl wanted her bike on the road now! It was a warm, sunny day, ideal for learning to ride a bicycle.

Parenthood is a long series of events, each of which falls on one side or the other of a basic parental dichotomy: We want our children to grow up to be independent, yet we want our children to depend on us. We seem reluctant to accept that the love our children have for us is based on what they feel, not what we do for them.

I can see my little girl sitting atop her new bike. She is so small, yet so eager. Her husky voice begs me, "Don't let go, Dad!" Her teeth are clenched. The dimpled pink hands display white knuckles. I keep one hand on the seat and the other on a handlebar. I jog slowly alongside the bike and rider. Occasionally, I remove one hand, but I hear, "Don't let go, Dad!"

Even allowing for the inaccuracies of my memory, she seems to have mastered this complex activity as she would later learn other skills and knowledge—quickly, but only after some frustration over her lack of instant expertise. She executed her characteristic, methodical attack on the challenge with a strong, almost heartbreaking, desire for success. Tentatively, I again removed my hand. "Don't let go, Dad!"

She bubbles with excited anticipation over her lunchtime sandwich. We rush back outside to the sidewalk test track. In spite of her anxiety about falling, the wobbling front wheel is beginning to stabilize. It won't be long now. I can feel her growing confidence. I have to jog a little faster. Her legs pump with newfound strength and confidence.

What event in child rearing presents a more poignant picture of growing independence? Learning to walk is a beginning of independence. Learning to talk and express original thought is also a step along that road. But these steps are gradual, and allow for some adjustment time for the parents. Learning to ride a bike is learning to fly—an experience that almost instantly gives the recipient a new, permanent and irrevocable freedom.

The moment has come. I've known for several minutes that she has acquired the magic "it" that makes this improbable form of transport possible. My daughter finally realizes it, too. Now, my hand no longer steadies her efforts; it is holding her back. My body lumbering alongside is not comforting—it is distracting.

"Let go, Dad!"

She takes off like a shot! Little pigtails flying in the air. She goes at least fifty feet before coming to a gentle stop in the grass adjacent to the sidewalk. She beams. She glows.

She has a grin that could only have come from self-satisfaction. I smile, too. Not just because I share her sense of accomplishment, but because I realize that she has begun a journey. She's on it, still.

Parenthood harbors sorrows and joys. Some events, inexplicably, bring both simultaneously. A holding on and a letting go. A little push on a bike. A hug and a blessing at the door before school. We are bound, as parents, to do both: hold and release, each in its own time. I willingly release my children to their futures. I encourage their independence to discover their strengths and talents. But let go? Never.

Richard H. Lomax

Daddy's Little Girl

"Will you tell Daddy for me?"

That was the worst part. At seventeen, telling my mom I was pregnant was hard enough, but telling my dad was impossible. Daddy had always been a constant source of courage in my life. He had always looked at me with pride, and I had always tried to live my life in a way that would make him proud. Until this. Now it would all be shattered. I would no longer be Daddy's little girl. He would never look at me the same again. I heaved a defeated sigh and leaned against my mom for comfort.

"I'll have to take you somewhere while I tell your father. Do you understand why?"

"Yes, Mama." Because he wouldn't be able to look at me, that's why.

I went to spend the evening with the minister of our church, Brother Lu, who was the only person I felt comfortable with at that time. He counseled and consoled me, while Mom went home and called my dad at work to break the news.

It was all so unreal. At that time, being with someone who didn't judge me was a good thing. We prayed and talked, and I began to accept and understand the road that lay ahead for me. Then I saw the headlights in the window.

Mom had come back to take me home, and I knew Dad would be with her. I was so afraid. I ran out of the living room and into the small bathroom, closing and locking the door. Brother Lu followed and gently reprimanded me.

"Missy, you can't do this. You have to face him sooner or later. He isn't going home without you. C'mon."

"Okay, but will you stay with me? I'm scared."

"Of course, Missy. Of course." I opened the door and slowly followed Brother Lu back to the living room. Mom and Dad still hadn't come in yet. I figured they were sitting in the car, preparing Dad for what to do or say when he saw me. Mom knew how afraid I was. But it wasn't fear that my father would yell at me or be angry with me. I wasn't afraid of him. It was the sadness in his eyes that frightened me. The knowledge that I had been in trouble and pain, and had not come to him for help and support. The realization that I was no longer his little girl.

I heard the footsteps on the sidewalk and the light tap on the wooden door. My lip began to quiver, opening a new floodgate of tears, and I hid behind Brother Lu. Mom walked in first and hugged him, then looked at me with a weak smile. Her eyes were swollen from her own tears, and I was thankful she had not wept in front of me. And then he was there. He didn't even shake Luther's hand, just nodded as he swept by, coming to me and gathering me up into his strong arms, holding me close as he whispered to me, "I love you. I love you, and I will love your baby, too."

He didn't cry. Not my dad. But I felt him quiver against me. I knew it took all of his control not to cry, and I was proud of him for that. And thankful. When he pulled back and looked at me, there was love and pride in his eyes. Even at that difficult moment.

"I'm sorry, Daddy. I love you so much."

"I know. Let's go home." And home we went. All of my fear was gone. There would still be pain and trials that I could not even imagine. But I had a strong, loving family that I knew would always be there for me. Most of all, I was still Daddy's little girl, and armed with that knowledge, there wasn't a mountain I couldn't climb or a storm I couldn't weather.

Thank you, Daddy.

Michele Campbell

Grandpa Pinch-Hits

I raised three children. Time to spectate. Time to watch the next generation of parents. So I thought. Then, my daughter Mary-Kim informed us of her pregnancy. She asked, "Dad, would you be our natural childbirth coach?" I rubbed my eyes and waited a moment. Salty liquid flowed from my face as Mary-Kim explained the plan. Since her husband Steve's new coaching job took him a thousand miles away, and since her mother traveled a great deal as a business executive, my job as a high school teacher tethered me to one home base.

I persisted, "How about Steve?"

"Daddy, the baby is due in February. That's basketball season. We decided that I live here." Sounds logical. The young man couldn't serve as a childbirth coach from another section of the country. Yet, I'd retired from this baby business a score of years past. "Dad," she said, wringing my hand, "you studied natural childbirth when my little brother Jon was born. You pioneered."

Anxiety—with perhaps a tinge of horror—grudgingly gave ground to anticipation and excitement. "Sure," I said bravely, "be glad to."

The next morning, we visited the gynecologist. My last

trip to this type of specialist took place in another lifetime. Waiting-room frowns and snickers seemed to accompany our arrival. Not a trace of paranoia in me. It appeared that the half dozen women and three men occupying the holding room scrutinized us with a collective raised brow.

Was my salty beard a problem? The seated men looked like players on the last Little League team I coached. Fatherhood awaited them. They peeked at me furtively. Insulted, I glared. Did I look so ancient?

The receptionist called. "Mr. and Mrs. S., come in."

I pleaded, "No, I'm Mr. . . ."

My comment ignored, the woman ordered my daughter to the scale. "Step on this!" So much for my correcting the record.

This lady in white then squeezed us into a room the size of my poolside shower. Directly above the paper-cloaked examination table hovered ivory-tinted plastic gulls. I started spinning the birds. Someone entered. She smiled broadly as she watched the acrobatic birds.

"Doc," my daughter said, "this is my dad."

This doctor looked like a teenaged Susan Lucci. She said, "He doesn't look old enough." That flippant comment fueled my ego for several months. The doctor attached a futuristic-looking device called a fetal monitor to my daughter. A tiny, flashing heart winked at me. I heard my grandchild's heartbeat in quadraphonic stereo. The doctor said, "Put on a good show for Grandpa, kid. This could be worth big bucks." My first coaching hurdle ended successfully.

That night, I visited the library. I piled volumes describing natural childbirth on the floor. They described methods of childbirth, fearless childbirth and natural childbirth. Passersby stared at my leaning tower of books.

I studied long hours. I took extensive notes. I knew all about breathing and contractions. Bring on baby.

The week before my first refresher course on natural birth, my wife and daughter began rethinking my coaching. I sensed it in their whispering huddles. Eventually, I was told how they agonized about releasing me gently from the project. Watching these two women in my life share the experience, and weighing their delicate words resounding in my mind, I said on the eve of my first class, "Why don't you two take that lesson without me?"

"But Dad, you were so excited."

Trying to make my dismissal easier for them, I said, "It's better as a mother-daughter thing. Besides, with Mom's beeper, you can get her." They accepted my suggestion with sympathetic smiles. Mother and daughter bonded. After every class, they sipped tea at a local diner. Endlessly, they spoke the jargon of contractions. They designed baby rooms. I accepted my benching. More time to relax.

The patient and primed women of the house boldly awaited the birth.

A day before the predicted birth date, Steve surprised us with a weekend visit. The following Monday, however, a road game required his flying halfway across the country. On that crisp February morn, I steered my car over crackling ice-plated asphalt and left him at the local airport. Four hours later, I followed that same trail, sloshing through melting ice. I took Mary-Kim for her routine checkup.

The office protocol changed. The doctor's inner chamber opened immediately. Again, the nurse weighed my daughter. I tried to peek at the scale. Then another nurse led us into another phone-booth–sized waiting room. *No gulls flying here,* I thought. No one smiled. My daughter was ordered to lie down. The familiar stereo attachments of the past were plugged and pasted all around her tummy. Baby's heartbeat resounded. I sensed a problem knitted in the nurse's brow as she recorded the heartbeat numbers.

A hurried nurse brushed by me and disconnected the monitor. She whisked us to a second-floor room. This time, sonar-type paraphernalia—something you might see in a nuclear submarine—was connected to the expectant mother. When finished, we returned to the reception area to await instructions. The nurses scurried out. One took my daughter's hand blurting, "Mrs. S., Doc wants to give you an internal right now."

"I'll wait here," I said.

Ten minutes later my Mary-Kim returned. She said, "We're going to the hospital, Grandpa. I lost amniotic fluid. They'll induce birth."

I was a veteran. I watched when my middle child, Peter, was induced. Still, our original script never included this. "Just a routine checkup" replayed in my mind. I opened the car door and helped Mary-Kim in. "Dad," she said, "I'm a little scared."

A little scared. My body quivered. I refused to reveal my panic. "Baby, don't worry. I've been here before with your mom," I rasped out.

The hospital expected her. An attendant stood at the entrance. I felt like a VIP. Some forms required signatures. Emerging baby or not, signing these documents provided her admission ticket. Characters in World War II spy movies generated fewer documents.

After filling them out, I excused myself and jogged toward the telephone at the end of the hall. A phone warden leaned on it. He looked like a Russian power lifter. In Homer's time, he might have entertained himself by rolling boulders off cliffs at unsuspecting seamen.

I pleaded, "May I use the phone? My daughter is having a baby." The man's pencil smile, swamped by bulbous jowls, grudgingly nodded in the affirmative. I made three frantic calls. The Cyclops watched. I called Adele at home.

I called her office. I beeped her. No answers. I thanked the behemoth and sprinted back.

In the delivery room, my attitude changed. Immersed in Coach Dad spirit, I prepared to offer my expertise. She needed Dad now. The delivery nurse said, "Mr. S., we'll dress her and give you clothes to take to the car. Then come right back." I gave up my fight on the Mr. S. label.

Back in the game, I sprinted to the elevator and pumped the down button. Later my daughter told me that she corrected the nurse. "He's my dad, not Mr. S." The nurse answered, "Dad must be nervous. He dropped your bag of clothes near the elevator." They both laughed.

I continued my dash to my car. Coach Dad lived again. I huffed back to the waiting room. Adele startled me. Disappointment braked my walk. With her arrival, my coaching day ended. I briefed my wife and wistfully watched as she took the elevator. With drooping head, I drove home.

Two hours later my daughter called from the delivery room.

"Dad," she said, "bring my black makeup kit."

"Still in labor?"

"Yes. Nothing yet. Love ya, Dad."

An hour after that, Coach Mom also retired. Steve, the head coach in this arena, returned after several connecting flights. Moments after his appearance, my granddaughter Alee was born. So much for my rerun as a natural childbirth coach. None of that mattered. I became a granddad.

F. Anthony D'Alessandro

THE FAMILY CIRCUS   By Bil Keane

©2001
BKI

"When I grow up and have kids,
how would you like the job as grandparents?"

Reprinted with permission of Bil Keane.

Catch and Release

Every son, at one point or another, defies his father, fights him, departs from him, only to return to him—if he is lucky—closer and more secure than before.

Leonard Bernstein

An old hurt lay buried between father and son, watered with silence, fertilized by time. It grew strong, as such hurts do, when left neglected by forgiveness.

Sarah warily watched it grow between her husband and his father. She was there when it was planted and continually sought a way to uproot the ugly old thing.

The only balm she had found so far was Joshua, her son. Each man showed the child unrestrained love—as if the feelings they used to have for each other needed an outlet, a beneficiary, an heir.

Joshua loved Grandpa Bill and his stories of growing up way back in the woods. And for two weeks every summer, Sarah would take Joshua to Grandpa's house by the lake.

There on the dock, Grandpa Bill and Joshua would sit, fishing from sunup until she called them in for supper. Yet,

Sarah never let Joshua go out in the boat—he was too little, she'd say.

One summer, after much pleading by Grandpa Bill and Joshua, Sarah finally agreed to let the boy go out on the boat. The one condition Sarah set was that Joshua would have to wait until after his seventh birthday later that month.

Ted never came along on the visits to his father's house. But Sarah insisted Joshua get to know his grandpa, for Sarah regretted never knowing her own grandparents.

For Joshua's birthday, Ted gave him his first fishing pole. It was just a lightweight rod with a foolproof reel, but Joshua couldn't wait to go out on Grandpa Bill's lake.

Before the birthday dishes were done, Sarah had called Grandpa Bill and arranged for Joshua to go out in the boat. When Ted found out, he was furious!

"It's the boy's first fishing trip, Sarah, and I wanted to take him out myself," Ted said.

"Then go with them," Sarah said, as she dried the last of the dishes.

"You know that's not possible," Ted replied flatly.

Sarah threw down her dishtowel and turned on Ted. Glowering she said, "I know no such thing, Ted Wilkins! All I know is that Joshua wants nothing more than to go fishing with his grandpa and his father. What kind of man are you to let an old argument stop you from making your son happy?"

Ted's indignation deflated before Sarah's logic. She had a point, and it struck him to the heart.

"Well, he won't let me on his property, let alone in the boat," Ted said under his breath, as he turned away.

"He will after I'm through with him!" Sarah replied, as she headed for the phone.

It was a long conversation, but a fruitful one, as Grandpa Bill reluctantly agreed to let Ted join their party.

Their greeting, after so many years, was cool and conducted under the watchful eye of Sarah—but one look at Joshua's face set both men in their place. The boy was positively glowing. This had been his secret birthday wish!

They loaded the boat with enough fishing gear to sink the *Titanic*, as each man took his own tackle box of secrets. Sarah securely wrapped Joshua in a bright orange life vest, which came all the way up to his nose when he sat down in the wide aluminum boat.

As Sarah released the bowline and pushed the boat away from the dock, Ted and Grandpa Bill called out, "Aren't you coming along?"

"No, fishing is a guy thing," she replied, as she waved them off. "Have fun!"

Ted sat in the bow stubbornly facing due starboard, with Joshua in the broad middle seat by the rods. Grandpa Bill ran the outboard, looking everywhere but at the bow.

Each man took turns showing Joshua how to spinner fish for walleye, how to troll for trout, how to work a bass plug. But never once did either man speak to the other— only to Joshua.

They tried the rock banks, the deep shaded pools, the underwater shelves, even along the sheer granite wall. But after a full day they were snookered, not one fish among them. Finally they tried floating worms off the bottom near the reed-choked sandbar.

"This isn't what I thought it would be like," Joshua pouted, as they sat rocking in silence. He could sense the tension between his father and his grandpa, but he didn't understand it.

"Well, Joshua, some days are like this," Ted explained.

Just then, Joshua's line took off—in an instant both men were talking to him.

"Keep your pole up!" Grandpa shouted excitedly.

"Reel, Son, reel!" Ted said, with equal enthusiasm. "Check your drag."

Joshua didn't have a clue what that meant. He'd never really caught anything big enough to take out much line.

"Dad, reach over and check his drag, he doesn't know how," Ted quickly added.

The fish paused in his battle for freedom and Grandpa Bill reached over the struggling boy's hands. With practiced skill, he took the line between his forefinger and thumb; one tug told him the drag was way too tight.

The old trout was not tiring; in fact he had other ideas. Angrily, he rose to the surface, jumping into the hot summer air some forty feet from the boat. He flashed a rainbow of silver and green, as the water flipped from his powerful body.

Then came the sound both men knew meant disaster—the twanging sorrow of line separating under too much strain.

Grandpa Bill still had a tentative hold on the line between his fingers, but not for long.

"Grab the line up the pole, Ted," he shouted.

Ted dove for the rendered line whipping through the pole guides.

Joshua fell backward into the bottom of the boat, as the tension on the pole suddenly ceased. Grandpa Bill grabbed the monofilament line and began hauling it in hand over fist.

Bill took in as much line as he could before getting his hands caught up in knots, then Ted would take over until he, too, was entangled. By then his father would be free to take over once more. Palms were cut and fingers sliced by the struggling line, yet each man continued without complaint, for it was Joshua's first fish.

"I see him! Get the net, Joshua, get the net," Ted hollered.

Joshua reached over the tipping boat's side and scooped the bright green net under the trout. But the fish was not done just yet.

With a powerful thrust of his tail, he jumped three feet straight up. Thinking fast, Joshua stood on his seat and swirled the net after him, catching the fish mid-air like a butterfly!

Together, Ted and Bill grabbed Joshua's life vest, hauling the boy inboard to safety.

The two men and the boy laughed hysterically, as a five-pound trout slimed the bottom of the boat. Joshua had caught his first fish—and set more than the boat to rights.

All the way home, the three relived their part in the triumph like old friends.

Sarah was absolutely amazed when they neared the dock, for each of them vied to recount the story. The cold distant manner was gone from their voices, as each man cut into the story to compliment the other for some daring act in the tale; while Joshua, his chest lifted with pride, held the stringer with one single, but very important, fish.

Sarah took a photo of the three of them, arms about each other, with Joshua and his fish in the middle. All were grinning like they had caught the biggest fish in the world.

"Hey, Dad, let's go show him how to clean it," Ted said, as they headed for the dock.

As they walked away, Sarah smiled to herself. All it had taken was one boy and one fish to make them a family again.

Dee Berry

THE FAMILY CIRCUS® By Bil Keane

©2001 BKI

"Let me sit there, Daddy."

Now I Understand My Dad

On this day last year, on Father's Day, my father died. He had gone into intensive care only the day before, his heart not working right. As word went out, each of his six grown children sped toward Venice Hospital in Florida, where he lay on a table in a small room, attached to various monitors and machines. Late that night, we stood around him with our mother, holding his hands and grasping his arms and speaking close to his face as he strained against some powerful force that kept on pulling him sway.

"Good-bye, Dad," we said. "We love you, Dad. Thank you, Dad. Oh, no . . ."

A breath left his body under our hands, and we turned to watch the graphs and numbers on the machines, and then we made an involuntary collective sound, a great groan, and he was gone. It was early morning and eerily quiet, and we gripped each other's hands around him and someone whispered, "Hey, you know what day it is? It's Father's Day."

He was seventy-five years old. With his passing, I was abruptly stripped of any illusions of my own immortality, no longer might I comfort myself with the thought that he was next in line ahead of me. For any boy, that is one of his father's silent function; to stand as a shield between his son and the abyss. With that mythical protection gone, I was newly alone and vulnerable and, more so than ever, responsible for my life.

I remember being five years old when, one morning after a snowstorm, he carried me on his shoulders for a mile from our apartment into town. As he marched bravely through the snowdrifts, I put my hands around his head to hold on, inadvertently covering his eyes with my mittens. "I can't see," my father said, but he walked on nevertheless, a blind hero making his way with me on his back through a strange, magical landscape of untrodden snow.

He had returned recently from World War II, and this ride would become my first experience with him to take hold as a genuine, lasting memory.

As he was buried, there were other memories that flooded in, but later I found myself trying to put my feelings about him into perspective. How much of a father, really, had he been? Why hadn't I grieved more over losing him? Had I ever forgiven him for his shortcomings and faults? Had I been able to recognize, and truly appreciate, what he gave me? What was the actual journey that he and I had taken together?

From my teenage years onward, I had expected a great deal from my dad in terms of encouragement. I had assumed that he would help me defy certain traditions or conventions and give me courage; but that kind of assistance, in whatever way I was demanding it, seldom came. Over the years, I had learned to accept this gap between expectation and reality, to adjust to it, but it had taken even longer to put my silent resentment to rest.

I remembered telling him, after senior year of high school, that I wanted to be an actor. He launched into a speech about the instability of such a career: "The odds are you'd wind up holding a tin cup on the corner."

One time, while I was still living at home, we argued over my decision to take acting lessons in New York. He stormed up to my room, where I met him at the doorway. We stood toe-to-toe and I held up my fist and glared at him, trembling, and said the issue was settled unless he wanted to fight. The red fury drained from his face, and he turned, shoulders slumped, to walk slowly back downstairs.

Ever since that moment, I have wondered what would have happened if he had slugged me. I never knew if I had won too easily. A rite of passage had taken place in a second, leaving me on my own without his resistance.

But, general attitude of caution continued. After I did become a professional actor, for example, he came to see me in a Broadway show and later remarked, "Of course, it would be wise to have something else to fall back on."

I fell back, so to speak, on newspaper work, only to quit when my first book was published a few years later. We had a family celebration during which he took me aside and said. "Now is the perfect time, with this credential, for you to apply to a corporation." When I told him I intended to remain self-employed for as long as possible, he fell silent.

As the years went by, in response to my unspoken pleas for a father's blind enthusiasm and faith, his expressions of doubt and fear became predictable. As late in the game as 1990, when a book of mine about Ted Turner and CNN was about to be published, he was still worrying about my security: "Hey, I've got an idea. Why don't you ask Mr. Turner for a job?"

Long before then, I'd realized that my father's warnings and his talk about safety were his means of relating to me. I knew, also, that while I might have wished to hear him discuss some detail of my work, even to hear him say he hated this or that about it, he felt unable to do so. In earlier years, I had thought he didn't care; but, over time, I came to understand that he was offering what he could.

I also began to realize that in some ways he had even inspired me—not by words, but by what he had done. He had come home from a terrifying war to raise six kids in a house with a yard. He had returned, with so many other young men of his generation, to create order and stability and safety for those in his care, and to give them a future.

He spent two decades in advertising and longer in real estate, meanwhile always taking us on vacations, sending us through college and, as we grew up and scattered, writing frequent letters to us and finding excuses to plan reunions. He and my mother had created and sustained a family. My father had provided a foundation, with continuity, enabling his children to feel strong enough to go their individual ways.

Just two weeks before he died, my father held a celebration for Mom on her birthday. We flew from our separate homes to Florida and, during our stay, joined him on a fishing trip. It was one of many such outings that we had shared with him over the years. Aboard the chartered boat Dad was happy to be with us, but he did not look well, and soon we began to wish that he had stayed on land.

We had no idea then how badly he felt or how perilous his condition had become. Looking back, it's clear that he had deliberately kept all of that hidden from us to avoid spoiling our fun.

The morning we were about to leave Florida, he pulled me aside and pointed to a mysterious box about three feet long and two feet deep. I looked inside and found, to my astonishment, hundreds of clippings related to almost everything I had done in my life.

"I figured you might like to have this," my father said.

We hugged each other, not knowing it was the last time,

but he must have sensed that he would not be around much longer to give it to me in person. I lifted that heavy box, with so much of myself inside, and carried it away.

All of a sudden I understood—no matter how negative his words had seemed to me—that nothing could erase his concrete act of having filled that big old box, piece by piece, ever since I had left home in the sixties. Through all that time, it turned out, he had been there—sharing that part of my life.

Then two weeks later came word that he was dying, and it happened on Father's Day, and then came the weeks and months of thinking about him until now, when a full year has gone by without having him around, and I miss him beyond words. What I miss most, ironically, is that time long ago when I was a boy trusting his father to carry him blindly through life and to protect him. The security, it turned out, lay in simply knowing he was there.

And the other day I found myself walking along with my own son, Benjamin, who is five years old. When I lifted him onto my shoulders, he reached his hands reflexively around my head so they covered my eyes. "I can't see," I said, but his little fingers maintained their grip. I walked on in the sudden darkness, feeling his weight above me, groping, the way my father had done for me when I was exactly the same age. And I felt, then, the first surge of hot tears since Dad died, and found myself becoming a new blind hero in the strange, magical land of fatherhood where the journey always begins, in hope and uncertainty, over again.

Hank Whittemore

4

BALANCING WORK AND FAMILY

The happiest days of my life have been the few which I have passed at home in the bosom of my family.

Thomas Jefferson

A Handful of Blackberries

A man's rootage is more important than his leafage.

Woodrow Wilson

Just as I began a new job in New York, I had to learn another important job: father. At the office, we had three new projects in the works, and at home, I had a young son who was growing fast and needed me. To say I felt stretched is an understatement. This was never more clear than one Thursday when, for the second time in a week, I was packing for a business trip.

"I know how important your job is," my wife, Ellen, said. "But it would be nice if you could be home more often."

I knew she was right. My son, Luke, was turning three, and I didn't like being away so much either.

"Yesterday," Ellen said, "Luke wandered around the house saying, 'Where is my daddy? Where *is* he?'"

Ellen wanted to discuss this further, but there wasn't time. "Honey, I really have to make this plane," I said. "Let's talk tomorrow when I get back."

In Chicago my meeting ended early, and I suddenly had a couple of hours to kill. So I called on Dan, an old family friend who had retired to the area to be near his grandchildren.

Dan had once farmed in Indiana, where my father was a country doctor. Now, as we sat at his kitchen table, he began to reminisce about what a fine man my dad had been. "He'd get you well no matter what it took," Dan said. "I don't think there was a soul in that county who didn't love your father."

Then, to my surprise, Dan confided that after he'd recovered from prostate cancer, he had developed a serious depression that he just couldn't shake. "I didn't care about getting better," he said. "But your daddy got me through it."

His remembrance touched me, and I put my hand on his shoulder. "He cared about his patients a lot," I agreed.

Indeed, I knew how devoted my father was to his patients. But I also knew that his devotion and hard work came with price—a price that seemed high to his family.

Dad was a tall, lean man whose sky-blue eyes could see straight through anything. But despite his no-nonsense gaze and way of speaking, he was always easy to talk to.

We lived on a farm, not because we were farmers, but because many of Dad's patients were. They often paid in livestock instead of cash, so he found a farm to put his fees out to graze.

There was no denying my father's love of hunting, however, and he always kept bird dogs. I would train them until they were ready to hunt. He left that chore to me, he said, because he didn't have the patience. Yet what he did or did not want to do, often seemed to hinge on what I might learn from doing it myself. My dad taught me everything. He showed me how to use a handsaw and mark a right angle, for instance—skills that enabled me to cobble together a raft for the pond beyond our meadow. One corner ended up out of line, but Dad helped me launch it without comment on its fault. His best way of helping was to ask questions that allowed me to realize things myself. When I was afraid I'd have to fight a guy at school he asked, "Can you take him?"

"I think so."

"Then you don't have to. Here, stand up and give me a shove."

He made me push him until I nearly knocked him down. "See, you just have to give him an idea of how strong you are. What if you try that and see if he doesn't back off?" I did, and it worked.

That was the kind of help I needed from Dad. But the summer I turned thirteen, he virtually disappeared from my life, and I didn't know what to do.

So many people were sick, and Dad was gone most of the time seeing patients. He was also building a new office and trying to earn enough to pay for an X-ray machine. Often the phone would ring while we were at supper, and I'd hear him say, "Be right there." Then Mom would cover his plate with a pie tin and put it in the oven to wait.

Many times he'd be gone for an hour or more. Then his car would crunch on the gravel drive, and I'd run downstairs to sit with him while he ate. He'd ask about my day and give me whatever advice I had to have about the farm. But that was about all he had energy for.

As that year went on, I worried about him, and I worried about me. I missed his help. I missed joking around and just being together. *Maybe he doesn't like me as much as he did,* I thought. *Maybe I've done something to disappoint him.* He'd been helping me become a man, and I didn't think I had a prayer of getting that done without his guidance.

The pond beyond the meadow was ringed with reeds and cattails. I liked to fish there. I'd never caught a big one, hooking only sunnies and a few catfish. But big fish were in there. I'd seen them jump, making a glistening turbulence in the mist of early morning. Sometimes the ripples would carry so far they'd reach the shore.

That summer I used to sit on my raft and think of ways to lure my father back. My mother wanted us to take a vacation, but he nixed that because he had so much work.

One day my mother and I stood in the kitchen and talked about him. "See if you can get him to go fishing," she finally said. "Even just one evening off will help."

The next day I began my campaign to get Dad down to our pond. I planned to make a fire, roast ears of corn and fry up whatever we could catch. The problem was getting my father to change into old clothes and take off a few hours.

Finally, one Friday I simply bullied him into it. I met his car when he came home and pulled him into the mudroom, where we changed our work clothes. "We're going fishing," I said. "And that is that."

And we did! As we stood on the pond's edge casting into the fading sunlight, I was still amazed that I'd persuaded him to do it. Soon I went to gather wood for a fire. We hadn't had any luck yet, but we could still roast the corn and talk.

While I worked, I watched him cast into a deep hole near a fallen red oak. "Please let him catch a fish," I whispered to myself. "*Any* fish—just let him catch something."

Almost as if my thought had raised the fish to the lure, a bass struck his line. "Whoa, boss!" he yelled, and the moss-colored fish took to the air. It looked humongous and put up a good fight as Dad expertly reeled it into his net, then brought it to me by the fire.

"Hey, Dad," I said. "How about that!"

He looked young, happy and proud. I dredged his fish

in cornmeal and fried it over the fire. We sat on a stone eating our supper.

"That was some meal," he said when he finished. "I don't know when I've liked anything more."

My father made a pot of coffee, while I went to the edge of the meadow where the briers were borne down with ripe blackberries. I picked our dessert and carried it back in my baseball cap. We had the berries with our coffee and watched the sun make dazzling colors in the western sky. My father ate slowly, one berry at a time, savoring each. Then out of the blue, he began telling me how much he cared about me.

"You know, Son, you're going to be a success in life," he said. "I know that because I never have to ask you to do something twice. But more than that, you're a good kid."

The expression on his face was of such warmth and pride that I felt utterly blessed.

Times like this were all too rare as my father's practice grew ever larger. But whenever I needed it, I'd reach back to that moment by the pond, remembering how good it felt when Dad was with me.

"Yes, sir," Dan said, interrupting my memories. "Your father was some fine man. And his medicine wasn't just pills and shots. He thought a lot about people. He could always understand what someone was going through."

"Yes. Sometimes he did," I said, looking momentarily away.

Then Dan told me, "When I was at my worst, I said to him, 'Doc, give me one reason to beat this depression.' And do you know what he said?"

Dan stared across the table until I reestablished eye contact. "He said, 'Blackberries. Think of a handful of blackberries and how wonderful that is. To pick a handful of blackberries, sit down with someone you love very much and eat them. Think of that and tell me life's not worth the fight. You have a wonderful wife and three fine kids. Take some time with them. It's family we live for—not just ourselves.'

"That's what he said, and I've never forgotten it," Dan finished. "I think it saved my life."

My hands were quivering. All I could do was stare back at him. I was feeling so many emotions that I could muster not one word.

On the plane home, I closed my eyes and thought about me and my dad. I knew what that day by the pond had meant to me. But I had never known what it meant to him. Now, in my mind's eye, I could see him standing at the edge of the water, the bass on his line, so full of joy. *How wide the ripples spread,* I thought. *How far they reach.*

Suddenly, I found myself staring out the airplane window, hoping that the flight would get in on time. I planned to be home before dark for a change—to play in the yard with my son in the fading light of day.

W. W. Meade
As appeared in Chicken Soup for the Country Soul

Family Picture

No one on his deathbed ever said, "I wish I had spent more time on my business."

Paul Tsongas

I was sitting in my favorite chair, studying for the final stages of my doctoral degree, when Sarah announced herself in my presence with a question: "Daddy, do you want to see my family picture?"

"Sarah, Daddy's busy. Come back in a little while, Honey."

Good move, right? I was busy. A week's worth of work to squeeze into a weekend. You've been there.

Ten minutes later she swept back into the living room. "Daddy, let me show you my picture."

The heat went up around my collar. "Sarah," I said, "come back later. This is important."

Three minutes later she stormed into the living room, got three inches from my nose and barked with all the power a five-year-old could muster: "Do you want to see it or don't you?" The assertive woman in training.

"No," I told her, "I don't."

With that, she zoomed out of the room and left me

alone. And somehow, being alone at that moment wasn't as satisfying as I thought it would be. I felt like a jerk. (Don't agree so loudly.) I went to the front door.

"Sarah," I called, "could you come back inside a minute, please? Daddy would like to see your picture."

She obliged with no recriminations and popped up on my lap.

It was a great picture. She'd even given it a title. Across the top, in her best printing, she had inscribed: "OUR FAMILY BEST."

"Tell me about it," I said.

"Here is Mommy [a stick figure with long, yellow, curly hair], here is me standing by Mommy [with a smiley face], here is our dog Katie, and here is Missy [her little sister was a stick figure lying in the street in front of the house, about three times bigger than anyone else]." It was a pretty good insight into how she saw our family.

"I love your picture, Honey," I told her. "I'll hang it on the dining room wall, and each night when I come home from work and from class (which was usually around 10:00 P.M.), I'm going to look at it."

She took me at my word, beamed ear to ear and went outside to play. I went back to my books. But for some reason I kept reading the same paragraph over and over.

Something was making me uneasy.

Something about Sarah's picture.

Something was missing.

I went to the front door. "Sarah," I called, "could you come back inside a minute, please? I want to look at your picture again, Honey."

Sarah crawled back into my lap. I can close my eyes right now and see the way she looked. Cheeks rosy from playing outside. Pigtails, Strawberry Shortcake tennis shoes. A Cabbage Patch doll named Nellie tucked limply under her arm.

I asked my little girl a question, but I wasn't sure I wanted to hear the answer.

"Honey . . . there's Mommy, and Sarah, and Missy. Katie the dog is in the picture, and the sun, and the house, and squirrels and birdies. But Sarah . . . *where is your daddy?*"

"You're at the library," she said.

With that simple statement, my little princess stopped time for me. Lifting her gently off my lap, I sent her back to play in the spring sunshine. I slumped back in my chair with a swirling head and blood pumping furiously through my heart. Even as I type these words into the computer, I can feel those sensations all over again. It was a frightening moment. The fog lifted from my preoccupied brain for a moment—and suddenly I could see. But what I saw scared me to death. It was like being in a ship and coming out of the fog in time to see a huge, sharp rock knifing through the surf just off the port bow.

Sarah's simple pronouncement—"You're at the library"— got my attention big-time.

I hung the drawing on the dining room wall, just as I promised my girl. And through those long, intense weeks preceding the oral defense of my dissertation, I stared at that revealing portrait. It happened every night in the silence of my sleeping home, as I consumed my late-night, warmed-over dinners. I didn't have the guts to bring the issue up to Barbara. And she had the incredible insight to let it rest until I had the courage to deal with it. I finally finished my degree program. I was "Dr. Rosberg" now, and I guess should have been a big deal for me. But frankly, there wasn't much joy in my life.

One night after graduation, Barbara and I were lying in bed together and I found myself working up the nerve to ask her a few questions. It was late, it was dark, and as I murmured my first question, I was praying Barbara had already fallen asleep. "Barb, are you sleeping?"

"No," she said. *Rats!* I thought to myself. *Now I'm committed.*

"Barbara, you've obviously seen Sarah's picture taped on the dining room wall. Why haven't you said anything?"

"Because I know how much it wounded you, Gary." Words from a woman wise beyond her twenty-something years. At that point, I asked the toughest question I've ever asked anyone in my life.

"Barb . . . I want to come home. Can I do it?"

Twenty seconds of silence followed. It seemed like I held my breath for an hour. "Gary," Barb said carefully, "the girls and I love you very much. We want you home. But you haven't been here. I've felt like a single parent for years."

The words look cold in print, but she said them with restraint and tenderness. It was just plain, unvarnished truth. My little girl had drawn the picture, and now her mom was speaking the words. My life had been out of control, my family was on automatic pilot, and I had a long road ahead of me if I wanted to win them back.

But I had to win them back. Now that the fog had lifted, it suddenly became the most important thing in my life.

Gary Rosberg

A Father's Interpretation of
1 Corinthians 13

The only rock I know that stays steady, the only institution I know that works, is the family.

Lee Iacocca

Though I manage a staff of many but have not managed my family, I have managed nothing.

And though I have negotiated the deal of deals while neglecting my children, I have negated the opportunity of a lifetime—in fact, my God-appointed duty as father.

Though I become a head of state but fail to assume my role as head of the household, I am but unemployed.

And though I have trained personnel, enduring hours, days and years but have not trained my child in the way he/she should go, I may claim not the title of teacher.

Though I consult executives, yet have not been available to my own children for consultation, I remain the misguided one.

Though I prioritize my workday/career, and do not prioritize my home life, I have prioritized a progressive distancing of those who in fact mean the most to me.

Though I earn great wealth and respect among my

peers through business accomplishment, yet I fail to earn the respect of my wife and children, I am reduced to a very poor man.

Though I travel the world pursuing my goals, yet am not available to drive my son to a ballgame or my daughter to her recital, I have indeed boarded the wrong plane.

And though I bestow all my accomplishments to provide for my family, and though I work until utter exhaustion, but do not make time with my family a priority, it profits me nothing.

And yes, I must keep in perspective that if a man won't work, neither shall he eat, and if a man won't provide for his family he is worse than an infidel.

Should I choose, however, to tolerate the devastating demands society has placed on family values, God help me, for I have failed to recognize that toleration is the first step to deterioration.

Time can never be recaptured once it is passed. Time will not even pause for a moment. Nor will Time be forgiving as it is fleeing away.

Time spent together cannot be measured, for those precious moments become priceless memories to the beholder.

When I was a child, I thought like a child, cherishing each moment together when I took my daddy's hand. When I became a daddy, I recaptured that moment each time my little girl took her daddy's hand.

For now those memories seem as fresh as yesterday, and had I known then what I have learned until now, might I have spent just an extra minute at home instead of at the office?

And now abide Time Management, Quality Time, Quantity Time, these three; but the greatest of these is TIME itself spent with your children!

John G. "Giovanni" Grippando

Statistics

The wife of a statistician, determined to find a job, cajoled her husband into staying home for a day to take care of their children.

When she returned, he handed her the following report:

Dried tears, nine times
Tied shoes, thirteen times
Toy balloons purchased, sixteen
Average life of a balloon, ten seconds
Cautioned children not to cross street, twenty-one times
Number of times children crossed street, twenty-one
Number of times I will do this again, zero.

Bits & Pieces

THE FAMILY CIRCUS ® **By Bil Keane**

©2001 BKI

"I'm passing the torch to you."

Working from Home

My family recently had the bright idea that I should spend a day working from home.

When I mapped out such a day, I had imagined working diligently in my den until I took a mid-morning cookie snack with the kids. After that, I'd return to my computer until my wife prepared a picnic in the backyard.

Later, I would sit at my desk watching my kids play with the neighbors on our front lawn. Finally, I'd knock off an hour early and go for a family walk around the block.

This is how I imagined it. I even joked to myself that if I liked it so much, I just might telecommute for the rest of my life.

Yeah . . . . right!

During the first hour of my workday at home, I barely touched a shred of work. The children kept running into my den to tell me important things like:

1. Knock-knock jokes.
2. Who touched whom first.
3. Why Mommy screamed really loud when she saw the mess in the playroom, and is now lying down in the back-seat of the car . . . with the doors locked.

Sometime, around 10:30 A.M., I decided to take that mid-morning cookie break.

Moments later, I walked into the garage, banged on the car door, and asked my wife what happened to the Oreos.

"I told the kids to leave you some," she said through the closed car window.

"There's one."

She shrugged. "That's something."

"It would be," I said, "if the creamed filling wasn't scraped out of it."

I held the cookie to the glass. "Who's teeth-marks do these look like?"

She wasn't any help, so I returned to my den and began writing. That is, until my wife walked in.

"What's the matter," I asked. "Couldn't find anything to do in the glove compartment?"

She frowned. "Are you busy?"

I collapsed my shoulders.

"I need to run to the store," she continued.

"So?"

"And, I need you to jump the car battery . . . it ran down in the middle of 'A Bridge over Troubled Water.'"

I mumbled to myself all the way to the garage, and back to my desk. Then, I think I managed to paperclip some papers together before my children inquired about lunch . . . thirty-eight times. After telling them over and over again to wait until their mom gets home, I finally tacked a sign to my door that read: Go Ask Someone Else!

And that worked really well, up to the point that the neighbor called to ask me where my kids might find their mother, and did I really have amnesia.

I told him to send my kids home. Frustrated, I slapped together peanut butter and jelly sandwiches for the kids and myself. We ate in front of the TV. Just as I was cleaning up, my wife walked in.

"Sorry I'm late," she said.

"Where were you?" I huffed. "I haven't done a single thing today!"

"The grocery store."

"For two hours?"

"I ran into Barb from Toddlercize," she explained. "She's really depressed—her baby has crib head."

"And?"

"And, she needed to be held."

I headed for the door. "That's it, I have to go back to work," I announced.

"Why?"

"I left something there."

"What?"

"My sanity."

Ken Swarner

My Biggest Fan

A famous singer once contracted to appear at a Paris opera house. Ticket sales boomed, and the night of the concert found the house full and every ticket sold.

A feeling of anticipation and excitement was in the air as the house manager stepped out on the stage and announced, "Ladies and gentlemen, thank you for your enthusiastic support, but I have news that may be disappointing to some. An accident, not serious in nature but serious enough, will prevent the man you have come to hear from performing tonight." He went on to give the name of the understudy who would step into the role, but the crowd groaned and drowned it out. The excitement in the audience turned to bitter disappointment and frustration as the opera began.

The stand-in artist gave the performance everything he had. Throughout the evening, there had been nothing but an uneasy silence. Even at the end, no one applauded.

Then from the balcony, the thin voice of a little girl broke the silence. "Daddy," she called out, "I think you were wonderful."

The crowd broke into thunderous applause.

Bits & Pieces

Where Am I Going So Fast?

Most days go by like torpedoes as I drive to work. Yellow lines slip under my wheels while the trees rush past my car. Where am I going so fast?

To my left then my right, I can count the smiles on one hand. I'm not one of them. All of these people, maybe looking forward to lunch and getting home. And they haven't even started the day. Why? Where are we going so fast?

Are they what they wanted to be when they grew up? Do they walk out front doors and look up in wonder at the sun? Could they tell you how the wind felt against their skin as they picked up the newspaper? If you asked them to describe the exact color of their children's eyes, what would they say? As for me, I also often move through life with dollar-bill wings, needing to win but forgetting to smile.

Finally, I'm at work. Fourteen phone messages, needing fourteen different pieces of me. I swear to myself that I'll take a day off soon, but "soon" has a sneaky way of becoming "someday."

Run to a meeting with an armload of hurry. Projects crammed in pockets, knowing I want to, need to, must do well. For lunch, I slam down a sandwich. Then, off again, through the halls, jockeying for position in a corporate race, with too few pit stops and too much fear. And, many faces going by look how I feel. I consider stopping them to ask if they're happy. But, of course, I don't. Further down the hall, I wonder how many would have said, "Yes" or just lied.

As I said, most days go by like torpedoes. But not yesterday. Because, through it all, this quick, chaotic moving, I saw it, finally glimpsed the lesson when ... Matthew, my two-year-old, woke up at 5:17 A.M. His cries urged me from hard dreams. And, when you're tired and worn, waking up to your child's cries can be nails on a chalkboard. Long jagged nails that keep getting louder until you throw off the sheets and curse the alarm.

So, I made my exhausted way into his room though I couldn't have told you the color of the carpet. Because, I was already thinking about the day ahead. I walked over to Matthew's crib and picked him up. But I may have missed his first smile of the morning because I was thinking about morning meetings.

Then, I sat and held him. He put his head down against my chest. But I may have missed him looking up at me while I was trying to find the remote to catch the news. And, that's when I realized the only news that mattered was the child in my arms.

For, in that moment, I realized I'd been far away, missing my son, missing my life. Because, as I searched for the remote control, Matthew reached his hand out and touched my lips. I was about to move it, but then my eyes couldn't leave his fingers, couldn't deny the fact that I saw the future there. Those hands dipping in fingerpaints, scooping out pumpkins, throwing a baseball, wrestling with his brother, hugging his mom, wiping awkward teenage tears, signing a driver's license then a marriage

license, holding his sleeping baby daughter, helping his
father out of a chair when I'm older. I saw those gentle fingers become a boy's then a man's. It happened quick . . .
and was gone. Like a firefly.

I saw all of that at 5:37 A.M. Could easily have missed it.
Again, I ask, "Where am I going so fast?"

Jim Warda

Employee of the Year

I have been enjoying my job a whole lot more now that Larry Johnson packed his belongings and moved out of our department. I don't want to appear insensitive, but you can't have someone with that much free time, and a calm disposition, dragging down you or your coworkers.

For years, my associates and I attended to our jobs just fine, and we all planned to stay there until we retired.

Then, Larry arrived last December. I took one look at him and called an emergency meeting in the break room.

"I don't want to panic anyone," I said, "but there's something peculiar about the new guy."

The staff looked concerned.

"Did anyone notice his clothes? They're pressed." A wave of fear spread across their faces.

"His complexion is clear. His hair is combed. His shoes are shined." People started to weep.

"You mean to tell us . . . ," Steve from accounting started to say.

"Yes," I interrupted. "I don't think he has kids."

Everyone screamed.

We sent a reconnaissance squad to Larry's desk to confirm my suspicions. "Sure enough," the squad leader reported back, "but it's worse than you thought. He's not even married."

The problems started immediately. While we were doing what we always did—shuttling kids to doctors' appointments, rushing home for forgotten school lunches and hawking Boy Scout fundraisers in the elevator—Larry was working late, arriving early and eating his dinner at his desk.

Then, the inevitable happened. The boss noticed.

"Has anyone noticed how hard Larry is working?!" he barked.

How could we tell our leader from the "Leave It to Beaver" generation that we had responsibilities to our children? He'd never understand.

"Maybe Larry would be a good candidate for that new job in Department Six," I suggested to the boss. "You'd look good, sir, for recommending him." And that's how we got rid of Larry "No Kids" Johnson.

The next day, Larry's replacement showed up with a hint of baby formula behind each ear and a dried macaroni necklace as her only accessory. I was the first to greet her. "So, do you plan to work overtime here?" I asked nervously.

She winced. "Do you see these dark circles around my eyes? I was up at the crack of dawn digging a pacifier out of the compost pile, and when I leave here, I have to drive ten giggly Brownies clear across town to the slaughter-house so they can earn their farming badge. Who has time to work?" She has my vote for Employee of the Year.

Ken Swarner

You Can Do Anything

You can't learn how to be strong and patient and brave, if you've only had wonderful things happen to you.

Mary Tyler Moore

Many years ago, my dad was diagnosed with a terminal heart condition. He was put on permanent disability and was unable to work at a steady job. He would be fine for quite a while, but would then fall suddenly ill and have to be admitted to the hospital.

He wanted to do something to keep himself busy, so he decided to volunteer at the local children's hospital. My dad loved kids. It was the perfect job for him. He ended up working with the terminally and critically ill children. He would talk to them and play with them and do arts and crafts with them. Sometimes, he would lose one of his kids. In certain instances, he would tell the grieving parents of these children that he would soon be with their child in heaven and that he would take care of them until they got there. He would also ask the parent if there was a message they would like to send with him for their child.

My dad's assurances seemed to help parents with their grieving. One of his kids was a girl who had been admitted with a rare disease that paralyzed her from the neck down. I don't know the name of the disease or what the prognosis usually is, but I do know that it was very sad for a girl around eight or nine years old. She couldn't do anything, and she was very depressed. My dad decided to try to help her. He started visiting her in her room, bringing paints, brushes and paper. He stood the paper up against a backing, put the paintbrush in his mouth and began to paint. He didn't use his hands at all. Only his head would move. He would visit her whenever he could and paint for her. All the while he would tell her, "See, you can do anything you set your mind to."

Eventually, she began to paint using her mouth, and she and my dad became friends. Soon after, the little girl was discharged because the doctors felt there was nothing else they could do for her. My dad also left the children's hospital for a little while because he became ill. Sometime later after my dad had recovered and returned to work, he was at the volunteer counter in the lobby of the hospital. He noticed the front doors open. In came the little girl who had been paralyzed, only this time she was walking. She ran straight over to my dad and hugged him really tight. She gave my dad a picture she had done using her hands. At the bottom it read, "Thank you for helping me walk."

My dad would cry every time he told us this story and so would we. He would say sometimes love is more powerful than doctors, and my dad—who died just a few months after the little girl gave him the picture—loved every single child in that hospital.

Tina Karratti

Taking the Time

I vividly remember some time back being caught in the undertow of too many commitments in too few days. It wasn't long before I was snapping at my wife and our children, choking down my food at mealtimes, and feeling irritated at those unexpected interruptions through the day. Before long, things around our home started reflecting the pattern of my hurry-up style. It was becoming unbearable.

I distinctly recall after supper one evening the words of our younger daughter, Colleen. She wanted to tell me about something important that had happened to her at school that day. She hurriedly began, "Daddy, I wanna tell you somethin' and I'll tell you really fast."

Suddenly realizing her frustration, I answered, "Honey, you can tell me . . . and you don't have to tell me really fast. Say it slowly."

I'll never forget her answer: "Then listen slowly."

Charles R. Swindoll

5

SPECIAL MOMENTS

When you're drawing up your first list of life's miracles, you might place near the top the first moment your baby smiles at you.

Bob Greene

Riding Tandem

In 1998, my father and I set out from Denver, Colorado, to take part in the Vietnam Challenge—a sixteen-day, twelve-hundred-mile bicycle trek from Hanoi in the north to Ho Chi Minh, a city in the south. It was my first time to Vietnam and my dad's second. He had been a fighter pilot in the Vietnam War, flying over a hundred missions, and he hadn't been back since.

Since I am blind, my father and I rode a tandem bike. I wasn't always ecstatic, however, to be connected nine hours a day to my dad.

Not only did we have to ride together, our feet spinning on the pedals at an identical pace, but we also dressed the part. We wore the same tight uniforms and helmets and, when my sunglasses broke early into our trip, my dad came to the rescue with an extra pair of his "coke-bottle" prescription sunglasses.

"We're twins," my father needled.

"Yeah, right," is all I could muster. Regularly, a team-mate would pull up beside us and yell, "Weihenmayer squared, how you doing?"

"I feel like a square in these dorky glasses," I'd mutter back.

And yet, for all my misgivings about my father, as we cycled forth, I learned more and more about this rather private man.

While passing the former DMZ, the demilitarized zone, my dad remarked, "I know this sounds corny, but even after all these years, when I hear President Kennedy's speech, 'Ask not what your country can do for you but what you can do for your country,' I still get choked up." He spoke the words as if he were admitting a precious secret. And maybe he was. I was astonished at my dad's ability to hang on to his optimism, his faith in country, when others around him became jaded.

I come from a generation of cynics. We were taught that patriotism was for the naive, and that it had died in the battlefields of South Vietnam. Even when I was younger, and the *Star Spangled Banner* played before a football game, my father would bellow out the words with unabashed gusto, his bass, ex-Marine Corps voice drowning out the mumbled sounds of me and my brothers. I'd feel my brother's elbow in my ribs and we'd both share an embarrassed chuckle.

In college, after completing a history of war class, I would argue with him, "You can't just blindly do what your country tells you to do. You have to follow your own conscience. You have to ask whether your country's cause is also your cause."

"Patriotism isn't learned in a textbook," he shot back angrily. "What if every American put his own concerns above those of his country? Where would we be now?" While I had made the argument more out of an exercise in historical debate, I was taken aback by the ferocity of his defense.

Halfway through the Vietnam Challenge, my dad and I faced our own challenge as we pedaled our tandem toward the Hai Van Pass. Rising 3,280 feet out of the coastal plains, this six-mile stretch of road with a ten-percent grade, separated the former North from the South. It was, by far, the most physically demanding part of our entire ride; on this hot and humid day, despite our differences, we would need to be a team.

My father had been the captain of the Princeton football team. He admitted that he wasn't the best athlete, but perhaps the most "enthusiastic." Twice, on kick-offs, he had hit his opponent so hard he had knocked himself out. My dad loved a challenge, and the Hai Van Pass was that and more.

For a while, we climbed gradually, but then the road became progressively steeper. As I pedaled, I couldn't stop thinking of our experience the day before in the dusty parking lot of the My Lai War Crimes Museum. I recalled my father's words, his reluctant tears.

I had heard him cry only twice in my life, once when his father died and again after the death of my mother. But there he was, hot tears rolling down and burning into his proud face. "I am not a war criminal," he said. "I had a friend, Gus," he continued, his words coming in concentrated bursts, "He got married to the same woman three times. They kept splitting up and then getting married again. His tour of duty was done. He was going home, but on his last day he volunteered for one more mission." Dad took a deep breath. "Gus's plane was lost somewhere over North Vietnam. How can I believe that he died for nothing? I'm not proud of any war," he said softly, "but I am proud of my service to my country."

Listening to my dad against a backdrop of the Vietnamese anthem being piped out over loudspeakers, I was beginning to understand that, for my father, the meaning of patriotism was inextricably linked to the meaning of his own life. I awkwardly reached out and touched his shoulder. It was as though I were tenuously stepping out of one role and into another.

In the past, it had always been my father putting his hand on my shoulder. Just after I went blind at thirteen, our family started going on hikes together. My father would put his hand on my shoulder and inexpertly steer me over steep rocky trails. The system was imperfect and at times, after a poorly placed foot, we would find ourselves bouncing down the side of a trail. In spite of the jarring force of our falls, I could feel my father still hanging onto my shirt—refusing to let go.

On the back of our tandem bike, facing the steepest section of the Hai Van Pass, this would be my chance to do something for him. I wanted my legs to be the force that would power our small team up the steep switchbacks to the top. "We'll go as slow as you want, but we won't stop," I commanded. But hearing my father's heaving breaths, I backed off. "We can stop if you want." He kept pedaling.

Each time we reached a switchback, the road would steepen further and I'd feel my father purposely weave our bike back and forth, creating mini-switchbacks in the road. I'd pour my muscle and mind into pedaling until I felt the grade ease again. Then I'd attempt to relax and get into a new rhythm, waiting for the next rise. I wouldn't have to wait very long. Sometimes, I'd feel my father attacking the steep sections as he would attack an opposing lineman, exhausting himself in the effort. "Relax!" I'd coach. "Slow and steady until we get there."

"Another half mile," my father groaned, and I could tell he was barely hanging on. I was tired, too, and could feel my legs losing strength like a deflating tire. I could hear cheers carrying down to us from the top. It still seemed like a long way to go.

I maintained the rhythm of our pedaling. I wouldn't let us quit. "Only a hundred yards," I heard my father gasp, and I could hear the cheers growing nearer. It was only a few seconds after that exclamation of confidence that we hit a huge rock in the middle of the road. My dad had been concentrating so hard looking up the road to the finish that he hadn't seen it.

Our bike toppled over. Both of us were too tired to react. I hit the ground, rolling through the fall and was up in time to help my father, who didn't move quite so quickly. We pushed the bike the last few yards. "I feel a little dizzy, just a little dizzy," he admitted, as we walked the bike through the flock of people who had gathered to greet our team.

Away from the crowd, I stood beside the tandem with a single, persistent thought in my head. The bullheaded optimism that had kept my father charging along through the years, even against a torrent of cynicism, had also burrowed itself into my life and had given me strength. My father and I do not have a "touchy-feely" relationship. Rather, in my family, love is expressed in subtler ways.

At the top of the pass, for only the second time on the trip, I put my hand on my father's shoulder. "Good job!" I said. "*Great* job!" I was talking to him, to myself, to the both of us. We had done it together.

At our final team dinner, Diana Nyad, the world's great long-distance swimmer, recounted some inspirational words from a conversation she once had with my father.

"I have lived through a war," my father told her. "I watched my son go blind. I saw my wife die in a car accident. Some people think I'm unfeeling. But what am I supposed to do? How am I supposed to act? Should I have given up? Should I have quit? Life is too precious, and all I can do is live it."

As I listened to Diana share my dad's words, I felt like I was emerging from a long dream. For over two weeks now, I had been connected to my father by the frame of a tandem bike, but I hadn't always been connected to his story. Like my father, I, too, had struggled with my blindness and with the crushing sadness of my mother's death; like my father, I, too, had chosen to live, and in that way, I thought, my father and I were the same. Sitting at the dinner, reflecting on our bike ride across Vietnam, I was proud of my father, proud of myself, but especially proud to be my father's son.

Erik Weihenmayer

A Secret Promise Kept

Every time I pass a fire station, the red fire engines with shining chrome, the smell of drying hoses and freshly polished floors, the oversized rubber boots and helmets, all transport me back to my childhood, to the firehouse where my father worked for thirty-five years as head of maintenance.

One day, my dad let me and my older brother Jay slide down the sparkling gold fire pole. In the corner of the station was the "creeper" used to slide under trucks when men were repairing them. Dad would say "Hold on" and spin me until I was dizzy. It was better than any Tilt-a-Whirl ride.

Next to the creeper was an old soda machine that dispensed the original, green, ten-ounce bottles of Coca-Cola for ten cents. A trip to the soda machine was always the highlight of our visit.

When I was ten years old, I took two of my friends by the station to show my dad off. I asked Dad if we could each have a soda before we went home for lunch.

I detected just the slightest hesitation in my father's voice. But he said "sure" and gave us each a dime. We raced to the soda machine to see whose bottle cap might hold the illustrious star on the inside.

What a lucky day! My cap had a star. I was only two caps away from sending for my very own Davy Crockett hat.

We all thanked my father and headed home for lunch and a summer afternoon of swimming.

When I came home from the lake, I heard my parents talking. Mom seemed upset with Dad, and then I heard my name mentioned: "You should have just said you didn't have money for sodas. Brian would have understood. We don't have any extra money, and you need to have your lunch."

My dad, in his usual way, just shrugged it off.

Before I could be caught listening, I hurried upstairs to the room I shared with my four brothers.

As I emptied my pockets, ready to put my new bottle cap with the other seven, I suddenly realized how great a sacrifice my father had made for it. That night I made a promise: Someday I'd tell my father that I knew of the sacrifice he made that afternoon and on so many other days, and I'd never forget him for it.

Over the next twenty years, my father's lifestyle—working three jobs to support the nine of us—caught up to him. He suffered four heart attacks, finally ending up with a pacemaker.

One afternoon Dad's old blue station wagon was broken down, and he asked me to take him to his doctor's appointment. As I pulled up to the firehouse, I saw Dad outside with the other firemen, crowded around a brand-new pickup truck. It was a beauty. When I admired it, Dad said, "Someday, I'll own a truck like that."

We both laughed. This was always his dream—and it always seemed unattainable.

I was doing well in business, as were all my brothers. We had offered to buy him a truck, but he refused, saying, "If I don't buy it, I won't feel I like it's mine." When Dad stepped out of the doctor's office, his face was gray and pasty.

"Let's go," was all he said.

We rode in silence. I took the long way back to the station. We drove by our old house, the ball field, lake and corner store, and Dad started talking about the memories each place held.

That's when I knew he was dying.

He looked at me and nodded.

I understood.

We stopped at Cabot's Ice Cream and had a cone together for the first time in fifteen years. We really talked that day. He told me how proud he was of all of us, and that he wasn't afraid of dying. His fear was of being away from my mother. Never had one man been more in love with a woman than my dad.

He made me promise that I would never tell anyone of his impending death. I agreed, knowing it was the toughest secret I'd ever have to keep.

At the time, my wife and I were looking to buy a truck. I asked Dad if he would go with me to see what I could get for a trade-in.

As we entered the showroom and I started talking with the salesman, I spotted Dad looking at the most beautiful, fully loaded, chocolate-brown, metal-flake pickup truck I had ever seen. He ran his hand over it like a sculptor checking his work.

I suggested to Dad that we take the brown truck out for a ride. We pulled out onto Route 27, my father behind the wheel. He drove for ten minutes, saying how beautifully it rode.

When we got back, we took out a smaller blue truck, a better truck for commuting because of its lower gas consumption. We returned and completed the deal with the salesman.

A few nights later, I asked Dad if he would come with me to pick up the truck. I think he agreed so quickly just to get one final look at "my brown truck," as he called it.

When we pulled into the dealer's yard, there was my little blue truck with a SOLD sticker on it. Next to it was the brown pickup, all washed and shiny, with a big SOLD sign on the window.

I glanced at my father and saw the disappointment register on his face as he said, "Someone bought themselves a beautiful truck."

I just nodded and said, "Dad, would you go inside and tell the salesman I'll be right in as soon as I park the car?" As my father walked past the brown truck, he ran his hand along it and I could see the look of disappointment pass over his face again.

I pulled my car around to the far side of the building and looked through the showroom window at the man who had given up everything for his family. I watched as the salesman sat him down, handed him a set of keys to "his truck"—the brown one—and explained that it was for him from me, and this was our secret.

My dad looked out the window, our eyes met, and we both nodded and laughed.

I was waiting outside my house when my dad pulled up that night. As he stepped out of "his truck," I gave him a big hug and a kiss and told him how much I loved him, and reminded him this was our secret.

We went for a drive that evening. Dad said he understood the truck, but what was the significance of the Coca-Cola bottle cap with the star in the center taped to the steering wheel?

Brian Keefe
As appeared in A 3rd Serving of Chicken Soup for the Soul

What Any Father Would Do

The average parent will go through the full gamut of ups and downs and trials and tribulations. The key is developing close ties with your children, teaching them to perform and function effectively.

Earl Woods

Jim Redmond did what any father would do. His child needed help. It was that simple. The Olympic Games have the kind of security that thousands of policemen and metal detectors can offer. But no venue is safe, when a father sees his son's dream drifting away.

"One minute I was running," Derek Redmond of Great Britain said. "The next thing there was a pop. I went down."

Derek, twenty-six, had waited for this four-hundred-meter semifinal for at least four years. In Seoul, he had an Achilles tendon problem. He waited until a minute-and-a-half before the race began before he would admit he couldn't run.

In November 1990, Derek underwent operations on

both Achilles tendons. He has had five surgeries in all. But he came back. In the first two rounds, he had run 45.02 and 45.03, his fastest times in five years.

"I really wanted to compete in my first Olympics," Redmond said. "I was feeling great. It just came out of the blue."

Halfway around the track, Redmond lay sprawled across lane five, his right hamstring gone bad.

Redmond struggled to his feet and began hobbling around the track. The winner of the heat, defending Olympic champion Steve Lewis, had finished and headed toward the tunnel. So had the other six runners. But the last runner in the heat hadn't finished. He continued to run.

Jim Redmond (Derek's dad), sitting high in the stands at Olympic Stadium, saw Derek collapse.

"You don't need accreditation in an emergency," Redmond said.

So Redmond, a forty-nine-year-old machine-shop owner in Northampton, ran down the steps and onto the track.

"I was thinking," Jim Redmond said, "I had to get him there so he could say he finished the semifinal."

The crowd realized that Derek Redmond was running the race of his life. Around the stands, from around the world, the fans stood and honored him with cheers.

At the final turn, Jim Redmond caught up to his son and put his arm around him. Derek leaned on his dad's right shoulder and sobbed. But they kept going. An usher attempted to intercede and escort Jim Redmond off the track. If ever a futile mission had been undertaken . . .

They crossed the finish line, father and son, arm in arm.

Ivan Maisel

I'm Daddy's Girl

*P*ast experience indicated that the best way of
dealing with her is total attention and love.

Lyndon Johnson

One evening not long ago, my husband stayed home
with the children while I went to the grocery store.
Shopping for a family of six when four of them are males
takes a while, so it was late when I got home. When I
walked back into the house, all was dark and unusually
quiet. After setting down a bag of groceries, I tiptoed into
the bedroom, lighted by the soft glow of the moon sifting
through the window. Scott was lying there, his hands
folded behind his head, staring at the ceiling. He seemed
so pensive, I immediately thought something was bother-
ing him.

"Hey," I said softly and sat down on the bed beside him.
"What's the matter?"

"Aw, I was just thinking about my daughter," he
grinned sheepishly. "And how much I love her."

Evidently, it had been a very good evening. "What
happened with Rachel tonight?" I asked.

"Well," he sighed and searched for words to convey what he was feeling. "I had built a fire outside to burn some excess wood, and the telephone rang. It turned out to be a tough discussion with someone, and I was upset. So I went outside to unwind by the fire, and, before long, our little girl came out of the house and snuggled by my side.

"'Dad,' she told me, 'you look like you could use a hug.'" He paused briefly and breathed a contented sigh.

"She's my little sweetheart, you know."

"I know," I smiled as I rubbed the back of my husband's neck. "And I hope she always will be."

The next evening Scott came home from work and found me asleep on the couch. He woke me by tickling my nose with a long-stemmed red rose. Before I could properly gush over it, Rachel strolled in from her room, beaming from ear to ear, her strawberry-blond curls boing-yoinging happily as she plopped down on the sofa beside me. In her small, slender hands she held a lavender basket of fresh daisies and pink carnations. Tucked into the arrangement was a card in Scott's handwriting.

"Thanks for the hug," it read.

Rachel's brown eyes twinkled, and she smiled triumphantly in my direction. "You just got one flower. Daddy gave me a whole basket!"

Becky Freeman

The Walnut Tree

The ordinary acts we practice every day at home are of more importance to the soul than their simplicity might suggest.

Thomas Moore

For many autumns my father and I would get into his pickup truck and drive somewhere south of El Dorado to an old walnut tree, which he had found at some time unknown and unimportant to me. The first trip to the tree was to "pick up a few black walnuts for your mother to make a pumpkin pie and some candy," he had said. As time passed, this trek to the walnut tree became our tradition. At first, it was just fun for me to be with my father alone as we traveled to our destination, picked up a basketful of fallen nuts and made our way home. Never in a hurry. My dad would say sometimes, "We're in a hurry, but just a *slow* hurry." However, as the years passed, I went away to school, took a job teaching and was, in my mind, living a hurried life, but in all those years I still found time to come home for a weekend to go to the walnut tree with my father when he notified me "the walnuts are ready."

My father died suddenly and unexpectedly in June 1965, at the age of seventy-six. I was devastated. During that summer, after my dad was gone, I realized just how much I had taken him for granted. I realized that I wanted to tell him a thousand things that I had not told him when I had the opportunity. I really began to remember our trips to the walnut tree all those carefree, lazy, lackadaisical afternoons that were gifts from my dad, and I had just enjoyed them, never really appreciated them. I remember the weather on those afternoons—sometimes warm and balmy, other times simply hot, and a few times cold and damp and uncomfortable. I would say to him at times, "Gosh, it's hot!" or "Why does it have to be so cold and wet?" Regardless of what my comment was, his good-natured answer was always the same, "Beats no weather at all."

My father was not a highly educated man, but he was wise. "Son," he would say, "there will always be folks who know more than you—listen to them; and there will always be folks who *think* and *tell* others they know more than you, be polite—but in your mind, ignore them." He almost had disdain for pretentious people. He could "see through them with a quick glance." "Son," he would tell me, "when I was a baby in my crib, a friend of my daddy's came to visit, and the friend was talking about politics, and he was so slanted and narrow in his beliefs that I kicked the slats out of my crib because I couldn't talk back." He continued thoughtfully, "Son, when you read or listen, consider the source, and the source's credentials."

In the fall of 1954, the year that I had taken my first teaching job, I came home when the "walnuts were ready." The weather had turned unseasonably cooler. There had been a hard shower of rain around noon, but by mid-afternoon when my father and I headed the old pickup toward the walnut tree, the rain had stopped and the afternoon was shining. The leaves of all the trees were colorful, many of them falling into a slight breeze that sent them scurrying across the ancient dirt road as we neared "our" tree. As we approached the tree, the sun's rays were focused especially on the amber and gold leaves of the walnut, turning the leaves, hanging with great drops of rain, into the most majestic things of beauty that I had ever seen. When I pointed out the sight to Dad, he smiled and said, "Son, 'to everything there is a season.' You're older and wiser now. . . . You're no longer a boy. Now you will see these things and know that it has always been."

In silence we gathered our treasures into our basket, and when my father spoke again, it was with his gentle smile: "Son, you're a teacher now, and whether you like it or not, you will be an example to your youngsters, and you must remember that the shadow of your influence will fall across somebody's path every day of your life. . . . It's up to you what kind of example you will be—up to you what kind of influence you will have on your students."

At first, his words seemed so simple, almost *too* simple. As I thought about the words, I began to realize the full importance of what he had said. I broke the waiting silence by saying, "Dad, that's frightening. I'm not sure I can handle that."

"Of course you can, Son. Basically, you're a good fellow. You know the difference between right and wrong. You're wise enough, intelligent enough, to make the right decisions. A wise person, such as yourself, won't rush into a rash decision quickly, and by the time you think about it, you'll know what the decision needs to be—what right is. I know you will. I have faith in you."

I carefully clutched a golden leaf that had fallen while we were filling our basket, took it home with me and pressed it between the pages of a literature book that I was teaching from that semester. As my first year of school wore on, I began to use the drying leaf as a bookmark, always being reminded of what my father had said to me. There were times, as that and many more years passed, when the once-golden leaf from the walnut tree reminded and refreshed my memory of my dad's quiet wisdom. There were times when that leaf and his words kept me from making bad judgments. I never told my father. I wish I had, but somehow, I think he knew.

Another year, another autumn, and as we filled our basket with the nuts that would eventually end up in a pumpkin pie or a batch of candy, I was telling my dad how a piece of music had affected me. I had not felt free to discuss the impression with a friend, but talking about it with my father was easy.

Still clear to me, after all those years, I can hear him respond, "Son, music is something that, if it is worth anything, will speak to your heart. It shouldn't simply entertain you; instead, it should calm you, rouse you, move you to tears, give you peace or a joyful heart."

I was amazed. It was a wondrous and warming feeling to know that Dad felt as I did. It was as if he could read my mind.

My dad was highly successful in the dairy business. After many years of hard work, he owned an all-registered herd of Jersey cows. He took much pride in showing his cattle at county and state fairs, leaving me a sizable box of prize ribbons of purple, blue, a few red ones and three or four white ones. In other people's eyes he was successful, but, to him, attainment for himself—reaching a goal he had set for himself—meant much, much more than what others thought.

As the leaves were yellowing and the walnuts fell in the autumn of 1964, Dad and I made our last journey to the walnut tree, but we didn't know that then. As we enjoyed a late afternoon under the tree, we gathered the nuts and talked freely, as always. I spoke of my goals as a teacher, speaking of what I had done, what I hoped to accomplish, and then, smiling gently, my father said, "Son, I hope you will become a great teacher. I think you are already a *good* teacher. Only time will tell, but I ask you to remember . . . not to take *full* credit for anything you might accomplish that is worthwhile. Instead, remember all the people who contributed to making you what you are—what you might become. Give your parents a little credit; think of the long line of teachers who influenced and taught you; and you must remember your pastors and Sunday school teachers—all have contributed to whatever you are, or ever will be. And you've grown up with friends who have impressed you one way or another—hopefully, mostly good impressions. We don't reach our goals of attainment all by ourselves. And, yes, there are successful people who take full credit for each and every accomplishment, thinking, even saying, they reached the 'top' all on their own, by themselves. They are wrong.

"And, Son, if you have failures, and you have and will, accept the responsibility. Don't blame someone else."

Today, as I write this, my father lives vividly in my memory, and I remember him for what he was, for what he said, for his actions—and what a positive influence he has on me. He was like the biblical city on a hill. I miss him still, but the legacy he left me is a priceless treasure that cannot be bought with mere money.

And even after all those years, as I think about our treks to the walnut tree—each visit being a journey of love—I now know he planned them all from the beginning, for a reason. I strongly believe that he felt just as close to me as I did to him on those lazy, golden afternoons when we were in a *"slow* hurry," those leisurely trips that I now know my father did not have time for, but which he wouldn't have given up for anything.

Calvin Louis Fudge

THE FAMILY CIRCUS® By Bil Keane

"Can't wait until I'm grown up and I can do anything I want and not have anything to worry about."

A Different Perspective

A little girl was sent upstairs by her father to empty the wastebaskets, but she returned so quickly that her father said, "You couldn't have emptied all the baskets in this time."

"They didn't need emptying, Dad," the child replied. "They just needed stepping in."

Bits & Pieces

"Daddy, are you home?"

Golf Balls in Heaven

My dad first taught me how to golf when I was three years old. He was an accomplished golfer and had a room full of trophies to prove it. Unfortunately, I can attest that golf skills aren't always passed on genetically, though it wasn't for lack of trying.

Dad would take me out to the driving range on most Saturdays in my childhood, and he eventually started taking me out on the course with him as well. And while our driving-range experiences felt to me like forced practice sessions, the days I spent with him on the course were the ones I looked forward to. Since Dad ran his own business and worked long hours, he didn't have a lot of spare time, so it meant a lot to me when I would have him all to myself out on the course for nine or eighteen holes. So much of the best of our relationship, from the mutual encouragement to sharing the little victories together, was forged on the golf course.

I'll never forget one summer during my junior-high years. Twice a week Dad would wake me before dawn and we'd head off to Glendover, the local municipal course that my mom had helped save from developers a few years earlier. Those dewy mornings, when we were the first golfers to walk the course together, are things of beauty in my memories of Dad.

Dad died suddenly and unexpectedly of an aneurysm on June 9, 1999. My wife and I had a golf date set with him for the Fourth of July. It was a difficult time for the whole family, but arrangements for the funeral had to be made nevertheless. As we discussed what to do about my dad's final resting place, we weighed several options, including the cemetery outside of town where some of our family members were interred. Just then my mom and sister had the same idea: Wouldn't it be great if Dad was buried in a cemetery close by so we could visit him as often as we wanted? Well, the only place close by that we knew of was a private cemetery that we thought was full.

I called them on a whim the next morning. A delightful woman, whose family had managed the cemetery for years, informed me that contrary to popular belief, they had plenty of space. She went on to tell me of the beautiful mountainside setting, the amazing views, and "Oh, by the way, we're right next to a beautiful golf course." I took it as a sign, and made an appointment for all of us to meet with her the next morning at the cemetery.

The sky was a clear blue as we pulled into the picturesque grounds. We immediately noticed the golf course adjoining the property and the driving range that actually bordered one side of the cemetery. My eyes followed the fifty-foot-high net that protected the grounds as it ran up to the tee area of the range, and I noticed that it was devoid of life on this early weekday morning. As the caretaker reverently guided us through the headstones, we quietly talked about what a beautiful setting this was. What little doubt remained about this being Dad's perfect resting place was erased a moment later. As our guide brought us to a halt in what we later agreed was the most beautiful spot in the cemetery, she gestured to the area she had in mind. And as she pointed to the spot where my dad would spend the rest of his days, a single golf ball fell out of the sky and rolled to a stop. We all looked back up toward the tee area, and seeing it was still empty, knew that Dad had given us his approval.

After the funeral service a couple of days later, our family gathered for a very special and private final farewell. We opened Dad's casket and gave him back the golf ball he had used to let us know he was still with us. We love you, Dad, and hope you're in a place where the fairways are always green and your scores under par.

Mark Donnelly

The Confession

It was difficult raising my two stepchildren, Michael, age nine, and Mimi, age six, after the loss of their mother. They were rambunctious kids, so we worked very hard to make a go of it.

One evening when I returned from work, a broken lamp was lying on the floor with two wide-eyed kids standing over it.

"Who did this?" I asked.

Both immediately denied it.

"One of you did it, and I will tell you what I am going to do about it," I admonished. "Go to your rooms and stay there until the one who did it confesses. And remember, you are making the other one stay in his or her room for something you did."

About five minutes later, Michael came out and said, "Can I talk to you?"

I replied, "Sure, Michael, what's on your mind?"

He reluctantly said, "I want to confess. Mimi did it."

I broke out laughing, and after further reprimands, all was forgiven.

Gerald R. Winner
Submitted by Jo Rose-Winner

My Father, My Friend

The first time I met him, he was just "Mr. Cohan" to me. One Saturday afternoon my mother insisted I wash my face and hands and get dressed up so I could escort her out of our apartment house and meet some man waiting by his car. She'd gone out with men before. What was different about this one? Why did I have to stop what I was doing and change my clothes for him?

Why? Because he had asked her to marry him the night before, I later learned. He had already met my brother. Now he wanted to meet me.

"Hello, Mr. Cohan," I said, anxious to run back inside and return to my games. "Hello, Susan," answered a curly-haired, middle-aged man. He spoke softly, almost shyly, as he took my hand and shook it.

After he and my mother married, I didn't know what to call him, and for a long time I didn't call him anything. My friend called her new stepfather "Uncle," but that seemed phony to me. "Leo" didn't seem right, either. He called me Susan, or Sue, as my mother and brother did. He didn't have to call me "Daughter"; did I have to say "Dad"? Who was this man to me? He seemed kind and gentle, and he even liked to have me around. But a father? Would calling him "Father" make him a father?

Stepping into a family already containing a mother, a teenage boy and a twelve-year-old girl, Leo knew he wouldn't be treated like a father automatically. We were a long-established group; he was a new piece to be fitted in. It's not that he had to compete with any love we felt for our "real" father, a cold, self-centered man who had been anything but kind, anything but caring in all the years we had known him. Leo's job was harder—he had to compete with a fantasy, our unrealistically high expectations of what a perfect father should be: loving, caring, available, supportive, generous, clever and handsome. And, most of all, a perfect father would think his children were perfect, too.

He probably had his own fantasies. Orphaned as a young child, Leo had been raised by older brothers and sisters who, although they loved him, never put his interests first in their lives, the way a devoted parent would. His own first marriage had been sad and unsatisfying. Now, at the age of fifty, he had married a woman with two children, accepting all the responsibilities and financial obligations this would entail.

That first year the four of us lived together, Leo spent a lot of time fixing and building things in our new home. It was his way of putting down roots, I guess, of establishing a firm foundation on which our new family could stand. He stained the wood paneling in the den, hung wallpaper in the bathrooms and designed and constructed cedar closets in the basement.

But, at the same time we were becoming a family, I was becoming an adolescent: self-absorbed, defiant and rebellious. My mother and I, who had always been close, now seemed to argue all the time. "Why can't you behave?" she angrily asked me. "You won't let me do anything my way!" I countered, and stormed out of the room. I had to talk to someone. I found Leo in the basement, working on the closets. Slowly, methodically, he was planing a piece of wood. Then he sanded it carefully, letting me talk, offering me a piece of sandpaper to help him smooth the edges, giving me a few nails to hold while he positioned the wood on the wall, and having me help him hammer it into place. "She's impossible!" I told him. "She yells at me for every little thing. Whatever I do has to be perfect to satisfy her."

He nodded as I talked, and kept on working. I wished he would take my side—how could anyone not?—but he knew he was caught in the middle. "Your mother only wants you to *aim* for perfection," he said softly. "That shouldn't be too difficult for you. I think you're pretty exceptional."

Leo and I spent a lot of time together in the basement that first winter. He taught me how to work with tools so I, too, could build, paint and repair things. That "shop" time became a good outlet for a lot of adolescent frustrations. That basement—which my mother rarely visited— became a "safe haven" for me to escape to. Leo was there for me whenever I needed him. He didn't solve my problems, but encouraged me to sort things out for myself. What I needed—and what he gave me—was a sympathetic ear. "You know," he once remarked, "you and your mother have a lot in common. You're both energetic, spirited and strong-opinioned people. That's why you sometimes irritate each other. But that's also what I like about you . . . the two of you."

Leo was a calm man, slow moving and contemplative. He loved to fish, but what appealed to him more than the desire to catch anything was the peacefulness and serenity he'd find out on a lake in a rowboat. In fact, when he *did* catch something, he'd always chuckle, surprised that his "two-bit" lure actually worked. Then he'd hold the struggling fish gently in his hand, being careful not to squeeze it too hard. Very quickly, he would slip the hook out of the fish's cheek, wipe its mouth with a rag the way a parent pats a child, and toss it back into the water. I'd never seen a fisherman so concerned about his fish.

Dinnertimes, he often brought home small, inexpensive surprises—a flowered-china light-switch plate for my bedroom wall, a sports magazine for my brother. Conversations at the table were lively. He listened to our stories about school, complaints about homework, tales about victories on the athletic field and all our silly jokes. He always assumed we were smart and treated us as if we were. "Try this," he'd begin, and we knew what was coming: a new mind teaser he'd just heard at work or read in the paper. He'd laugh in the end after we had figured out the answer. "I knew I couldn't trick you!" he'd boast, shaking his head but beaming at the same time.

The first June I lived with Leo, I biked to a popular men's store in town, with two weeks' allowance and all my baby-sitting money from the past month. Heady masculine aromas of after-shave lotions and colognes intoxicated me as I entered the store. I had never been in a men's shop before. Pictures of hunting scenes were mounted on dark wood-paneled walls, and rich plaid carpeting covered the aisle floors. Men's suits, ties, bathrobes, pajamas, shoes, slippers and jewelry were displayed everywhere. At the age of thirteen I had come to purchase my first Father's Day gift.

Maleness was no longer something to shy away from. Now I knew a man who was gentle and loving. Father's Day was not just for other families. This year it would be our holiday, too.

I selected a blue silk tie decorated with rows of tiny fish, and carried it home pridefully. The next Sunday morning I gave it to Leo, who put it on immediately, right over his pajamas. "Thanks so much," he said. "I'll treasure this." He put his arms around me and kissed my cheeks.

"You're welcome," I answered. "Happy Father's Day, Dad." I said it as casually as possible, but I saw him smile and knew he heard me.

You might think that because my natural father had been so cruel, I'd have welcomed any other man who was halfway decent. But memories of my childhood practically destroyed any hopes I had of having a warm, loving relationship with someone who tried to be a father to me. Before Leo came into my life, I'd had it with fathers. It was the simplicity, honesty and constancy of his friendship that won me, and I have never forgotten how lucky I have been.

Gradually, over time, our new family has created its own common roots and traditions. It was Leo who sent my brother and me to college, saw us married and has now shared so much of his time and love with our children—his grandchildren. Sure, they've been told he's a "step"-grandfather, but what's it to them? "Pa" has loved them since the day they were born. He took them for strolls in their carriages, read to them and rocked them. Later on he taught them how to fish and work with tools. He's been a one-man cheering squad at their soccer games, baseball games, piano recitals and school plays. Just as he used to do with me. Just as he taught me to do with my kids.

Children, I have learned, are entitled to be cared for by kind, loving adults who are not only parents to them but friends as well.

Leo chose my mother, and he chose my brother and me, too. We are family and friends by choice—not by birth or blood. His friendship—and his love—has been a gift that I will never forget.

Susan J. Gordon

My Father's Day Card

For a couple of reasons, Father's Day has been a bummer for me for quite some time now. Having lost my father in an automobile accident fifteen years ago, I would just as soon forget Father's Day and move on with summer. Loving my dad the way I did, I always looked forward to being a father myself. Playing catch, shooting baskets and kissing children good night after tucking them into bed were the special acts of love I wanted to give to my children. After ten years of marriage, however, I realized that those special acts of love would have to remain memories of my father's treatment of me. Due to a medical condition, my wife Kathy and I could not have children. As a schoolteacher, I rationalized that even though I never had children of my own, I still was around them enough to satisfy my parental longings. But something was always missing.

In twenty years of teaching and coaching, I've had the opportunity to teach thousands of students. It is very rewarding for me to watch my students as they change from children to teenagers to young adults. I love when they come back to visit and tell me of their dreams. I still envy parents who visit me during open-house nights at school. I wondered what that would be like to check on a son's or daughter's grades. Still I have my students, and I just convince myself that is enough. But something is still missing. A friend of mine helped me find a part of it.

I had just suffered through another Father's Day, and for some reason this one was one of the worst. Kathy and I had spent the day playing a round of golf, and we were teamed up with a father and his daughter. At one point in the round I heard the daughter say, "Good shot, Dad!" I was saddened when I realized that I would never hear those words from a child of my own. Upon arriving home, I went to the mailbox where I discovered an envelope addressed to me from a young lady named Melanie. Melanie was a former Miss Missouri who had come to speak to my students at school. We had quickly become friends and began speaking together at school assemblies on the topic of "Believing in Yourself." As I opened the envelope, I discovered a Father's Day card with my name on it. On the inside was a note thanking me for being there for so many of my students and a simple inscription—"I Love You, Dad!" As I read those words, my heart melted. I just wanted to dwell in the feeling of warmth and love this simple message had produced. For a brief moment, I had experienced the joy of fatherhood.

To this day, I cherish that act of kindness by my friend. It helped fill a missing part of my life that is special to me. Thank you, Melanie. You're a true friend. It's the only Father's Day card I've ever received.

Tom Krause

My Wife Is Having a Baby

The sobs and tears of joy he had not foreseen rose with such force within him that his whole body shook and for a long time prevented him from speaking. Falling on his knees by her side, he held his wife's hand to his lips and kissed it, and her hand responded to his kisses with a weak movement of fingers. Meanwhile, at the foot of the bed, in the midwife's expert hands, like the flame of a lamp, flickered the life of a human being who had never existed before.

Leo Tolstoy

Most people remember the day their first child was born as being one of the most wonderful days of their lives. Everybody has their stories about how this day went. For most men middle-aged or older, this day was spent in the waiting room. Nowadays, though, men do not have to stay in the waiting room. We get to go right in and go through the whole thing, start to finish.

My wife and I even took a course on having a baby. Not only does this course teach the woman about the various aspects of childbirth, but also teaches the man how to be a coach and how to give good moral support. All of this knowledge sounded great at the time; however, looking back I can now see some serious flaws in the course.

For instance, I cannot recall anything about protective measures for the husband. They tell you to sit next to the bed, hold her hand, rub her back, remind her to breathe right during contractions and, in general, to just be there with a reassuring presence.

What they did not tell the men was that while you are sitting there holding her hand, she may decide to hold your hand (arm, shoulder or any other part of your body that is within reach) during major contractions, which brings up the point: never did anyone say anything about the damage a woman's fingernails can do while a major contraction is nearing its peak. As for rubbing the back, there was no warning here either.

Having been raised around animals, I should have seen this flaw coming from a mile away. Animals do not especially like being touched while in serious pain. Neither do women in the throes of labor. The response is not unlike that of poking a bear with a sharp stick.

Then there's the matter of the breathing. In class, we were told we might have to actually breathe right into our wives' faces in the manner in which they should be breathing at certain times. This maneuver can be extremely dangerous, somewhat like sticking your head in a lion's mouth—only in this case, the lion is in extreme pain and sees you as one of the main reasons for its discomfort.

Now as serious as these flaws were, they could not compare with the severity of the very first flaw I encountered on this day. Needles! No one said anything about needles! While growing up, I could never watch myself (or anyone else for that matter) get a shot. I would shut my eyes as tightly as humanly possible, then turn my head in the opposite direction. But here I was in the hospital, standing beside my wife and holding her hand, while a nurse was trying to insert an I.V. in her other arm. I should have gone with my first instincts: to shut my eyes as tightly as humanly possible and then turn my head in the opposite direction.

However, wasn't I here for support? Yes, I was! *I will hold back my fear and be strong and bold!* Bad move. After watching a two-inch-long needle being stabbed into my wife about four or five times, "strongness" and "boldness" turned to "weakness" and "queasiness." So much for support. I had to get out of there.

Thinking that if I could get some food in me I would regain some strength, I headed for the cafeteria. While getting on the elevator, things started getting a little fuzzy. Stepping out of the elevator, I started for the cafeteria.

Waking up lying half in and half out of a broom closet in a hospital with half a dozen health care workers bent over you is embarrassing enough, but their response to my explanation for being found this way did not help. The first thing I said when asked if I was alright was, "My wife is having a baby," to which they all smiled and in unison replied, "Ohh."

Robert D. McLane II

CLOSE TO HOME JOHN McPHERSON

Many first-time fathers take the job of videotaping the birth far too seriously.

The Color of Love

My ninety-eight-year-old grandfather, always called "Pa" by our family, likes to give his gifts in a big way.

When I was about ten years old, Pa gave me one of the most memorable, and definitely the largest, personalized gift I'd ever received. It taught me a lot about what love looks like.

My family went to visit Pa one July evening after supper. As the grown-ups admired his yard, we kids clambered up the granite boulder we had fondly dubbed "The George Washington Rock," our own mini-Mt. Rushmore. When the grown-ups disappeared behind the arborvitae hedge, we followed. That's where Pa grew his vegetable garden. I remembered from other years how extraordinarily tidy he always kept it. Straight paths separated neat rows of well-trimmed plants and set off a border marked by marigolds. Every year, Pa carefully staked and tied his tomatoes and built intricate moats and mounds around his gourds, winter squash and melons. Even to a child who despised vegetables, his garden was pleasing to look at: its variety of textures and vivid greens, its symmetry altered only by sun and shadows.

When we caught up to the grown-ups by the garden, I

gasped in surprise. This was not the model of vegetable geometry I had come to expect.

Instead, most of Pa's garden was covered with bicycle-tire-sized dusty leaves and vines as thick as handlebars. Pigs'-tail tendrils curled and stretched in every direction. Here and there star-shaped flowers bloomed, bright as orange California poppies. In a few places where the flower had puckered into a fist, I could see a green, tennis-ball-sized fruit growing.

With his arms akimbo, Pa announced he had only put in a "postage-stamp patch" of his usual garden produce this year because he was "going whole hog into pumpkins, *giant* pumpkins." He explained how he had started "Atlantic Giant" seeds indoors in paper cups ("Only one seed per cup, mind you"). About two weeks later, he had transplanted the most vigorous seedling into some specially prepared, extra enriched soil in his garden. He gave the vine plenty of room to spread out—a square at least twenty-five feet per side—and mulched the soil with straw. He said he planned to put white sheets over the pumpkins when they grew above their leaf-shade canopy. I laughed, imagining squatty ghostlike bumps haunting the garden at noon instead of midnight. But Pa explained that without a covering, the skins of the ripening fruit would get sunburned. I slipped away as my mother and Pa started discussing what he should put under each of his prodigies to keep their undersides clean and free of rot and scarring. With the rest of the summer ahead of me and fifth grade in the fall, I soon forgot about Pa's pumpkins. . . .

Until the middle of October, that is. Then Pa invited us for another visit. As soon as we tumbled out of the station wagon, he greeted us. Right away, I could tell something was up. Pa has never been the apple-cheeked, twinkly eyed, merrymaking kind of grandpa. He isn't demonstrative,

except with his gifts, and always looked rather professional with his wool vest and pipe. But that day, he was
different. It was as if he had a giggle bubbling in his chest
that he had to keep swallowing, so it wouldn't escape and
embarrass him. He took us straight back to his garden.

Huge as harvest moons, there they were: two behemoth
pumpkins.

"Wow!" we said.

"Oh, my goodness sake!" my mother said.

Convinced we had been adequately awed from a distance, Pa took us in to get a closer look. My younger
brother and I stepped tentatively over the prickly vines
and through the scratchy leaves. We touched the smooth,
cool skin of the pumpkins and tried to nudge them with
the heels of our hands. We might as well have tried to
move The George Washington Rock. Those bruisers would
probably have sent the scale's arrow spinning to at least a
quarter ton each.

But it was the silver scrawl across the top of one of the
pumpkins that caught my attention. As the fruit grew, Pa
had scratched my full name and birth date into its skin.
The other pumpkin was inscribed with my younger
brother's name and birth date. As a lower-middle child in
a large family, I never assumed that anyone knew who I
was or recognized me as an individual; I was just part of
the passel, usually just the little sister of one of my older
siblings. I often felt lost or left out, or simply overlooked.
So when I discovered that Pa knew my whole name and
exact birth date—when I realized he had grown that
pumpkin thinking of just me, planning to surprise me at
just the right time—I whooped for joy. I think I even dared
to hug the old curmudgeon, or at least his legs. Later, the
thought of how much effort and time he had joyfully and
secretly poured into that pumpkin touched me, too.

Carved into the jack of all jack-o'-lanterns and then

made into spice-scented pies and muffins, that pumpkin was definitely one of the most unusual gifts I've ever received. But more than that, it was just the right size to express Pa's giant generosity and fill a little girl's heart with the surprise of being loved.

Red may connote mere passion, but for me, orange is what real love looks like. For me, orange—bright, pumpkin orange—is definitely the color of love.

Allison Harms

A Piece of Chalk

In our home, it was natural to fear our father.

Even our mother was afraid of him. As children, my sister and I thought every family was like that. Every family had an unpredictable alcoholic who was impossible to please, and a praying mama who was there to protect the children. We thought God planned it that way.

We were good children; Mama was always telling us we were, even if Daddy couldn't see it. Part of this was because we dared not do anything. We were quiet, timid children who rarely spoke—and never when Daddy was home. People thought God had blessed Mama with the sweetest girls. She was always so proud!

Then came the day we found something new and fun to do.

We knew it would not upset anyone. We never took the risk of doing that. On our house, we had a wooden door. We discovered we could draw pictures on it with chalk and it would rub right back off. We could have lots of fun.

We set to work drawing and making lots of pretty pictures all over it. We had a great time. It surprised us to see how talented we were. These pictures were good! That's when we decided to finish our masterpiece. We were proud of our work. We knew Mama would just love it. She would want all her friends to come see it, and maybe they would want us to do their doors, too. We had found something we were really good at!

The praise we expected did not come. Instead of seeing the beauty in our work, all Mama could see was the time and effort she would need to clean it off. She was mad. We did not understand this, but we knew all about anger— and we were in big trouble!

Off we ran to find a place to hide. In our wooded yard, it was not hard for two small children to find safety. Together, we huddled behind a tree and did not move. Soon we heard the frightened voices of Mom and our neighbors calling out to us. Still we did not budge. They were afraid that we had run away or had drowned in the pond out back. We were afraid of being found.

The sun set, and it began to get dark. The people around us became more anxious, and we became more frightened. Time was slipping by, and the longer we hid there, the harder it was to come out. Mom was, by now, convinced something awful had happened to us, and she resorted to calling the police. We could tell something was happening, because we could hear all the voices drawn together in a group. Then the search was on again, this time with strong male voices overpowering the others. If we were frightened before, now we were terrified!

As we clung together in the dark, we became aware of yet another voice, one we instantly recognized with horror: our daddy. But there was something strangely different about his voice. In it, we heard something we had never heard before. Fear, agony, despair—we couldn't put a name to it then, but that's what it was. Then came the tears and prayers intermingled together.

Was that our daddy on his knees pleading with God? Our daddy, with tears running down his face, promising

God that he would give his life to him if he would safely
return his girls?

Nothing in our lives had prepared us for this kind of
shock. Neither of us remembers making a decision to
come out. We were drawn to him like a magnet, our fears
dissolving into the forest. We don't know yet if we actually
took steps, or if God somehow moved us out and into his
arms. What we do remember are those strong loving arms
holding us and crying, holding us like we were precious.

Things were different after that. We had a new daddy. It
was like the old one was buried that day in the forest. God
had taken him and replaced him with another, one who
loved us and was ever thankful for us.

Mama always told us that God was a God of miracles. I
guess she was right. He changed our whole family with a
piece of chalk.

Holly Smeltzer

Holding Hands

The best thing to hold on to is each other.

Anonymous

I was sleeping late. I had just published the first issue of my local newspaper, *Atlanta 30306*, and was recovering from three all-nighters earlier in the month. The phone rang.

The call was from either a brother or a sister. I don't remember which now. My dad had been walking down the hallway at the Northside YMCA on Roswell Road, going to his daily swimming aerobics class, when he had a massive stroke.

I drove quickly to Piedmont Hospital and ran into the emergency room. I thought about how Dad had cared for me there through broken bones, an appendectomy and so on. Now, I was going to see him.

I found him in a room, unconscious. It was so quiet. I just stood by his side, helplessly. A nurse I hadn't seen standing in the corner told me I could touch him.

Touch him? I thought. *How?* I looked at his hands. I remembered grasping them in handshakes for years. I remembered how later, after our family discovered affection, hugging him, and even in recent years, kissing him. But I had no memory of ever just holding his hand, as a child might grab a parent's hand to cross the street.

I placed his hand in mine and just held it. It felt so large; bony, yet soft. *Why have I never done this before?* I thought. *Was it my insecurities or his?* Perhaps both. It was the last time I touched my father. He never regained consciousness and died later that evening.

I revisit that image often and have drawn much comfort from remembering that simple act of holding hands with my dad during the last hours of his life. A seemingly small gesture, but one that allows two people to connect so quickly, so closely.

My own eleven-year-old son knows this and is, thankfully, not bound by the inhibitions of earlier generations. One time, after my dad's death, I was walking in a mall with him and his cousin of the same age. His cousin asked him why he was holding my hand. He said nothing, but quickly released my grasp. *That was it,* I thought. *The defining moment.* Even though I had felt a little self-conscious holding his hand there in the mall, I knew I would miss his touch more than he would ever know. Yet, a few weeks later during another weekend together, he quietly slipped his hand in mine. I felt connected again.

This summer in Paris, we walked along the Seine as I led him and his thirteen-year-old sister to cathedrals and museums. He grabbed my hand, and we walked together for several blocks. My daughter, who had stopped holding my hand at age nine or ten, sped up and looked over at the clasp. I knew she was going to say something as only a sister, much too cool for such a display, would. Then she caught my eye and my smile. Uncharacteristically, she retreated and said nothing.

And so we continued along the riverbank, a family of

three, she comfortable in her detachment, my son content with his innate instinct to connect with others, and me, somewhere in between.

Sometimes, we have a choice of when to let go. Sometimes, we don't.

Chris Schroder

More Than a Friend

We may find some of our best friends in our own blood.

Theodore Roosevelt

Louisville, Kentucky, is a place where basketball is an important part of life, and taking my son to an NBA exhibition game is very special. Little did I realize how special the evening was going to be! It was a biting winter cold that was blowing some mean wind, as Josh held my hand as we crossed the Kentucky Fairgrounds parking lot headed for famous Freedom Hall. Being eight years old, he still felt it was okay to hold his father's hand, and I felt grateful, knowing that these kind of moments would pass all too soon.

The arena holds nineteen-thousand-plus fans, and it definitely looked like a sellout as the masses gathered. We had been to many a University of Louisville basketball game and even a few University of Kentucky games in this hallowed hall, but the anticipation of seeing Michael Jordan and the Chicago Bulls against the Washington Bullets (with ex-University of Louisville star Felton

Spencer) made our pace across the massive parking lot seem like a quick one, with lots of speculation about how the game was going to go.

The turnstile clicked and Josh hung on to his souvenir ticket stub like he had just won the lottery! Climbing the ramps to the upper elevation seemed more an adventure than a chore, as we got to the upper-level seats of the "true" fans. Before we knew it, the game was underway and the battle had begun. During a time out, we dashed for the mandatory hot dog and Coke and trotted back so that we wouldn't miss a single layup or jump shot. Things were going as expected until halftime. I started to talk to some friends nearby when there was a tug on my sleeve, my arm was pulled over by a determined young Josh Frager, and he began putting a multicolored, woven yarn bracelet around my wrist. It fit really well, and he was really focused intently as he carefully made a double square knot to keep it secure (those Scouting skills really are handy). Being a Scoutmaster with a lot of teenage Scouts, I recognized the significance of the moment, and wanting him to be impressed with my insightful skills, I looked him squarely in the eyes, smiled the good smile, and told him proudly how I knew this was a "friendship bracelet" and said, "I guess this means we are friends."

Without missing a beat, his big brown eyes looked me straight in the face, and he exclaimed, "We're more than friends. . . . You're my dad!"

I don't even remember the rest of the game.

Stanley R. Frager

A Young Man's Odyssey

"Dear Dad," I wrote, "I want to come home." After many minutes of thinking as I sat by the side of a busy highway, I tore the page in half and wadded it into a small ball. I'd started this letter many times, but had never really finished. I wanted to go home—home to my parents and sisters, but . . .

I had run away from home after finishing high school. My parents had insisted I go to college, but I was tired of school. I hated it. I was determined not to go. And, besides, my father was too strict on me. I had too many chores to do around the farm. I hated the work!

There had been a quarrel between my father and me. I threw some things into a bag and left angrily, as my father shouted after me, "If you leave, don't come back!" My mother cried openly, and I have seen those tears during a hundred sleepless nights.

The letter had to be written.

Dear Dad,

It's been more than a year now. I've traveled east to west. I've had dozens of jobs. None of them amounted to very much. Always the same questions: "How much education have you got?" It seems they always want college men for the good jobs.

Dad, you and Mother were right about everything. I know now that the work on the farm didn't hurt me, and I'm convinced I need college. I'm also convinced that both of you loved me. That was not easy for me to write, and I couldn't have written it a year ago. I've met some nice people since I've been away, as well as rough and tough people. I thought I could take all kinds, but sometimes it wasn't so easy, especially not having a good home to come to at night, where there was love and security. I wasn't really aware of what a home means until I'd been away for a few months.

Dad, I've learned a lesson. I want to come home. I know you said if I left, that I couldn't come back, but I'm praying you'll change your mind. I know I made you terribly angry that day—and hurt you, too.

I wouldn't blame you if you refused me, but I must ask you. I know I should have written before, but I was afraid you wouldn't want to hear from me.

I want to come home and be a part of the family again. I'd like to go to college and learn how to be a successful farmer, and then, if you'll let me, maybe I could farm with you.

I'm on the road now, so you can't answer me by letter. But in a few days (I don't know what day because I'm hitch-hiking), I'll be passing the farm. And, Dad, if you'll let me come home, please leave the porch light on. I'll make it a point to pass at night. If there is no light, I'll just keep on going, and I won't have any hard feelings if the porch is dark. I'll understand.

Give my love to Mother and the girls.

Love,
Your son

As I folded the letter and put it into an envelope, I felt a refreshing relief. It was as if a heavy load had been lifted from my shoulders. I put the letter into my shirt pocket and lugged my beat-up suitcase closer to the side of the road, and held out my thumb to the first passing car. I had a long way to go before I'd know the answer.

Night came and I'd gotten only fifty or sixty miles since noon. I had mailed the letter in a little, insignificant post office. After I dropped the letter into the out-of-town slot, I was a little nervous. Perhaps I shouldn't have mailed it, but it was done, and I had to be on my way.

Sometime the following day, the rides had gotten few and far between. I hadn't any sleep the night before, and I was weary as well as tired. Crossing over the road to a giant oak at the edge of a field, I stretched out on the grass and tried to sleep. But sleep did not come easily. In a nearby field a tractor hummed pleasantly, two dogs chased a rabbit within a few yards of me. From the farmhouse, nestled in a clump of trees on a hill, I could hear small children engaged in play; a rooster crowed and a hen cackled. I imagined I could smell fresh apple pie. Then, with closed eyes, I could vividly see my own home, the one that I had so recklessly left in a moment of anger. I wondered what my little sisters were doing. They could be such pests, but in their eyes, I could do no wrong. And, oh, how my mother could cook, and she was always saying as we sat down to eat, "I fixed this just for you, Son."

I couldn't bear my thoughts any longer. I got to my feet, and with the refreshing smell of fresh-cut hay in my nostrils, I started down the desolate road—the long road home. But was it still my home? My father was fair-minded, but he was strong-willed.

A car picked me up, and it was good to have someone to talk with. The driver was a salesman and very pleasant. "Where you going, Son?" he asked good-naturedly.

There was a long silence before I said, "Home."

"Where have you been?" he asked.

I knew he wasn't prying. There was something about his face that told me he was interested. "All over," I said.

"Been away from home long?"

I smiled, a little self-conscious, and said, "A year, one month and two days."

He didn't look at me, but he smiled, and I knew he understood. He told me about his family. He had two sons, one was my age and one was older.

As darkness approached, he found a place to eat and insisted that I join him. I was dirty and told him I would shame him, but he wouldn't take no for an answer. He was going to spend the night there, and after we had eaten, he talked me into spending the night, too. He reasoned that I could get cleaned up and get some rest before going on. Somehow, he reminded me of my father. I told him I had very little money, and after he had bought my supper, I couldn't let him spend any more on me.

However, I stayed. The next morning, after breakfast, I tried to thank him, but he said, "You're a fine boy. You see, my older son ran away from home two years ago—two years and fifteen days." He looked away and then said, "I hope somebody will be nice to my son."

I didn't know what to say. He shook my hand and smiled warmly.

"Thank you, sir, for everything," I stammered. "And, I hope . . ."

"Thank you," he said, "and good luck."

Two days later, I was within fifty miles of home. I hadn't had a ride for hours. Darkness came slowly. I walked, not waiting for anyone to stop. Some inner force was driving me forward—homeward. But the faster I walked, the more doubts I had. Suppose the porch would be dark? What would I do? Where would I go?

A big truck and trailer slowed and stopped. I ran and got in.

"How far you going?" the dark, burly driver asked.

"About forty or fifty miles from here. Are you going that far?" I asked.

"Farther," he muttered.

There was very little conversation. He was not easy to talk to. I pretended to be sleepy and leaned back and closed my eyes.

Thirty minutes later rain began to fall, slowly at first, and then it was coming down in sheets. I dozed, awoke and dozed again.

Then, with the rain pouring, we were nearing my father's farm. I was wide awake. Would there be a light on the porch? I was straining my eyes to see through the darkness and the rain. Suddenly, we were there. I couldn't look. I couldn't bear to look and not see a light. I closed my eyes tightly, and my heart pounded.

The driver chuckled and spoke roughly, "Look at that, would you! That house there, the one we just passed. Must be some kind of nuts! Three or four chairs were settin' on the porch with lighted lamps in every one of them, and an ol' man was out there with a flashlight aimed toward the road—and the porch light was on, too!"

Calvin Louis Fudge

6

OVERCOMING OBSTACLES

The task ahead of us is never so great as the power behind us.

Ralph Waldo Emerson

Perfection

In Brooklyn, New York, Chush is a school that caters to learning-disabled children. Some children remain in Chush for their entire school careers, while others can be mainstreamed into conventional yeshivas and Bais Yaakovs. There are a few children who attend Chush for most of the week and go to a regular school on Sundays.

At a Chush fund-raising dinner, the father of a Chush child delivered a speech that would never be forgotten by all who attended. After extolling the school and its dedicated staff, he cried out, "Where is the perfection in my son Shaya? Everything that God does is done with perfection. But my child cannot understand things as other children do. My child cannot remember facts and figures as other children do. Where is God's perfection?" The audience was shocked by the question, pained by the father's anguish and stilled by his piercing query.

"I believe," the father answered, "that when God brings a child like this into the world, the perfection that he seeks is in the way people react to this child."

He then told the following story about his son Shaya:

"Shaya attends Chush throughout the week and Yeshivah Darchei Torah in Far Rockaway on Sundays. One Sunday afternoon, Shaya and his father came to Darchei Torah as his classmates were playing baseball. The game was in progress and as Shaya and his father made their way towards the ballfield, Shaya said, 'Do you think you could get me into the game?'

Shaya's father knew his son was not at all athletic, and that most boys would not want him on their team. But Shaya's father understood that if his son was chosen, it would give him a comfortable sense of belonging.

"Shaya's father approached one of the boys in the field and asked, 'Do you think my Shaya could get into the game?'

"The boy looked around for guidance from his teammates. Getting none, he took matters into his own hands and said, 'We are losing by six runs and the game is already in the eighth inning. I guess he can be on our team, and we'll try to put him up to bat in the ninth inning.'

"Shaya's father was ecstatic, as Shaya smiled broadly. Shaya was told to put on a glove and go out to play short center field, a position that exists only in softball. There were no protests from the opposing team, which would now be hitting with an extra man in the outfield.

"In the bottom of the eighth inning, Shaya's team scored a few runs, but was still behind by three. In the bottom of the ninth inning, Shaya's team scored again and now with two outs and the bases loaded and the potential winning runs on base, Shaya was scheduled to be up. Would the team actually let Shaya bat at this juncture and give away their chance to win the game?

"Surprisingly, Shaya was told to take a bat and try to get a hit. Everyone knew that it was all but impossible, for Shaya didn't even know how to hold the bat properly, let alone hit with it. However, as Shaya stepped up to the plate, the pitcher moved in a few steps to lob the ball in softly so that Shaya should at least be able to make contact.

"The first pitch came in and Shaya swung clumsily and missed. One of Shaya's teammates came up to Shaya, and together they held the bat and faced the pitcher waiting for the next pitch. The pitcher again took a few steps forward to toss the ball softly towards Shaya.

"As the next pitch came in, Shaya and his teammate swung the bat and together they hit a slow ground ball to the pitcher. The pitcher picked up the soft grounder and could easily have thrown the ball to the first baseman. Shaya would have been out, and that would have ended the game.

"Instead, the pitcher took the ball and threw it on a high arc to right field, far and wide beyond the first baseman's reach. Everyone started yelling, 'Shaya, run to first! Shaya, run to first!' Never in his life had Shaya run to first.

"He scampered down the baseline wide-eyed and startled. By the time he reached first base, the right fielder had the ball. He could have thrown the ball to the second baseman who would tag out Shaya, who was still running. But the rightfielder understood what the pitcher's intentions were, so he threw the ball high and far over the third baseman's head, as everyone yelled, 'Shaya, run to second! Shaya, run to second.'

"Shaya ran towards second base as the runners ahead of him deliriously circled the bases towards home. As Shaya reached second base, the opposing shortstop ran towards him, turned him towards the direction of third base and shouted, 'Shaya, run to third!'

"As Shaya rounded third, the boys from both teams ran behind him screaming, 'Shaya, run home! Shaya, run home!'

"Shaya ran home and stepped on home plate, and all eighteen boys lifted him on their shoulders and made him the hero, as he had just hit the 'grand slam' and won the game for his team.

"'That day,' said the father who now had tears rolling down his face, 'those eighteen boys reached their level of perfection. They showed that it is not only those who are talented that should be recognized, but also, those who have less talent. They, too, are human beings; they, too, have feelings and emotions; they, too, are people; they, too, want to feel important.'"

Rabbi Paysach J. Krohn

Nonstop

On August 4, 1992, my daughter Susy and I boarded a nonstop flight from Chicago to Oakland, California. When the plane touched down in Oakland that evening, Susy and I were not among the passengers.

It was to be a vacation. We were going to visit my parents, who live in Berkeley. My wife and our older daughter were taking the cross-country train. They had a three-day head start. The plan was to meet that night at my parents' house.

That didn't happen either.

Susy, age fourteen months, was traveling in my arms; no ticket necessary because she was under two. She was just getting over a cold, which had made her fussy. The trip thus far had been trying.

Then, not long out of Chicago and to my inexpressible relief, she fell asleep.

I pulled out my Tom Clancy novel, flagged the flight attendant and bought two beers. One must make the most of such intervals.

Susy, in my lap, slept deeply.

The man in the next seat was a pleasant fellow with an outgoing manner. He was a candy salesman for Schraft's and, though it was August, he was working on his Valentine's sales promotion.

He motioned to my sleeping bundle and asked about Susy: "How old? Does she do any tricks? Can she talk?"

"She is fourteen months," I replied, "and has just learned pat-a-cake. Her sole word was, 'dada.' Experience has demonstrated that 'Dada' is some kind of universal noun, not a reference to me.

The candy salesman nodded sagely.

"All children say 'Dada' and it doesn't mean anything special," he said.

After an hour, Susy stirred. I couldn't see her face because she was sitting on my lap, face forward, head against my chest. But she felt hot, damp and limp, like a bath mat. She started whimpering. Break time was over.

I cradled her in my arms and rose from our seat, intending to walk her up and down the aisle, cooing and cuddling. I looked at her face and nearly cried out.

Susy was having a grand mal seizure. I didn't know this right off, of course. The formal diagnosis came later. All I saw was her eyes popping out of her head while one side of her mouth was pulled and released by a grotesque leer. As the seizure intensified, her face was wrenched by one immense tic after another. She began to buck in my arms.

To say the least, I didn't know what to do. We were at 30,000 feet somewhere over Nebraska in a United Airlines 727 full of people. A passenger, a pleasant man I recognized from the waiting area in Chicago, observed my distress.

"Do you want me to call the flight attendant?" he asked.

"Please!" I said, and he tapped the call button over head. It lit up and made a sound like a "bong." A woman of about forty, sitting a couple of rows ahead and facing us, took us in. She had half noticed my frantic state but hadn't realized there was a big problem until the call button sounded. She stood up and demanded, "Is there something wrong with that child?" She had a Southern accent. The last word came out "chile"; rhymes with "while."

"Yeah," I said. "I think she's having a seizure."

And then this miracle woman says, "I'm a neonatal intensive care nurse. Can I help?"

The nurse, Peggy Moyers—late of Tennessee, now of Oakland—took Susy from my arms and hurried down the aisle into first class where it was roomy. She laid Susy on the floor of the galley. At that moment, Susy had a second grand mal seizure.

There were two doctors in first class; one an orthopedic surgeon and the other a retired cardiologist. They offered their opinions but were pleased to defer to nurse Peggy.

We got Susy down to her diaper. I held an oxygen mask over Susy's mouth. The mask covered most of her face. She was passed out, and she felt really hot. A stewardess had provided Peggy with a stethoscope and Peggy was listening to Susy's heart, looking very sober, very intense. I looked down at the unconscious Susy. *Just don't die*, I thought. *Anything else I can deal with. Just, please God, don't let her die.*

The head flight attendant squeezed in to the galley and asked if there was anything she could do.

Peggy whipped around and spoke rat-a-tat. "Yes. Tell the captain to land the plane right now in a really big city with a really good hospital."

The astonished stewardess had probably expected drink orders. She asked Peggy if she had any identification. Peggy told her where she'd been sitting. Her wallet was in her purse, her nurse's ID was in the wallet.

The stewardess carried Peggy's wallet into the cockpit. She emerged almost at once, went down on one knee and asked Peggy, "How's Denver?"

Peggy said Denver would be fine.

And then things started to happen.

The captain got on the PA system and told everybody that a child was ill and we were going to make an emergency landing in Denver. Peggy, Susy and I were jammed into a couple of seats in first class. The captain must have made a straight drop because we landed in what seemed like ten minutes.

The captain had radioed ahead. Two emergency medical techs scrambled onto the plane and took Susy from my arms. I was right behind them. I turned at the cabin door. Peggy gave me a wave. Several passengers whispered "Good luck." Very worried, with no clear idea of what was happening or where we were going, I followed the techs down the steps that had been wheeled across the tarmac to the plane. Our carry-on bags and all Susy's baby stuff were in the overhead compartment. There was no time to collect them. My Tom Clancy novel was on the floor next to the candy salesman. I have never finished reading it. It was his current bestseller, *The Sum of all Fears*.

An ambulance was waiting on the tarmac. It took us to a good-sized hospital in the middle of Denver. I carried Susy into the ER. It was about 3:00 in the afternoon when we arrived; maybe an hour had passed since Susy's seizure. She was alert now, though still pretty hot. The people in the ER were calm and focused. They needed to determine the source of the seizure: family history, poison, epilepsy, encephalitis, fever? They X-rayed Susy and examined her eyes and prodded her stomach. She had gotten some of her strength back and was spectacularly uncooperative.

When they tried to take blood, Susy was so dramatically contrary that it took three of us to hold her down. I had her legs.

As a nurse tried to get the needle in her arm, Susy pulled loose, sat up and pleaded to me, "Dada, Dada."

Which, of course, broke my heart.

Later, I thought about the candy salesman. He might be interested to learn that I had amended my assessment of the word "dada." They sent me out of the room so they could administer a spinal tap. But she was extra, extra uncooperative, they told me later: twisting and struggling so they couldn't get the needle in. The pediatrician in charge, a woman whose nameplate said "Dr. Smith" came into the waiting room and had a corridor conference with me.

She said Susy was so strong and forceful that she probably wasn't in such bad shape after all. Dr. Smith had come to the conclusion that Susy might have had a febrile seizure—one brought on by a sudden high fever that spikes at maybe 105 and shuts the brain down, literally causing it to seize. The fact that she was just getting over a cold pretty much confirmed the diagnosis. Dr. Smith said that about 2 percent of all kids have a febrile seizure sometime in their infancy. Nobody knows why. It doesn't mean trouble down the road. It just happens.

Playing it safe, the doctor hooked up an IV. It was after 9:00 at night. The day's events finally had taken the fight out of Susy and she didn't fuss too much when the big needle went in a vein in the crook of her left arm. They taped her arm to a board so that wouldn't bend it.

She was admitted for observation, and I was allowed to stay with her in the nursery. I called my wife, who was, at that point in their train trip, in Santa Fe visiting her sister. I was sobbing so hard that it was a couple of minutes before she understood what had happened. She and our older daughter would fly to Colorado the next day.

The United Airlines plane had long since landed in Oakland. Peggy told me later that a message had been relayed to the pilot from the hospital. Just before the plane touched down in California, he got on the PA and announced, "We just got word from Denver. Little Susy Fay is going to be okay." The plane errupted with applause.

There was a rocking chair in Susy's room in the pediatric wing. We rocked for hours. Her little books and toys were on the plane so, for entertainment, I sang. Torch songs, patriotic songs, spirituals, musicals. For some reason that, even today, I cannot explain, one song completely did me in. I was crooning the Jiminy Cricket version of "When You Wish upon a Star." And when I hit the words, "Like a bolt out of the blue, Fate steps in and pulls you through," I began to weep.

Susy, cradled in my arms, studied my face as I cried and cried.

I had only the clothes on my back in a large city where we knew no one. But I had Susy. From that trip I learned how much she means to me. And I learned that when a child needs help, you must give it. You must find a way, even if it means commandeering an airplane full of people.

That trip, that close call, that unplanned descent on Denver, was full of discovery. To have the privilege of being a parent is one long course of discovery.

At midnight, still awake, Susy tried to do pat-a-cake. But the board that secured her left arm to the IV had rendered it useless; it was like the flipper of a seal. She took my left hand, hauled it up, and positioned it so she could play pat-a-cake . . . her right hand against my left.

As the new day of discovery arrived, I listened to the sound of one hand clapping.

Stephen Fay

Babies and Restaurants Are the Chernobyl of Parenting

Taking care of a newborn baby means devoting yourself, body and soul, twenty-four hours a day, seven days a week, to the welfare of someone whose major response, in the way of positive reinforcement, is to throw up on you.

Dave Barry

If you're a new parent, there will come a time when either you or your spouse will say these words: "Let's take the baby to a restaurant!"

Now, to a normal, sane person, this statement is absurd. It's like saying: "Let's take a moose to the opera!"

But neither you nor your spouse will see anything inappropriate about the idea of taking your baby to a restaurant. This is because, as new parents, you are experiencing a magical period of wonder, joy and possibility that has made you really stupid. You are not alone: All new parents undergo a sharp drop in intelligence. It's nature's way of enabling them to form an emotional bond with a tiny human who relates with other humans exclusively by spitting up on them. Even very smart parents are affected, as we see from these two quotations:

Albert Einstein Shortly Before The Birth Of His Son: "To know that what is impenetrable to us really exists, manifesting itself as the highest wisdom and the most radiant beauty which our dull faculties can comprehend only in their most primitive forms—this knowledge, this feeling, is at the center of true religiousness."

Albert Einstein Shortly After The Birth Of His Son: "Daddy's gonna EAT THESE WIDDLE TOES!"

After a month or so of bonding with their baby, the typical parents have the combined IQ of a charcoal briquette. This is when they decide it's okay to take the baby to a restaurant. I know what I'm talking about: My wife and I have a baby daughter, and we have repeatedly taken her to restaurants, even though by now experience should have taught us that it would be far more pleasant and relaxing for us to stay home and play tic-tac-toe on our foreheads with a soldering iron.

But we cannot help ourselves, and neither can you, if you're a new parent. That's why today I'm presenting these Helpful Tips For Dining Out With A Baby:

1. THE INSTANT YOU GET TO THE RESTAURANT, ASK FOR THE CHECK. You want to be able to pay and get out of there as quickly as possible when your baby screams, or decides—as babies instinctively do in restaurants—to grunt out an impossibly large output, such that you experience a dreaded condition known to diaper scientists as Projectile Huggies Leakage (PHL). So it's best to pay your bill as you enter the restaurant, adding a little extra (say, eight hundred dollars) to compensate for the fact that after you're finished, your table may have to be burned. Some parents never actually enter the restaurant: They simply drive up to the front door,

hurl money out the car window, then speed off, their baby wailing like an ambulance siren in the night.

2. REQUEST A TABLE IN A LOCATION THAT WILL NOT DISTURB OTHER DINERS. For example, if you want to eat at an elegant restaurant in New York City, you should try to get a table on the roof. Or, better still, at a Bob's Big Boy in Cleveland.

3. SELECT AN APPROPRIATE CUISINE. Of the wide variety of cuisines available today—Italian, French, Chinese, Tiny Portions Of Meat With Some Kind Of Inedible Decorative Stuff Dribbled On The Plate In A Pattern As If It Were An Art Project Instead Of A Meal—I would say that the best kind of cuisine, for the parent of a small baby, is a cuisine that you can eat with one hand. You, of course, need the other hand to keep putting things into your baby's mouth, so your baby can spit them out (a baby is not happy unless it is emitting something from somewhere). In fact, you may need both hands for this activity, so you might want to order an entree that you can eat with no hands, sporadically lunging your face down to your plate and snorking up food Labrador-retriever style. You will not have time to taste anything. Restaurant employees know this, and sometimes, for fun, they serve prank entrees to new parents, to see if they'll notice. A Boston restaurant recently got a new father, distracted by a small baby, to eat a whisk broom covered with melted cheese.

At least he ate something. Sometimes, I spend the entire meal carrying my daughter around the restaurant, crossing paths with other nomadic parents carrying their children around, each of us leaving a trail of drool. Our big night out! It may not sound like fun to you, but we parents of newborns are able to enjoy it, because of our philosophy of life, which can be summed up by the immortal words penned by William Shakespeare shortly after the birth of his first child: "Woogum woogum WOOGUM WOOGUM WOOGUM!"

Dave Barry

If You Love Me, Say That!

Expressed affection is the best of all methods to use when you want to light a glow in someone else's heart and feel it in your own.

Ruth Stafford Peale

Jerry couldn't forget the snowy winter day that his first-born son almost had a serious accident. Jeff was in his first year of driving, which made Jerry nervous to begin with. The close call with disaster only heightened his anxiety.

One day following the near-accident, Jeff told his father he was getting ready to leave the house.

"Drive carefully, now!" Jerry warned.

Jeff turned to his father with a look of chagrin and asked, "Why do you always say that?"

"Say what?"

"'Drive carefully.' It's like you don't trust me driving."

"No, Son, that's not it at all," Jerry explained. "It's just my way of saying, 'I love you.'"

"Well, Dad, if you want to say you love me, say *that!*" Jeff said. "That way I can't mix up the message."

"But . . . ," Jerry hesitated. "What if your friends are here with you? If I say 'I love you,' you might get embarrassed."

"In that case, Dad, when you're saying good-bye, just put your hand near your heart, and I'll do the same," Jeff offered.

Jerry was touched that his son wanted, as badly as he, to express his love. "You've got a deal," he said.

A few days later, Jeff was getting ready to leave again, this time with a friend. "Can I have the keys, Dad?" he asked his father.

"Sure," Jerry answered. "Where are you headed?"

"Downtown."

Jerry tossed him the keys. "Jeff," he said, pausing before adding, "have a great time." He subtly placed his hand near his heart. Jeff did the same. "Sure, Dad," he said.

Jerry winked.

Jeff walked back to his father and whispered, "Winks weren't a part of the deal." Jerry was slightly taken aback.

Jeff headed for the door. "Okay, Dad, see ya," he said. Just before he shut the door, he turned back—and winked.

Mitch Anthony

Night Moves

In the middle-of-the-night pecking order, I'm chomped.

At 10:30 P.M.: my wife and I—too exhausted to floss, occasionally penciling in a kiss but typically making only eye contact like two tortured lab animals—slump off to sleep, sometimes with the stove burner left on.

12:30 A.M.: My son trudges off to the bathroom, misses the large hole I have strung with runway lights, pelts the cat in the eye, then knees my groin as he climbs onto my side of the bed.

1:00 A.M.: Trapped in the middle and asphyxiated from bad first-grader breath, I burrow under my wife and pop up at the edge of the bed barely alive. The rapid movement of fresh air knocks me back to sleep.

1:45 A.M.: Dreaming of climbing to the top of an Ivy League football dog pile, I awake to discover my son trapped under my pillow.

2:15 A.M.: My daughter, who I never heard come into my bed, yells as if possessed: "Daddy, get out. It's too crowded." I nudge my wife to move, she won't, so I leave.

2:25 A.M.: After removing seven layers of toys with a snow shovel, I climb under my daughter's Barbie comforter and with my feet sticking out, fall back to sleep.

2:40 A.M.: I wake up with my daughter's foot in my face. I push it away and she cries, "Daddy, stop it. I'm trying to sleep." I get out of her bed and limp to the kitchen to de-ice my toes over the stove burner.

2:55 A.M.: I slump off to my son's Ferrari bed and dive into three feet of water. I grab a leaking water pistol to stay afloat and hoist myself out.

2:57 A.M.: Drying off with a Tickle Me Elmo, I land on the lumpy living-room couch, my head sloping a foot below my feet. As the blood rushes to my eyeballs, I start my mental to-do list. Number one: Make appointment with chiropractor.

3:30 A.M.: The phone rings. With my brain swimming in blood, I reach for it and fall off the narrow couch and onto my daughter who is curled up on the floor.

"Daddy! I'm trying to sleep!" she yells. The phone stops ringing before I can get to it.

3:34 A.M.: I slip under a pile of laundry on the family-room couch and I'm lulled to sleep by chirping birds and passing traffic.

5:00 A.M.: Peeking through my son's Batman underwear, I watch as my children peel the clothes off the pile until they reach my exhausted body: "We're hungry. Make us breakfast!" they chime. Before I can answer, they begin to cry, which inspires all of the dogs in the neighborhood to bark.

6 A.M.: The paperboy pelts my sleeping face with the morning edition and I fall off the milk box. My head crashes to the cement and I finally get the sleep I deserved.

You think I'm making this up, don't you?!

Ken Swarner

The Gag Gift

A person's a person no matter how small.

Theodor Geisel (Dr. Seuss)

It was our turn to open presents this particular Christmas morning. The living room was already covered with torn wrapping paper from the onslaught of the children's eagerness to unveil the hidden treasures that had tormented them for nearly a month. Now we adults sat around the room with our presents at our feet, slowly removing the paper while at the same time holding back the child within ourselves and maintaining our dignity in front of each other.

My wife, Brenda, and her family have a tradition of buying each other gag gifts. This always makes me a bit uneasy at Christmas or my birthday, never knowing what form of embarrassment lies waiting for me under the thin confines of the wrapping paper.

One of my daughters, Christy, who at the time was six years old, was standing directly in front of me. The excitement of the moment just beamed across her face. It was everything she could do to keep herself from helping me rip the paper from each present. Finally, I came to the last gift. With my natural Sherlock Holmes ability, I deduced that this had to be the gag gift, because with them it was never a question of *if*, it was a question of *when* you came to it. So, with everyone looking on, I decided to go ahead and get it over with—just let them have their laugh—and I ripped off the paper. And there it was . . . a toy airplane about two inches long. Our holiday guests started giggling to themselves as I looked up to my wife with a smirk on my face and blurted out, "A toy airplane, give me a break!"

Brenda gave me the look: that look that always tells me I have just put my foot in my mouth and am in the process of thoroughly chewing it. I had failed to look at the name tag before I opened the present to see who it was from. As I picked up the paper from the floor and read the name tag, my heart sank. On the tag were scribbled block letters that read, "To Dad, Love Christy." I have never felt as low at any time in my life as I did at that moment. One of the most agonizing experiences of my life was having to look down into my daughter's little face to find the joy that had once been there replaced with a look of total embarrassment and humiliation. The fear in her eyes spoke her thoughts of hoping no one would find out that the gift her father found so repulsive had come from her.

This loving child had taken her spending money that she could have spent on herself, but instead had chosen to buy her daddy a Christmas present. And it wasn't just any present. She knew from watching me play computer video flight-simulator games that I was fascinated with airplanes.

I quickly knelt down and grabbed her up in my arms and held her as tight as I possibly could, willing to give anything to be able to take back those words. I made a feeble attempt to explain that I thought it had come from

Mom, but since I found out it came from her, that made it different. It was obvious that nothing I could say was going to change the hurt in her little heart. I had to find a way to prove I meant what I said.

And I did. I took that toy airplane in my hand and began making airplane noises. I taxied onto the runway, which was the counter, and throttled to full thrust and was soon airborne. My mission goal was to remove the hurt from my baby's face—that *I* had caused—and to continue until her smile returned. I played all day with that airplane. I put so much excitement into that airplane that the other children left their new Christmas toys and wanted a turn playing with my little two-inch airplane. And just like a little selfish kid I said, "No, this is mine!" It wasn't very long until Christy's face was beaming with a smile again. But I didn't stop there. That little plane became a treasure of great wealth to me, and still is, for I still have that little two-inch plane.

I keep that plane mainly because it came from my little girl's heart with love. But it's also a reminder to me of the power of words.

George Parler

THE FAMILY CIRCUS By Bil Keane

© 2001 BKI

"Daddy! You forgot these Father's Day drawings
for your office wall!"

For My Grandson

There is nothing like having grandchildren to restore your faith in heredity.

Doug Larson

I heard a story in church one Sunday about a family of Eastern European refugees, driven from their home by invading soldiers, who decide their only chance of escaping the horrors of war is to make it through the mountains that surround their village. They are sure they will find safety in a neighboring neutral country, if only they can make it over the pass. The grandfather is not well, however, and the days of his mountain hiking are long past.

"Leave me behind," he pleads. "The soldiers won't bother with an old man like me."

"Yes, they will," warns the son. "It will mean your grave."

"We can't leave you behind, Grandpa," implores the daughter. "If you won't go, then we won't either."

The old man finally relents, and the family, which numbers some ten people of varying ages, including the daughter's year-old baby girl, sets off after dark toward the blue-black mountain range in the distance. As they walk along silently, each takes a turn carrying the baby, whose weight makes travel more difficult, as they wind their way up the steep mountain pass.

After several hours, the grandfather sits down on a rock and hangs his head. "Go on without me," he says in a low voice. "I can't make it."

"Yes, you can," his son implores. "You have to."

"No," says the old man. "Leave me here."

"Come on," says the son. "We need you—it's your turn to carry the baby."

The old man looks up and sees the tired faces of the others in the group. He looks at the baby wrapped in a blanket and being carried now in the arms of his thin, thirteen-year-old grandson.

"Yes, of course," says the old man. "It's my turn. Come, give her to me." He stands up and takes the baby in his arms and looks into her small, innocent face. Suddenly, he feels a renewed strength, and a powerful desire to see his family find safety in a land where war is a distant memory.

"Come on," he says with a note of determination in his voice. "Let's go. I'm fine now. I just needed to rest. Let's keep moving." They all headed up the hill again with the grandfather carrying the baby.

The family reached safety that night, and everyone who started the long journey through the mountains finished it, including the grandfather.

Floyd Wickman and Terri Sjodin

When Life Throws a Hardball

Either you master your emotions, or they master you.

Loretta Young

It's 1955. I am nine years old and standing in the alley near my family's home in Columbus, Ohio, rubbing spit into the pocket of my new fielder's glove. Bare-handed, twenty yards away, my father crouches in the gravel, demanding, "Burn it in there! Make it sting! You won't hurt me."

Afraid of doing just that, I lob a marshmallow.

"Hard! Put something on it!" he commands, loosing the epithet he knows will redden my neck and bring him just the sort of pitch he wants. "You pantywaist!"

Knuckles whitening from the grip, I study my target with a look of unbridled malevolence. I wind up and deliver, less muscle than anger, more shame than control, aiming not for his cupped hands, but rather for a spot right between his eyes. The pitch is wild, six inches above his head, when it pops his palms. He nonchalantly tosses it back, saying, "That's better. Now get it down a little."

For my father, I learned to play baseball—with a vengeance. I threw myself at the sport and broke five bones before realizing—at age thirty-six, watching yet another emergency-room physician grimace at my X-rays—that I was still back in that Columbus alley trying to impress my dad.

Few sons truly understand their fathers. We thrash and flounder just below the tide of paternal expectation, suffocating in self-doubt, clawing for adulation. As children, we avenge the sting of criticism, the absence of praise, in fantasy. We imagine ourselves the sons of more appreciative fathers. We daydream of heroic deeds, as though compelling our fathers to kneel in contrition might be the only way to make them see us eye-to-eye.

Fathers don't will themselves to be as enigmatic as they appear to their sons, however. My own father, a miner's son, grew up as uncertain as I of where he stood in his father's eyes. Yet he could no more stop himself from making his birthright my legacy than he could change his blood type. He toughened the hides of his sons with ridicule, chastened their shortcomings. He fully expected that we'd eventually prove we were growing up by raising fists to his authority.

My time came the year I turned sixteen. I was seated at the dining-room table when some flip comment I'd made provoked my father to rise and strike me; then came his dare to finish the matter outside. He used the "pantywaist" taunt again, but this time I looked at him not with anger but with pity. Anger he could deal with, but not pity.

After that, Dad gave grudging acceptance to my coming of age. But even as I graduated from high school two years later and was about to enter the navy, it was awkward for my father and me to absolve ourselves and each other of both real and imagined transgressions. Still etched in my memory is an autumn afternoon in 1968 when we went hunting together and tried to make our peace.

Had it been an earnest search for game, the afternoon would have been wasted. But in reality we were saying good-bye. I was leaving for Vietnam, and although terms of endearment came as hard to my father as ordering from an Arabic menu, he was trying to say something.

We sat in a clearing in the woods, watching dusk sponge the last light from the October sky. The tension was unbearable. When it became too much, we headed back to the car and started home. Nothing was said for a while. Then, gripping the wheel, staring at the bumper of the car ahead, he managed, "I want you to know I'm proud of you—always have been. If there were a way I could take your place, I'd do it. I'll miss you."

I never understood how much he meant what he said until years later, when a friend recalled an incident that had occurred in a tavern while I was away. "Your old man was shooting pool," the friend recounted, "and some loudmouth—a big strapping guy—was talking about Vietnam. Finally this guy, who had a boy your age in college, said, 'Well, you've got to keep the smarter ones home so they can run the country.' He never knew what hit him. Your dad came across the pool table before I could grab him. He was half this guy's size, but your father had him pinned on the shuffleboard machine with a pool cue across his throat, trying to choke him. It took four of us to pull your dad off of him.

"The year you were gone," he added, "a piece of your father died every time a military car came down the street."

My father hid from me his fears that I might not return. He was silent as well about his disappointment when I parted company with the navy after my hitch was up, instead of making it my career. It wasn't until recently that

I learned why he had taken such pride in seeing me in uniform.

Earlier this year a cousin gave me a letter Dad had written to her father over fifty years ago, shortly after Dad had enlisted in the navy. Written from the Naval Air Station at Corpus Christi, Texas, the two-page missive brimmed with his hopes of becoming a Navy pilot and making that a career.

"We fly with the pilots any time we want," my father boasted in the letter. "We swim out in the bay and fasten wheels on the seaplanes, then fasten them to a tractor onshore and pull them up the runway and wash the salt water off them. We change the oil and monkey with the engines." In the following paragraph, he detailed goals for the military career he intended to follow.

He was nineteen and single. His father had been forced by family necessity to quit school and work in the coal mines at age thirteen. In the Navy, Dad glimpsed the bright brass ring of a future better than his father's.

Shortly after he wrote the letter, however, he was turned down for flight training. He applied for submarine school and was accepted, but a rigorous physical detected a heart murmur. He was handed a train ticket home.

The letter explained a lot. When my father left Ohio for the Navy, he had no intention of returning. It was not his life's dream, as fate eventually ordained, to spend thirty years repairing garbage trucks while struggling to feed six children. His thwarted dreams made him bitter, and in his misguided eagerness to brace his offspring for similar reverses in life, he had tried to temper us with withering criticism. *So that,* I thought, folding the letter, *is where the "pantywaist" business came from.*

I was out of town when he passed away. The unfamiliar voice on the phone was his neighbor, calling to tell me Dad had suffered a fatal heart attack and that my mother wanted me to come home immediately. I recall cradling the phone in my lap long after it clicked silent.

Heading to Ohio the next morning, I remembered that game of catch we had played twenty-three years before. How I wanted to put a lump on his head as big as the one he had put in my throat. Why did two people who loved each other so deeply find such devious, childish ways to hide it from one another? I wonder if he died knowing how much I cared.

Pantywaist, I thought, half-smiling, my knuckles whitening on the steering wheel of the car taking me home, one more time, to Dad.

Mike Harden

A Year of Firsts

First and foremost, they are our fathers; and whatever magic we had with them, even if it is for just a few of our very early years, profoundly affects us for the rest of our lives.

Cyra McFadden

I call it a "Year of Firsts." Whenever someone you love passes away, the first year without them becomes a collection of moments and memories brought on by a holiday, birthday or special event.

My pop, Charles Perks, passed away on July 6, 1998. Less than two weeks later, I celebrated my forty-eighth birthday ... without him. The year of firsts began.

Of course, all of the typical events—his birthday, Christmas and New Year's Eve—were hard. But Sunday dinners, picnics and trips to the park also became painful reminders that he was gone.

As a professional inspirational speaker, I often told stories about my father that he knew nothing about. Now every time I told one, I felt he was watching and hearing them for the first time. Like a child, I thought I would be in trouble when I got home. Of course, upon returning home, I missed the phone call from him that would come to make sure I returned safely. "I asked God to protect you!" he would tell me. I'd reply, "He did, Pop. Thanks."

But of all the firsts in this first year, the most difficult one was Father's Day. The past several years, it was near impossible to find just the right gift for Pop. We almost always ended up giving him a gift certificate. Kind of a one-size-fits-all gift. But it always seemed inappropriate and lacked imagination and heart.

So what would I give him this year? Flowers on his grave seemed so cold and empty. I could hear him telling me not to throw money away like that. Then it dawned on me. The perfect gift.

Early Father's Day morning, I drove out to the cemetery. I knew this would be a difficult moment for me. A hundred people must have been there visiting their loved ones. At first, I sat in my car and just watched them. Some cried as they knelt down in prayer. A few drove up, placed the flowers near the headstone and left without hesitation. I sat in my car parked right next to my Pop's grave, remembering the good times and crying. Then as planned, I stepped out of the car leaving the door wide open. I reached over and popped in my CD that I had recorded recently at a professional studio. I think he would have been proud of my accomplishment. Pop loved to sing in his younger days. It was a gift he gave to me. I often sing during my presentations. But Pop stopped singing after Mom died of cancer in 1972.

I walked over and stood at the foot of his grave as the music began pouring out from my car. With all my heart, I sang his favorite song, "Danny Boy." In reality, whenever he heard this song, he thought of my brother Tom. In fact he left a handwritten version of it for Tom entitled, "Oh,

Tommy Boy." I discovered it in his belongings and read it as a surprise at the funeral. But today I sang for Pop.

"And I shall hear though soft you tread above me." He finally got to hear my music.

"For you will bend and tell me that you love me." With tears pouring down my face I said, "I love you, Pop. Happy Father's Day."

I couldn't continue and returned to my car and wept like a lost child.

Yesterday was July 6, 1999. My year of firsts has ended. But my love for him will live forever.

Bob Perks

My Father, the Hero

I cannot think of any need in childhood as strong as the need for a father's protection.

Sigmund Freud

My father was a good and honest man who was incredible at managing conflicts. Wise. The type that only spoke when he had something important to say. At least this is how I see him now. His power was in his quiet strength. He didn't have to tell anybody he was powerful. He showed it.

But when I was a teenager, I remember thinking as he sat between my brother and I wordlessly and watched us fight—with a slight grin on his face, head turning from side to side as if watching a tennis match—that he was powerless. The only thing he said was, "You have to learn to choose your battles." I thought he was crazy. *Why doesn't he do something? Can't he help me? What's the matter with him? He's my father, he should do something, not quote tired clichés!* But he held to his silence. I held to my opinion for many years, somehow believing, despite the evidence, that he was, indeed, powerless. Recently, however, my older brother Mitch told me a story that reawakened me to what I had known as a child and forgotten as a stubborn adolescent: My father was a hero.

My father had taken Mitch and several of his friends to a Golden Gloves boxing match. The event was filled with excitement for this fourteen-year-old boy. Before each match began, he watched people in the crowd. Blacks, whites, Hispanics, Asians. But as soon as the match started, his attention was on the ring. He did not even get distracted by the fights that were breaking out in the stands.

When the event was over, Dad, Mitch and his friends piled into the car in the parking garage. The kids asked Dad if they could go get ice cream. He said resolutely, "No, it's a school night." They began to pull out of their parking space and realized they couldn't go far, because random fights began to develop among people in the garage. "Random" because it appeared that no one knew whose side they were on. Black people punched black people; whites punched whites; Hispanics hit other Hispanics; and anyone who got stuck in the crossfire got punched. The next day the papers called it a "race riot," but those in attendance knew it was a free-for-all: a bunch of people who had gotten pumped up by the boxing matches and wanted to hit someone, anyone.

My father and brother, both of whom were sitting in the front seat of the car, found themselves as spectators again. Next to Mitch's window, several people were fighting and falling against the side of the car. Mitch watched, spellbound, until he saw one of the fighters pull out a blade that was as large as a butcher's knife. The blade was headed toward a victim leaning against Mitch's window.

Mitch looked over toward my dad hoping for reassurance, only to find Dad's seat empty. He had bolted out of the car, locked then slammed the door shut and was running around the car, headed straight for the man with the knife. He got so close to the man that they stood face-to-face, Dad yelling, yet completely controlled, "Put that knife away, get into your car and leave before someone gets hurt." The man looked shocked, but actually complied. Dad yelled to the rest of the crowd, again in a commanding voice, a voice that sounded like reason, calm in the midst of chaos, "All right, break this up! Everyone get in your cars and go home." Amazingly, the fighting ceased. All but one man moved toward their cars. Dad moved toward the last offender, and although Dad was six inches shorter and weighed a good fifty pounds less than the angry man, my father did not falter. They made direct eye contact, and Dad repeated, "I said, stop the fighting, get in your car now and leave." The man made a move toward my father. In a whisper, audible in the silence of the garage, he repeated himself, "I want you to take your son, get in your car and leave. And I don't want to have to say this again." The man turned, grabbed his son and grunted profanities as he went to his car. My father returned to his car and as he drove out of the garage, he turned to the kids and said, "Let's go get ice cream."

I don't know for sure, but I suspect that the blade of a knife in close proximity to his son triggered a value that shook my father to his core. I suspect that in that moment of decision—the decision to go out and face the knife—he was willing to give his life to protect his son. I suspect that this was not a conscious thought, but rather the selfless act of a man who lived from Love, and called on God in such a manner that there was no doubt in his mind that his efforts would succeed.

I understand my father better now that I know this story. I laugh at myself when I remember the day I decided my father was powerless. The truth? I was young, and he possessed wisdom that was barely a whisper at my level of understanding. It was his wisdom that gave him his power. He knew that the fight between my brother and me in my adolescence was trivial, that it was our battle and that we must learn to work it out. He was honoring our right to "learn to choose our battles." He is gone now, and I honor him by choosing to adopt a value that he would have died for: Battle is a choice, and it is the choice of the powerful to choose not to battle.

Beth Clark

Hello . . . Good-Bye, Daddy

I was not close to my father. But he was very special to me. Whenever I did something as a little girl—learn to swim or act in a school play, for instance—he was fabulous. There would be this certain look in his eyes. It made me feel great.

Diane Keaton

The plane's engines groaned in defiance as it tried to escape the gravity that was holding it to the earth. Once free, it settled into a gentle hum that was almost a comfort to hear. I hated flying because it scared me so. It was a fear of not being in control of my life. Someone else had the helm, and I was just a bystander.

But today was different. It was a very special thing that made me hop on a plane and fly to California. I was going to see my father. As I watched the clouds beneath me protect the earth in a blanket of pristine white, my thoughts drifted back to my childhood when I was seven.

"Victoria," Granny called from the front door. "There's mail for you." My heart almost stopped with excitement. I had never gotten mail!

I ran as fast as I could and almost ran right into Granny. "Slow down," Granny said with a smile. To my surprise there was a package, not just a letter, but a package! All for me! I sat down on the couch and ripped the brown paper wrapping as fast as l could. I didn't even know who it was from, but it didn't matter. It was something for me and me alone!

The tissue paper rattled as I threw each piece to the floor, and when I had the last piece almost off, I saw it. Oh, my eyes could not believe it! A beautiful red jumper with lace ties on the side and a white blouse with puffy sleeves. I screamed and stood up and something dropped to the floor. I stopped and looked down at my shoe. It was something shining and round. A silver dollar laid at my feet. "Oh Granny ... look, Granny, look, a silver dollar." I picked it up and felt the cold metal in my hand. It almost covered my entire palm!

I caught Granny staring at me, arms folded and her head shaking back and forth with amusement. Finally, she spoke, "That's from your daddy. He sent you a birthday present," she stated flatly. "Really, Granny? Really! This is from my daddy?"

I had not seen my father since I was eighteen months old, and I didn't really remember him at all. But I had my fantasy of him that I had dreamed up in my head. A white knight on a beautiful horse and he always, always called me Princess.

And I would let no one talk badly about my father, because he was The Prince I had manufactured in my own little world and I loved him more than anything in life. After all, he was always close because I carried his picture with me and we had grand conversations.

The plane rocked as we hit turbulence and the seat belt sign came on. I fastened my seat belt and was hurled back into reality. The flight attendant touched my shoulder and

I jumped, which frightened us both, and we exchanged a strained laugh. "May I get you anything?" she asked with a smile.

"No, no thank you," I managed with a slight bit of embarrassment.

"Thirty minutes and we'll be landing," she said and walked away.

I closed my eyes and thought, *Thirty minutes and I'll be seeing my father.* After twenty-five years, I was going to actually meet the man I called Daddy. I had never in my life wanted to see someone as much as I wanted to see and know him. I loved him even if I had not seen him. He was my father.

I stepped off the plane and the sun was warm on my face. I took a deep breath and went to catch a taxi to finally meet my father face-to-face.

I opened the door to the church and stood there for what seemed like an eternity. The red carpet under my feet, I thought, *How beautiful.* I walked to the front of the church and the small talk around me stopped, and there was silence that filled the entire room.

"Daddy? Hi, Daddy, it's your little girl, Victoria." I touched the casket where my father lay and felt the cold metal in the palm of my hand. I fought the emotions that were so near the surface. *I just wanted to tell you I loved you and have missed you so much.* I reached to touch his hair and the face I would never forget.

"Daddy, I brought something to give you. Do you remember my birthday? Oh, you made me so happy that day." My voice cracked and I choked back the tears that I knew were coming.

"I've kept this all these years, but I want you to have it now."

I placed the silver dollar under his hands. *It's okay, Daddy, I had enough love for both of us.*

"I guess this is hello and good-bye, Daddy. I just wish I could have felt your arms around me and heard you call me Princess just one time."

I knew I was falling apart at that moment, as someone touched my shoulder and asked, "Are you Victoria? You're Harold's daughter, right?"

I fought back the tears and answered, "Yes."

The man hugged me and said, "I have known you all your life, although I never met you. Your father spoke of you often with such pride. He carried a picture of you around in his pocket and referred to you as his little Princess."

Victoria Robinson

The Most Precious Gift

It is almost impossible to smile on the outside without feeling better on the inside.

Anonymous

I'll never forget that warm summer day in July 1965, when my mother unexpectedly died of a still unexplained illness at the young age of thirty-six. Later that afternoon, a police officer stopped by to ask my father's permission for the hospital to use my mother's aortic valve and the corneas from her eyes. I was absolutely stunned. *The doctors want to dissect Mom and give her away to other people,* I thought as I ran into the house in tears.

At fourteen, I could not understand why anyone would take apart a person I loved. To top it off, my father told them, "Yes."

"How can you let them do that to her?" I screamed at him. "My mom came into this world in one piece and that is how she should go out."

"Linda," he said quietly, putting his arm around me, "the greatest gift you can give is a part of yourself. Your mother and I decided long ago that if we can make a difference in just one person's life after we die, then our death will have meaning." He went on to explain they had both decided to be organ donors.

The lesson my father taught me that day became one of the most important in my life.

Years passed. I married and had a family of my own. In 1980, my father became seriously ill with emphysema and moved in with us. For the next six years, we spent many hours talking about life and death.

He cheerfully told me that when he died, he wanted me to donate whatever was in good condition, especially his eyes. "Sight is one of the greatest gifts a person can give," he said, noting how wonderful it would be if a child could be helped to see, and draw horses the way my daughter Wendy did.

She had been drawing horses all her life, winning award after award. "Just imagine how proud another parent would feel if her daughter could draw like Wendy," Dad said. "Think how proud you would feel knowing that my eyes were making it possible."

I told Wendy what her grandpa had said, and, with tears in her eyes, she went into her grandpa's room and gave him a big hug.

She was only fourteen years old—the same age at which I was introduced to the donor program. What a difference!

My father died April 11, 1986, and we donated his eyes as he had wanted. Three days later Wendy said, "Mom, I'm so proud of you for what you did for Grandpa."

"That makes you proud?" I asked.

"You bet! Have you ever thought what it would be like not to see? When I die, I want my eyes donated just like Grandpa."

At that moment, I realized that my father gave much

more than his eyes. What he left behind sparkled in my daughter's eyes—pride.

What I couldn't know that day, as I held Wendy in my arms, was that only two weeks later I would be once again signing papers for the donor program.

My lovely, talented Wendy was killed when a truck hit her and the horse she was riding along the roadside. As I signed the papers, her words echoed over and over: "You bet! Have you ever thought what it would be like not to see?"

Three weeks after Wendy's death, I received a letter from the eye bank.

> Dear Mr. and Mrs. Rivers,
>
> We want you to know that the corneal transplantation was successful and now two people who were blind have regained their sight. They represent a living memorial to your daughter—a person who cared enough about life to share its beauties.

If somewhere a recipient discovers a new love for horses and sits down to sketch one out, I think I'll know who the donor was. A blond-haired, blue-eyed girl will still be drawing.

Linda Rivers

A Favorite Recollection

Laughter is the best communication of all.

Robert Fulghum

When I started dating, about the age of eighteen, my mother always waited up for me to come home. As soon as I would walk in the door of the apartment, she and I would go into my bedroom, she would sit herself down on my bed and we would hash over the whole evening. Usually at this hour Daddy would be about to doze off for the night, but our talking would filter into his bedroom, which was very close by. "Are you girls going to talk all night?" he would call out. "Can't you wait until morning to have this discussion?" My mother would shush him and tell him to go back to sleep. He would grumble and be quiet for a while and then start all over again. "Lillian, come back to bed. When she's ready to marry the guy, you'll ask all those questions." Eventually, Mom and I would kiss each other good night, and she would go back to her room to pacify my dad.

As a young man my father started out as a comedian and tap dancer in vaudeville and burlesque. When vaudeville died, his dreams of show business died, too. Through the years, though, he never missed a chance to tell a few jokes, sing a song and do a little soft-shoe. He produced shows for his lodge and later for his condominium in Florida. He was a warm and outgoing person who always had a smile and kind word for everyone.

One weekend my mother went out of town to visit some relatives, and I had a date for that Saturday night. I promised Daddy I would not be home too late and that he really didn't have to wait up for me. My date picked me up, he and Dad met, they shook hands and off we went.

Well, the evening ran a little later than I had promised and as we walked to my house from the subway station, I could see my daddy hanging out the window of our third-story apartment, watching for me. I kept talking to my date hoping to distract him so that he wouldn't see my father, because I would have been terribly embarrassed. As soon as we reached the door of my apartment, I bid my date a real fast good night and waited until I heard the lobby door close before I opened the apartment door with my key.

I tiptoed in and saw that the door to my parents' bedroom was closed. "Good," I said to myself, assuming that Daddy had gone to bed. I was relieved not to have to give any explanations about why I was late coming home. I opened the door to my bedroom, walked in and almost fell on the floor.

There sat my dear daddy on my bed, wearing a big smile on his face and dressed in one of my mother's dresses. His curly hair was pouffed up, his legs were crossed, and with one hand on his knee and one on his hip he started speaking in a high-pitched tone. "So," he said, "How did the date go? What did he say and what did you say? Where did you have dinner? Did you go to a show? Will you see him again? By the way, what does he do for a living? Did he treat you nicely? I certainly hope he was a gentleman. Do you think he's serious about the relationship?"

"Daddy," I said, "slow down, one question at a time. This was only our third date."

"Well, I just want to make sure I get all the information that your mother gets when you talk to her."

We must have talked and laughed for almost an hour. Finally, I was the one who said, "Time for bed, we'll talk in the morning. I'm the one who's tired now."

Daddy gave me a hug and kiss good night and said, "Don't forget, we have to remember every little detail to tell your mother when she gets home, so she won't feel left out."

Rosalie Silverman

The Turtle

A tall man full of smiles bent down and patted my tousled-blond head and stuck something green and wiggly in my small, eager hand. I'm sure I smiled, too, just then, though maybe not back at him, my attention directed at the lively thing clutched tightly in my tiny fingers. It was one of those little turtles sold in pet shops, and quite popular I suppose, in the early 1950s.

The round, hard shell fit perfectly in the cup of my hand. I marveled at the various shades of green and yellow and red, the lines of which curved and angled around its head, which poked out inquisitively at my face. When I turned the turtle over, its short, fat legs moved oddly, each out of sequence with the other, as if this action might help propel it somewhere even in its upside-down position. I'm sure I laughed and thought all those things that little boys do and named it, too, though I can't remember exactly what.

Of course, I didn't know where it originally came from or why it was given to me at the time, nor did I care. I simply set about to do what any number of three-year-olds would do. Sifting around I found a plastic knife in my sandbox and began to saw happily upon its shell. Good thing for my new pet that I soon grew weary of the task and decided to play with it instead.

The tall man, as it happened, was not so tall after all. I was to find that out later in life when I came to size myself. He had been my present height exactly as a matter of fact—five-feet-six. But for the standards that I judged back then, at the age of three, he was quite the giant of a man, at least to me, and a nice one.

I remember that day, the day of the turtle, if little else of my toddler years. That was the day that this man walked into the house where my mother was. I know now that if I hadn't been busy with my newfound friend, perhaps I would have noticed him leave a few moments later. Maybe I would have waved. Maybe I did, I don't remember. But even so, how was I to know that, when he left that day, I would never see him again?

I'm speaking of my father, of course. To this day at the age of forty-eight, I find it hard to write about the man without a tear running down my cheek.

You see, he died before I came to know him, though I desperately wanted to. It had been my desire in life to find him, to knock on his door, to share some life with him. I was not angry, nor am I now. My heart ached for him and still does.

Ironically, I did find out where he was and even that he was a great writer. These things were kept quiet through my boyhood, what with the scandals and wherewithal of divorce being even greater back then. But I managed to pick up bits here and there, slips of the tongue, things kindly spoken by nostalgic grandmothers. I made up my mind, and my heart as well, that I fully intended to see him when I left the Marines. I didn't care what anyone thought, but it was not to be. My heart was effectively broken in half when I learned he had died two months before my discharge.

Twenty-five years went by, and I still carried with me the desire to simply know him. I never once remember a period when I hadn't thought of him, and still I grieved privately and found an emptiness that couldn't be filled. And I had in me this strange driving compulsion to write. But I didn't.

Then one day, I heard from my late father's widow. She said she would like to meet me and had pictures and things if I was interested. Still searching for my father, I packed up my wife and our young son and we headed for the Chicago area.

It was a wonderful meeting that day, the first moments of it culminating in a gathering silence as the lady, in somewhat of a happy shock, saw the resemblance of her late husband walk in to kiss her on the cheek. And though it was only me and we both knew it, she was quite satis-fied with this and delighted still. She invited us to her home. There I began to know my father, not only through his wife and his two other sons (a wonderful union in itself), but in the things he left unknowingly for me. Perhaps he somehow knew I'd be there someday, and for that I thank him now.

She had me remove from the attic a large, dusty box full of papers and letters and pictures, fragile treasures that I began to sort through with the misty blue eyes that my father had given me. Everyone lent me privacy in this. There were mementos of love and life, complete with notes and articles, including his obituary. Many things in that box led me along the trail of his life and helped me to understand him.

I pored over his manuscripts, both awed and amazed by his talents and accomplishments. It was obvious, right there in black and white, that he was a well-respected and prolific writer with high standards and many credits to his name who made quite a handsome living at his chosen work. He taught creative writing, spoke at seminars, judged pageants. I felt the pride swell in my chest. My theory had been that all this knowledge would help somehow in diffusing the pain, but I found that my heart ached even worse. Secretly, I lamented even more having lost the chance to be father and son.

At the end of this visit, my life changed. For the first time, I emerged fully formed and unwrapped from life's chrysalis. When I left my father's wife, I had two things in my hand that I pressed to my heart. One was a manuscript that both inspired and motivated and released in me everything that I am. With words he had pounded out long ago on his old Royal, he spoke to me on ancient yellowing paper in a fatherly tone that went straight down into my heart and helped me realize suddenly who I am and what I must do. Simply put, he said, in his still-living voice: You are a writer and now you must write!

Those words from my father have changed my life, and for that I am grateful.

As I turned to leave with this parchment in one hand, his widow pressed something into the other. It was a small cloth box.

"He would have wanted you to have this," she smiled. "He wore it on his tie."

I opened it slowly. It was a small green turtle.

Steven M. Wheat

Down Suicide Hill

An old-fashioned, blustery snowstorm had brought the neighborhood kids out in force. I was the parent-on-watch as they shouted and scooted through the white. On everything from skis and toboggans to flattened cardboard boxes, the little ones whooshed down a gentle slope. Older kids, including my son, Josh, braved a far steeper path, a trail that disappeared into the woods called Suicide Hill.

Every so often a survivor would emerge from below to tell his tale and offer steering tips. "Aw, man, I missed The Death Tree by an inch!" Or, "Go left of the rock, then over The Rapids. It's awesome!"

Little mittened surfers they were—reckless and all fired up. Not me. I was simply trying to stay warm until I could get back in front of the fireplace. Now and then I'd describe the wonders of cocoa to anybody who'd listen.

"All chocolatey and delicious," I said to my daughter, Rebecca, as she zipped down the safe slope on a plastic surfboard.

But the day changed when a wild kid I'll call Randy,

who looked to be about ten years old, burst out of the woods and added his account of Suicide Hill.

"I lost it at The Cliff," he said, wide-eyed. "I bailed." Something in Randy's voice summoned long-forgotten feelings—and right then and there, I knew. I was going down Suicide Hill.

And why not? I'd followed the children onto roller coasters, water slides and go-carts. Fatherhood for me had featured plenty of high-speed conveyances—from skateboards to Rollerblades. Suicide Hill was a logical progression. Suicide Hill was my destiny.

Summoned by the siren call, I borrowed Randy's Flexible Flyer and, hefting it in front of me like a shield, headed in a trance-like state toward the crest. The kids fell silent. They knew that a father was about to test the limits, to boldly go where no grown man had gone before.

"Dad," Josh yelled, "careful of the ice by the pine tree."

"And the roots after Dragon Curve," added Randy with concern. At that moment, I stood for all fathers who had been accelerated by their children. I laughed at their caution. After all, Daddy is not about caution. Daddy is about risk.

At the crest, I took a deep breath, then two quick steps, dropped onto my thirty-something belly and headed into the jaws of danger: the ice by the pine tree. "Your father's gonna die," I heard Randy cry out.

"Hah!" I laughed into the steering bar of the sled.

"Becky quick, go get Mom," Josh yelled to his sister.

The trail fell away suddenly, and I plunged face first down an icy chute. I bottomed out with a thump and leaned on the tiller into a hard right. I was instantly euphoric and terrified. I kaboomed past a great oak that had to be The Death Tree, then turned quickly left, right, then left again through a narrow file of pines. It had been two years between sled rides—but it all came back. I was alert and ready. I could hear my pulse.

Zooming out of the left turn, I whacketed under a thorny tunnel of bushes and saw a giant boulder dead ahead. I remembered the cartoon gag where the tracks of a pair of skis go around both sides of a tree, and I made a hairbreadth high-speed decision: go left around the boulder. Then I made another instant and equally brilliant decision: go right around the boulder. Left. Right. Left. Right. I pulled the steering bar back and forth. I pictured the blood pulsing in and out of my heart. As I accepted the finality of death, I flashed on Mrs. Fitzgerald, my fifth-grade teacher, and that purple flowery dress she wore. It was pretty.

There was a sonic boom. And my sled and I were airborne, a mile or two off the ground. We were over the boulder and headed into orbit. In that gravity-defying instant, I understood the phrase "warp speed."

As I hit the ground, I wondered how long a man could live without air in his body. But this was no time for getting sentimental about oxygen. The trail banked quickly left. I hung my left leg off the sled's side and pulled hard on the rudder. Come hither, beckoned centrifugal force. Slow down, said my brain.

I desperately dragged my foot, trying to claw my toes into the unforgiving ice. My boot came off, and some ligaments in my left ankle gave way. But those extra ten pounds I was carrying around came in handy. They helped me hold the line as I rocketed through the turn.

Coming out of it, I fishtailed, showed some finesse through a maze of roots, then burst out of the woods into the flatness of someone's backyard. As I slid under a jungle gym, I reached up, grabbed a swing to slow down and tumbled sideways off the sled into the snow.

I lay there for a moment listening to my breath. Alive breath. Daddy breath. When I lifted my head, I saw a half-dozen kids in ski jackets running down the hill toward me like some quilted MASH unit. Randy was carrying my boot.

"You all right, Dad?" Josh yelled. I gave him the thumbs up. "He's okay, Mom," Josh shouted up Suicide Hill.

Later there was cocoa, a wrap for my ankle and lots of stories. "Daddy, you were funny," Rebecca said, as though I had done a clown act for the kids instead of having flirted with the Grim Reaper. At bedtime Josh murmured sleepily, "Dad, you were awesome on Suicide Hill."

"Thanks, pal," I said, rubbing his head. "Awesome" might not have been my choice. A single word wouldn't do to describe my run down the hill. The phrase nearly hospitalized came close, as did "in mortal danger." But I couldn't blame Josh for being impressed. I had shown some world-class Daddy moves.

Josh closed his eyes, smiled and headed back to dreams of his cat-quick father. As I watched the moonlight stream onto his face, I neared the edge of yet another precipice.

I let myself go and surrendered to a Daddy swirl of sentiments. I could have told Josh that fatherhood was even more awesome than that ride down Suicide Hill. I could have told him that fatherhood was full of unexpected turns, all demanding major-league agility.

But sitting there in that bedroom, subject to no excessive gravitational forces, a Daddy at rest, I careered through the past and the future of this child. Proud of all the ways I'd served him, humbled by all the ways I'd failed. I was on that sled again, knifing back and forth through paternal gates of joy and dread. I swear I could feel the wind on my face.

Hugh O'Neill

7

A FATHER'S WISDOM

My prescription for success is based on something my father always used to tell me: You should never try to be better than someone else, but you should never cease trying to be the best that you can be.

John Wooden

A New Perspective

As a child, I could always depend on my father to put life's disasters into perspective, whether it was a broken leg or a broken heart. Years later, I was devastated by a series of personal crises. Feeling helpless and overwhelmed, I spent my last three hundred dollars on a trip to Florida to see Dad.

On the final evening of my visit, we stood at the end of a jetty watching the sun settle into the Gulf of Mexico. I could no longer contain my bitterness.

"You know, Dad, if we could take all of the great moments we experience in our lifetimes and put them back-to-back, they wouldn't last twenty minutes."

He responded simply, "Yup."

I turned to him, stunned. He was still studying the sun that sat on the horizon. Then, looking evenly into my eyes, he added quietly, "Precious, aren't they?"

Sean Coxe

Uncle Bun

Uncle Bun was a charmer. He didn't visit very often, but his occasional visits to my childhood home during the 1940s and 1950s changed everything for whatever period of time he was there. I was one of eight children, and most of our excitement came from making mud pies, playing with June bugs and lightning bugs and building a play-house in the former chicken coop.

In our eyes, Uncle Bun was a world traveler. Whenever he came for a visit, he would tell us stories about where he'd been and the people he'd met. He brought all of us a new perspective on life. He usually had a wonderful pres-ent for each of us and, sometimes, we would walk to the small country store in town where he would buy an entire brown bag of penny candy. That bag looked enormous when I was a little girl.

We never knew when we might hear from Uncle Bun. I attributed that to the fact that his "career"—whatever that was—kept him far too busy to plan ahead. Sometimes, instead of a visit, he'd send a huge box full of special sur-prises, things we'd never seen before. No children have ever been more delighted than we were as we unpacked those brown cardboard treasure chests of love.

I remember thinking how very rich Uncle Bun must have been to afford such fancy things. I couldn't help but compare this exciting and generous uncle with my own father: a simple man, with a simple life, working in the lead mines and taking on handyman jobs when he could in order to maintain a home for his wife and family. I loved my dad, and I knew he was a good man. But his life was unglamorous compared to his jovial brother with the twinkle in his eye, the wide grin and the fascinating stories.

Uncle Bun always phoned us a day or two before his visit, and as soon as Dad would hang up the phone and tell us who called, the excitement would begin to build. We adored Uncle Bun and looked forward to this welcome break in our routine.

What I didn't know as a child was that, when Uncle Bun called, Dad drove into town and wired money to him from the small savings he'd put aside. Every penny Uncle Bun spent on us actually came from my father. Over the years, the pieces started falling into place: Uncle Bun's many travels were by train—riding unticketed in the back of freight cars. His stories were of people who rode with him, and they were all slightly embellished.

I'll never know why Uncle Bun chose to live the way he did, or why my dad kept his secret all those years. What I do know is that, in a situation where it would have been easy to take the credit himself, my dad carried on an unselfish act for years. Through Uncle Bun, Dad gave us gifts from places he'd never travel. And through us, Uncle Bun was part of a family and received the love he didn't see in the lonely life he lived. From my father, who never said a word, I learned what selfless, unconditional love is all about.

Jan Nations

Once the Son, Now the Father

One winter evening as I sat reading, my young son, Luke, approached my chair in shy silence. He stood just outside the half-moon of light made by an old brass student lamp I cherish. It once lighted my doctor father's office desk.

In those days, Luke liked to approach me with his most serious problems when I was reading. The year before, he did this whenever I was working in the garden. Perhaps, he felt most at ease with difficulties when I was doing what he was getting ready to do. When he was interested in growing things, he learned to plant seeds and leave them in the ground instead of digging them up the very next morning to see if they had grown. Now he was beginning to read to himself—although he wouldn't admit to me that he could do that.

I looked up from my paper, and he gave me his wide-open grin. Then his expression turned abruptly serious, a not-too-flattering imitation of me. "I broke my saw," he said, withdrawing the toy from behind his back. "Here."

He didn't ask if I could fix it. His trust that I could was a compliment from a small boy to the miracle fixer of tricycles, wagons and assorted toys. The saw's blue plastic handle had snapped. My father, who treasured the tools of all professions, would not have approved of a plastic-handled saw.

I said, "There are pieces missing. Do you have them?"

He opened his clenched fist to reveal the remaining fragments. I did not see how the saw could be properly mended.

He watched me intently, his expression revealing absolute confidence that I could do anything. That look stirred memories. I examined the saw with great care, turning over the broken pieces in my hands as I turned over the past in my mind.

When I was seven, I'd gone to my father's office after school one November day. My father was clearly the best doctor within a thousand miles of the small Ohio River town where we lived. He always astonished me—and his patients—by the things he could do. He could not only heal whatever was the matter with anyone, but he could also break a horse, carve a top and slide down Long Hill on my sled, standing up! I liked to hang around his waiting room and hear people call me "little Doc," and I liked the way his patients always looked better when they left his office.

But on this day, when I was seven, my purpose was to see my best friend, Jimmy Hardesty. He hadn't been in school for three days, and his mother had sent word to my father's nurse that she just might bring Jimmy in to see the doctor today.

When the last of the afternoon's patients had gone, Jimmy had still not arrived. My father and I then went off to make house calls. He liked to have me with him, because he liked to tell stories when he drove. It was nearly seven when we finished. As we started home, my father said suddenly, "Let's go up and check on old

Jimmy." I felt squirmy with gratitude, certain that my father was doing this just to please me. But when we came in sight of the old gray stone house, there was a light in the upstairs back window and another on the back porch—the ancient beacons of trouble.

My father pulled the car right into the dooryard. Alice, Jimmy's older sister, came running out of the house and threw her arms around my father, crying and shaking and trying to talk. "Oh, Doc. Jimmy's dying! Dad's chasing all over the county looking for you. Thank goodness you're here."

My father never ran. He used to say there was no good reason to hurry. If you had to hurry, it was too late. But he told Alice to let go of him, and he ran then. I followed them through the yeasty-smelling kitchen and up the narrow, dark hall stairs. Jimmy was breathing very fast and made a high, airy sound. He had mounds of quilts piled over him, so that I could barely see his face in the flickering light of the kerosene lamps. He looked all worn out and his skin glistened.

His mother said, "Oh, Doc. Help us. It was just a little cold, then this afternoon he started this terrible sweat."

I had never seen Jimmy's mother without an apron on before. She stood behind me, both her hands on my shoulders, as my father listened to Jimmy's chest. He fixed a hypodermic and held the needle up to the light. I was certain that it was the miracle we all must have. My father gave Jimmy the shot. He then got a gauze pad from his black case and put it over Jimmy's mouth. He bent over him and began to breathe with him. No one moved in that room and there was no other sound except the steady pushing of my father's breath and Jimmy's high, wheezing response.

Then suddenly as lightning, there was the awful sound of my father's breathing alone. I felt his mother's hands tighten on my shoulders and knew, as she knew, that something had snapped. But my father kept on breathing into Jimmy's lungs. After a long time, Mrs. Hardesty went over to the bed, put her hand on my father's arm and said, very quietly, "He's gone, Doc. Come away. My boy's not with us anymore." But my father would not move.

Mrs. Hardesty took me by the hand then, and we went down to the kitchen. She sat in a rocker and Alice, looking as forlorn as I've ever seen anybody look, threw herself on her mother's lap. I went out onto the porch and sat down on the top step in the cold darkness. I wanted no one to see or hear me.

When Mr. Hardesty came back and saw our car, he went into the house and in a while I could hear voices. Then silence, then voices again. At last my father came outside, and I followed him to the car. All the lonely way into town, he said nothing to me. And I could not risk saying anything to him. The world I thought I knew lay sundered in my heart. We didn't go home. We went to his office instead. He began going through his books, looking for something he might have done. I wanted to stop him, but I didn't know how. I couldn't imagine how the night would end. From time to time, all unwilling, I would begin to cry again. Finally, I heard someone at the door and went out through the reception room, grateful to whomever it might be. News of the beginnings and endings of life traveled far and fast in a community like ours. My mother had come for us.

She knelt down, hugged me, rubbed the back of my head, and I clung to her, as I had not done since I was a baby. "Oh, Mama, why couldn't he, why couldn't he?" I wept and lay my head against her shoulder. She rubbed my back until I was quiet. Then she said, "Your father is bigger than you are, but he's smaller than life. We love him for what he can do; we don't love him less for what he can't. Love accepts what it finds, no matter what."

Even though I'm not certain I understood what she meant, I know I felt the importance of what she said. Then she went in to get my father. That winter seemed to have gone on forever when I lived through it long ago, but the memory played it out in seconds.

I sat turning over the pieces of Luke's broken toy. I said to him, "I can't fix it."

"Sure you can."

"No, I can't. I'm sorry."

He looked at me, and the expression of awesome confidence faded. His lower lip trembled, and he fought his tears even as they came.

I pulled him on my lap, and comforted him as best I could in his sorrow over his broken toy and his fallen idol. Gradually his crying subsided. I was certain he sensed my melancholy at seeing myself only an ordinary mortal in his eyes, because he stayed nestled against me for quite a time, his arm about my neck.

As he left the room, giving me a direct and friendly look, I could hear my mother's voice telling me in her certain way that love was not conditional. Once the son, now the father. I knew absolutely that out of the anguish of that discovery came the first faint light of understanding.

W. W. Meade

Dad, I Have a Beach Ball

I sat in the car in the driveway, listening to my daughter's pain. One of her "friends" had decided that her own self-worth needed a boost and that it would come at Betsy's expense. Every day at school, she would look for an opportunity to embarrass Betsy in front of the other kids. She would ridicule Betsy's clothes, her looks or something Betsy had said. She was making my kid's life miserable. Such are the ways of some teenagers.

"I can't go to school without worrying about what she is going to do! I don't understand why she is doing this to me. Sometimes, I wonder what she would do if I wasn't here anymore."

"What do you mean?" I asked, not wanting to know the answer.

"I mean, what if something happened to me and I wasn't around anymore? My life is miserable. If I wasn't here, nobody would care."

I held back my fears and told her, "I'd care. Your mom would care. We love you and think you're a wonderful kid. We would miss you." Our talk ended, as it was time to go in the house and get to bed.

That night, I talked to my wife, Nancy, about what

Betsy had said. Besides being the "mama bear" who wanted to take vengeance for the attack on her cub, Nancy said, "We have to keep her talking to us. We have to find a way to make sure she doesn't keep all this bottled up inside." We talked late into the evening about what we could do.

The next day at dinner, I told both Betsy and our son Andy that their mom and I wanted to talk to them about something. "Remember what Mr. Tewell [our minister] said last week about the beach ball?"

In Tom Tewell's sermon, he talked about a beach ball. He talked about how light it was, and how a small wind could just blow it away. He asked us to think about diving into the deep end of a swimming pool and trying to keep that beach ball between our legs, underwater. Sure, you can do it for a while. But, after succeeding for a time, two things can happen. You get so tired you let the ball slip and it pops up to the surface. Or, in the worst case, you get so tired trying to hide it, you might even drown.

Tom asked us to think of the beach ball as a problem, a lie or an act that we had committed that we didn't want anyone to know about. We try to keep it hidden. We use all our strength, and focus all our attention, on that beach ball. It ruins our life. But, if we let that beach ball pop to the surface, to the light of day, it just becomes the piece of plastic it is and eventually blows away.

I could see that the kids wondered what the point of this story was. I told them that sometimes, we all get into situations where we have our own beach ball we are hiding. We told them that from now on, whenever they had something they felt they could never tell us, that they should come to us and say, "I have a beach ball."

We promised that the only thing we would do for twenty-four hours was to listen. No yelling, no judgment, no advice, we would just listen. After twenty-four hours, we could talk to them about how they might get out of the situation they were in. But whenever they had a beach ball, we would just be there for them and listen.

Over the years, we had plenty of beach balls presented to us, usually late at night. Some were more distressing than others. Some were even funny, and we tried not to laugh as we listened. Some never reached our ears, but they did reach the ears of friends of ours whom our children trusted. We always abided by the twenty-four-hour rule. We never went back on our word, no matter how much we wanted to react to what they told us.

They are both young adults now. I am sure they will still have beach balls from time to time. We all do. But they know we will still be there to listen to them. After all, it's just a beach ball . . . a few pieces of light plastic glued together that blow away when you let it go.

Jeff Bohne

Pass It On

*My father never talked to me about how to treat
people. Every act of kindness I have ever shown
another person was because I was trying to imi-
tate him.*

Pamela McGrew

It was a bummer of a Friday, so I was relieved to know
the best part of the day would begin as soon as the school
bus dropped me off at my home. I ran quickly between
raindrops into the house.

"Dad, I'm here, I'm ready!"

My dad came from the basement with folded clothes
from the dryer and put them down. I searched for my
umbrella to cover the hair my mother, the beautician, had
styled the night before. Dad worked at Blue Cross and
Blue Shield and was always home one-half hour before
me. He was dropping me off at Darlene's, who was seventeen, a year older than me, and Darlene was driving us to
the mall.

"Jenna, come on."

"Okay!" I said, glad to get going. The umbrella covered

my hairdo as rain drizzled on Dad's long, loose blond hair.

"I got to get a pair of Nikes, and I just might as well get sandals, too," I told Dad, speaking over the radio.

"Jenna, you should limit yourself to a pair of sneakers."

"Geez, Dad. Mom like totally gave me her charge card. Why can't I just have 'em both?"

"Jen, you've got to stop being so selfish," he answered.

"But I'm an only child!" I joked with him as we went down I-490 toward Marketplace Mall, "Aren't I supposed to be selfish?"

"Don't try pulling that with me, Missy," he laughed.

My father knew me; I could have my way with Mom, but my dad was not an easy touch. He was always talking about responsibility and stuff like that. While I was running it through my mind how to finagle Dad into okaying the sandals, I felt the truck slow down, gravel spitting and spurting like popcorn in all directions, as he pulled the Toyota onto the shoulder of the expressway.

"What's wrong, Dad, why are we stopping?" I asked.

"Lady back there, looks like she's in trouble."

"What lady?"

"See the little S-10 pickup back there?"

I turned around, straining my neck to see what he was talking about. Then I saw it, a little white truck pulled to the side of the expressway.

"Yeah, I see it," I said, disgusted.

"There's a lady inside, she's having trouble with the truck and needs some help."

"Geez, Dad, like why do we have to stop and help her? Let somebody else do it." My dad gave me that look, and I knew I was in for a lecture.

"Look, little girl," he said with not a trace of a smile on his face, "you never pass up a person you can help. By me helping this lady, there's a great possibility that if my daughter, my spoiled only child, ever gets stranded or need help, someone just might stop and help her. Sit here and wait, I'll be right back!"

Though it was early June, I felt a chill go through me as my eyes followed my dad walking through the rain back towards the woman's S-10. Five minutes later he was back.

"She ran out of gas."

"Oh, what are we gonna do?" I asked, trying to show my dad I wasn't really such a spoiled, uncaring brat. It's just that it would be another week before I could get my learner's permit to drive the used Firebird Mom and Dad had bought for me and I just totally had to get to Darlene's to go to the mall.

"There's a plastic gas container in the back. Got to get to the gas station at the end of this exit."

"Okay, Dad."

We pulled into the gas station within two minutes; it wasn't far, the lady could have walked it. Dad parked the truck near the air pump, reached behind his seat and grabbed the container. He walked over to the gas pump, filled it up and paid the station attendant. As he walked back to the truck, his long blond hair waved through the breezy mist of the rain. I glanced at his ear and noticed the cross that he proudly wore on his earlobe. His neatly manicured hand reached for the door handle, and he hopped into the truck.

"Jen, Darlene's house is around the corner. I'm gonna drop you off, then come back here, park my truck and walk this gas down the ramp. You have fun at the mall, and be home by eight."

"Sure, Dad, okay." When we got to Darlene's house I gave him a peck on the cheek, then left to greet Darlene who was standing next to her Mustang.

The following week I had my learner's permit, then soon afterwards, my driver's license. I drove Darlene and

I everywhere during the summer, and I was thrilled when school started because I drove myself to school: No more bus for me. Autumn turned quickly into winter, and I was still loving the freedom the Firebird gave me. But my first winter of driving in the snow was a challenge. One clear winter morning I drove to school, but during the day it snowed like crazy, an unpredicted blizzard. By the end of school there was twenty inches of snow. I was lucky as I drove, making my way through the streets, but soon luck ran out and I found myself stuck at an intersection. A big burly guy in a four-by-four saw me struggling trying to rock my red Firebird free. He came up to my car and tapped the window.

"Miss, you need help?"

I rolled the window down just enough to keep the cold air from rushing in on me.

"Yeah, I keep spinning wheels in this stuff."

"I'll push while you give it a little gas," he instructed. "Okay," I heard him yell from behind the car, "Good. Now straighten your wheels. Miss, you gotta straighten the wheels." He pushed some more. "A little more gas, just a little." The car lunged forward, and I was free from the grip of the snow. He waved and nodded that I was okay.

"Thanks, Mister," I said, pulling five dollars from my purse. "Thanks! I really appreciate your help," I waved the money at him.

"Sorry, can't take that. Just saw you in trouble and needed a hand. My pay is knowing I could help you, and that you thanked me for helping. You can just pass it on by helping somebody else in a jam, that's how I see it. Go on, get yourself home and outta this stuff."

"Gee, thanks, Mister. Thanks again."

"You're welcome! Just remember, pass it on!" And with that he got back in his four-by-four and left. I got a great feeling inside as I drove home, thinking about my dad's talk about compassion. *Thank you, Dad, for helping that stranded lady last summer.* My father's lecture and the big burly man helping me suddenly made sense, and I'm proud to say I'm no longer that selfish, little brat anymore. I've learned to help others whenever I can, because by helping others, there's a great possibility that if my dad, my kind and loving dad, ever needs help, someone might just stop and help him.

Joan Lewis

A War Story

War stories. I was raised on them. Wrinkling my nose at oatmeal on a typical school-day morning, years ago, I can still recall my father's justifiable anger, as he began what I callously believed to be so much hot air. "You know Sandy, when we were in New Guinea, we would have given anything to have . . ." And so the story went. And there were many other stories, all equally unappreciated. When I decided to accompany Dad to his forty-fifth reunion of the 11th Airborne Unit, I thought I had heard them all.

Arriving early, I watched as Dad's former comrades assembled. Some were recognizable, others had been forgotten, for it had been many years since Dad had attended the last reunion in 1950, just five years after the end of World War II.

"Remember me, John?" called out a delighted-looking gentleman, approaching us and walking with a discernable limp.

"Why, Silent Yokem! Where the hell have you been?" my father answered. "After I got back to the states, I tried to look you up, but never had any luck."

"Well, I've always had a nonpublished number, John. That's why."

Turning to me, Rudy Kwiatkowski, alias "Silent Yokem" said, "I owe a lot to your old man. If it hadn't been for him, I wouldn't be alive. You see, when we were in Leyte, I smashed my knee and couldn't walk. Both the medics had just been shot down, and everyone was movin' fast with all the bombing going on. Your dad stayed behind, refusing to leave me. I kept saying 'Go on without me,' but your father wouldn't listen . . . he carried me out of there on his back."

"I didn't do it alone," interrupted Dad. "One of the other guys helped me. We traded off. I could've never done it alone."

Speechless, I eventually managed to ask Dad why he never told me this particular story.

"These kinds of stories are common. We all helped each other out," he said with a shrug.

For many veterans like my father, there are no medals to proudly display. The only reward for their honor and courage seems to lie within, only rising to the surface when the grateful recipients of such acts choose to speak of them. I smiled at my father, suddenly too proud of him for words.

War stories. I look at them differently now. And at the men who made them.

June Sandra Karshen

My Forever Valentine

The traditional holidays in our house when I was a child were spent timing elaborate meals around football games. My father tried to make pleasant chitchat and eat as much as he could during halftime. At Christmas he found time to have a cup or two of holiday cheer and don his holly-shaped bow tie. But he didn't truly shine until Valentine's Day.

I don't know whether it was because work at the office slowed during February or because the football season was over. But Valentine's Day was the time my father chose to show his love for the special people in his life. Over the years I fondly thought of him as my "Valentine Man."

My first recollection of the magic he could bring to Valentine's Day came when I was six. For several days I had been cutting out valentines for my classmates. Each of us was to decorate a "mailbox" and put it on our desk for others to give us cards. That box and its contents ushered in a succession of bittersweet memories of my entrance into a world of popularity contests marked by the number of cards received, the teasing about boyfriends/girlfriends and the tender care I gave to the card from the cutest boy in class.

That morning at the breakfast table I found a card and a gift-wrapped package at my chair. The card was signed "Love, Dad," and the gift was a ring with a small piece of red glass to represent my birthstone, a ruby. There is little difference between red glass and rubies to a child of six, and I remember wearing that ring with a pride that all the cards in the world could not surpass.

As I grew older, the gifts gave way to heart-shaped boxes filled with my favorite chocolates and always included a special card signed "Love, Dad." In those years my thank-yous became more of a perfunctory response. The cards seemed less important, and I took for granted the valentine that would always be there. Long past the days of having a "mailbox" on my desk, I had placed my hopes and dreams in receiving cards and gifts from "significant others," and "Love, Dad" just didn't seem quite enough.

If my father knew then that he had been replaced, he never let it show. If he sensed any disappointment over valentines that didn't arrive for me, he just tried that much harder to create a positive atmosphere, giving me an extra hug and doing what he could to make my day a little brighter.

My mailbox eventually had a rural address, and the job of hand-delivering candy and cards was relegated to the U.S. Postal Service. Never in ten years was my father's package late nor was it on the Valentine's Day eight years ago when I reached into the mailbox to find a card addressed to me in my mother's handwriting.

It was the kind of card that comes in an inexpensive assortment box sold by a child going door-to-door to try to earn money for a school project. It was the kind of card you used to get from a grandmother or an aging aunt or, in this case, a dying father. It was the kind of card that put a lump in your throat and tears in your eyes because you knew the person no longer was able to go out and buy a real valentine. It was a card that signaled this would be the last you would receive from him.

The card had a photograph of tulips on the outside, and on the inside my mother had printed "Happy Valentine's Day." Beneath it, scrawled in barely legible handwriting, was "Love, Dad."

His final card remains on my bulletin board today. It's a reminder of how special fathers can be and how important it has been to me over the years to know that I had a father who continued a tradition of love with a generosity of spirit, simple acts of understanding and an ability to express happiness over the people in his life.

Those things never die, nor does the memory of a man who never stopped being my valentine.

Pamela Underhill Altendorf

Dad's Squirrel

My memory is foggy as to whether I was sixteen or seventeen years old that sunny, autumn Saturday, but the memory is crystal clear when I think of that crisp morning. Dad and I were running errands when an encounter with a squirrel changed my life forever.

I am still sitting next to Dad in the front seat of our car, the passenger's side, but this isn't a past memory, dream-like. It's a vivid replay, over and over, as if it is happening to me today.

I was daydreaming out the window and singing with the music on the radio. I'm sure it was a hippie tune my dad didn't approve of. "One of those loud hippie songs" he grumbled that I should turn off. We were approaching the intersection of two side streets in this typical Chicago neighborhood. There was a park on our left side, with swing sets and slides abandoned at this wee hour. In front of a local bar, just outside my shotgun view, were brownish-green cubes of lawn between gray concrete city strips. "The Tavern" served great lunches all week to the factory workers and I thought, *How odd, there is no aroma of grilled onions and burgers coming from there.* The streets were so unusually empty. That's why I was startled when

Dad slammed on his brakes as we were turning left.

His right arm went up as usual, to be sure his passenger was braced and safe (these were pre-seat belt days). We weren't going fast at all, so I was surprised at his frantic reaction. Nothing was in sight. I stopped singing, sat upright and looked around for a clue as to what the heck he was doing! From that moment on, all I could do was observe.

Dad parked the car quickly and jumped out, never saying a word (which was also highly unusual). I watched him carefully pick up a squirrel. This small creature had just run into our car tire as it raced into the street. Perhaps it was gathering food for the winter chill on the way. But it never completed its task.

I watched my dad as he placed the tiny, gray, fuzzy body on a patch of grass under a maple tree. He looked around for just a second, and selected the largest golden-orange leaf he could find and covered the squirrel. Then I saw it. Dad had tears in his eyes. His bright blue eyes, usually sparkling with passion and life, had filled up and one teardrop escaped. As it dripped down his cheek, he wiped it away quickly, sniffled, got back in the car, and didn't allow another drop to be seen. It was as if this was the first time I saw my dad cry. I sat there stunned, realizing there was a side to Dad he kept hidden. My feelings were unexplainable at the time.

I had seen Dad cry at funerals, but everyone did that. These occurrences usually ended up in great reunions visiting with loved ones from afar. But cry over a squirrel? A lowly rodent with no sense at all? What would make anyone shed a tear, especially my father?

Here was a man I loved and feared. This was the man who made sure we went to church every Sunday and holiday, but religion was not for him. We did what he told us and knew there was no back-talk, ever. This was a strict man; no-nonsense, quick-tempered, but when he laughed, it emerged like a fiery volcano, loud and explosive from a bottomless shaft in his belly. There was nothing quiet about Dad. He knew everything and was often very intimidating. Why would roadkill make him cry? I think I was awestruck.

To see Dad cry pierced my heart. If he would have cried aloud, I would have joined him. I never knew sensitivity existed in my dad; he was strong, tough, hard. The remainder of the drive I sat just like him, completely silent. I don't recall if the radio was shut off or I just tuned it out. I only heard the silence of our hearts. I pondered the phenomenon I just witnessed. I was never quite sure what Dad's silence meant.

As an adult today, I wonder if Dad cried from all the sadness and loss he suffered in his lifetime. That Saturday morning, did his past heartaches lunge into the present at the jerk of his brakes from this unexpected accident? Was there any relation to his own subconscious grief at being motherless since thirteen months old and a squirrel that didn't make it home to waiting little fuzzy tails? Was he absorbed with stress from all his dedication and hard work invested in a thankless job as he was jolted into this mishap? Was he worrying about his four defiant children that he thought he didn't have much influence over anymore? (He was wrong!) Was he preoccupied with the fact he couldn't keep his children from growing up and his love could only be shown in strict protection and his desire to keep us eight years old forever? I'll never know where his thoughts were that day, but I saw a slight scratch beneath the rugged surface that changed how I looked at my dad forever.

There was a deep, reverent side to this man that he wanted to keep a secret. His respect for all life, even God's scurrying creatures, was deeper than I ever could have imagined. A glimpse of his true spirituality slipped between us that day. I think all the world was his church, though we never spoke of this incident.

Dad ceremoniously moved the animal off the street to keep this still body from being disregarded. The fact that a squirrel brought tears to his eyes brought tears to mine.

Dad's been gone so very long, yet to this day he affects my own driving. When I see a busy squirrel near the road, I stop. I let the little tree rat pass or retreat. I believe Dad is sitting next to me in the car. I glance at the passenger's seat and see him smile, telling me, "Good job."

I smile back, and brush away oncoming tears, still missing that overpowering presence, but grateful he unknowingly revealed a part of his inner soul to me. We share his secret, a part of him that few had seen and fewer knew existed. Who would think a squirrel with a large maple leaf for its grave could have such an impact on two bonded souls?

Loralee H. Hartje

My Father, My Son, My Self

I don't mind looking into the mirror and seeing my father.

Michael Douglas

My father still looks remarkably like he did when I was growing up: hair full, body trim, face tanned, eyes sharp. What's different is his gentleness and patience. I had noticed neither as a boy, and I wondered which of us had changed.

My son Matthew and I had flown to Arizona for a visit, and his sixty-seven-year-old grandfather was tuning up his guitar to play for the boy. "You know 'Home on the Range'?" my father asked.

"Yeah! I know that one," four-year-old Matthew said, bouncing on the couch and furtively strumming the guitar he wasn't supposed to touch. Then with a fierce pride he added, "My daddy taught it to me!"

My father and I were once at great odds. We went through all the classic resentful and rebellious teen stuff: shouting matches, my weird friends, clothes and beliefs. I still vividly recall the revelation that finally came to me one day that I was not my father and that I could stop trying to prove I wasn't.

When I was a boy, my father wasn't around much. He worked seven days a week as a milkman. But even when at work, he was the taskmaster in absentia. Infractions were added up, and at night he dispensed punishment, though rarely beyond a threatening voice or a scolding finger.

I believed that manhood required that I stand up to him, even if it meant fists. One day, some friends and I buried our high school's parking-lot barriers under the woodpile for the annual homecoming bonfire. We hated the things, because they kept us from leaving school in our cars until after the buses had left. I thought the prank was pretty funny, and I mentioned it to my father. He didn't think it was funny, and he ordered me to go with him to dig the barriers out.

Can you imagine anything more humiliating at age sixteen? I refused, and we stood toe-to-toe. Dad was in a rage, and I thought for an instant that the test had come.

But then, he shook his head and calmly walked away. The next day, my friends told me that they had seen him at the bonfire celebration. He'd climbed into the woodpile in front of hundreds of kids, pulled out the barriers and left. He never mentioned it to me. He still hasn't.

Despite our father-son struggles, I never doubted my father's love, which was our lifeline through some pretty rough times. There are plenty of warm memories—he and I on the couch watching TV together, walking a gravel road at dusk, riding home in a darkened car singing "Red River Valley."

He had this way of smiling at me, this way of tossing a backhanded compliment, letting me know he was proud of me and my achievements. He was a rugged teaser, and it was during his teasing that I always sensed his great, unspoken love. When I was older, I would understand that this is how many men show affection without acknowledging vulnerability. And I imitated his way of saying "I love you" by telling him his nose was too big or his ties too ugly.

But I can't recall a time my father hugged or kissed me or said he loved me. I remember snuggling next to him on Sunday mornings. I remember the strong, warm feeling of dozing off in his arms. But men, even little men, did not kiss or hug; they shook hands.

There were times much later when I would be going back to college, times when I wanted so badly to hug him. But the muscles wouldn't move with the emotion. I hugged my mother. I shook hands with my father.

"It's not what a man says, but what he does that counts," he would say. Words and emotions were suspect. He went to work every day, he protected me, he taught me right from wrong, he made me tough in mind and spirit. It was our bond. It was our barrier.

I've tried not to repeat what I saw as my father's mistake. Matthew and I cuddle and kiss good-bye. This is the new masculinity, and it's as common today as the old masculinity of my father's day. But, honestly, I don't believe that in the end the new masculinity will prevent the growing-up conflicts between fathers and sons. All I hope is that Matthew and I build some repository of unconscious joy, so that it will remain a lifeline between us through the rough times ahead.

It was only after having a boy of my own that I began to think a lot about the relationship between fathers and sons and to see—and to understand—my own father with remarkable clarity.

If there is a universal complaint from men about their fathers, it is that their dads lacked patience. I remember one rainy day when I was about six and my father was putting a new roof on his mother's house, a dangerous job when it's dry, much less wet. I wanted to help. He was impatient and said no. I made a scene and got the only spanking I can recall. He has chuckled at that memory many times over the years, but I never saw the humor.

Only now that I've struggled to find patience in myself when Matthew insists he help me paint the house or saw down dead trees in the backyard, am I able to see that day through my father's eyes. Who'd have guessed I'd be angry with my father for thirty years, until I relived similar experiences with my own son, who, I suppose, is angry now with me.

More surprisingly, contrary to my teenage conviction that I wasn't at all like my father, I have come to the greater realization: I am very much like him. We share the same sense of humor, same stubbornness, even the same voice. Although I didn't always see these similarities as desirable, I have grown into them, come to like them.

My father, for instance, has his own way of answering the phone. "Hellll-o," he says, putting a heavy accent on the first syllable and snapping the "o" short. Call me today and you'll hear "Hellll-o," just like the old man. Every time I hear myself say it, I feel good.

This new empathy for my father has led me to a startling insight: If I am still resolving my feelings about my father, then when I was a boy my father was still resolving his feelings about his father.

He raised me as a result of and as a reaction to his own dad, which links my son not only to me and my father, but to my father's father and, I suspect, any number of Harrington fathers before. I imagine that if the phone had rung as the first Harrington stepped off the boat, he'd have answered by saying "Hellll-o."

For reasons too profound and too petty to tell, there was a time years ago when my father and I didn't speak to or see each other. I finally gave up my stubbornness and visited unexpectedly. For two days we talked, of everything and nothing. Neither mentioned that we hadn't seen each other in five years.

I left as depressed as I've ever been, knowing that reconciliation was impossible. Two days later, I got the only letter my father ever sent me. I'm the writer; he's the milkman. But the letter's tone and cadence, its emotion and simplicity might have been my own.

"I know that if I had it to do over again," he wrote, "I would somehow find more time to spend with you. It seems we never realize this until it's too late."

It turned out that as he had watched me walk out the door after our visit—at the instant I was thinking we were hopelessly lost to each other—he was telling himself to stop me, to sit down and talk, that if we didn't he might never see me again. "But I just let you go," he wrote.

I realized that his muscles just hadn't been able to move with the emotion, which is all I ever really needed to know.

Not long ago Matthew asked me, "Sons can grow up to be their daddies, right?" This was no small struggling for insight, and I was careful in my response. "No," I said, "sons can grow up to be like their daddies in some ways, but they can't be their daddies. They must be themselves." Matthew would hear nothing of these subtleties.

"Sons can grow up to be their daddies!" he said defiantly. "They can." I didn't argue. It made me feel good.

All morning I am anxious. Matthew and I are about to leave Arizona for home, and I am determined to do something I have never done.

There is a time in every son's life when he resents the echoes reminding him that, for all his vaunted individuality, he is his father's son. But there should also come a time—as it had for me—when these echoes call out only the

understanding that the generations have melded and
blurred without threat.

So just before my son and I walk through the gate and
onto our plane, I lean over, hug my father and say, "I want
you to know that I love you. That I always have."

Walt Harrington

Thank You, Dad

The best thing to spend on your child is your time.

Arnold Glasgow

My father got his first job at eleven years old, cleaning up the garbage outside of the bowling alley. Two years later his dad died, and my father worked odd jobs to help put food on the table during the Depression. Ten years after that, Dad fell in love, married Mom and had a baby girl. Eight more children followed. During those years, Dad slipped into a routine he never broke. He woke up before six, took the train to work and wouldn't get home until after five-thirty. After supper, Dad spent the rest of the evening in the cellar making dental parts for extra money.

Two years ago, at the age of sixty-four, Dad retired. When I was young, Mom and Dad did well to hide the fact that we were poor. We all went to Catholic schools and always had plenty of school supplies. We slept in bunk beds, shared one bathroom and watched television from a tiny black-and-white set up in the living room. Mom and Dad never bought anything for themselves. They clipped coupons, wore the same pair of sneakers for twenty years and sewed ripped clothing together every Saturday afternoon.

At his retirement party, I wanted to thank Dad for all his hard work and sacrifice by buying him the best present I could think of. I wanted to buy him the big-screen television he could never afford or send him on a vacation he never took. As I shopped, I realized there was nothing I could buy that could thank Dad enough. Dad taught me through his own hard work and faith in God that the greatest gifts come from the heart and not the store. That night, I sat down and wrote a list of "Thank You's" to my father for all he had done for me. I left it on the kitchen table for Dad to read before going to work for the final day.

Thank you, Dad,

— for waking up every morning when it was still dark outside and going to work, while we slept in our warm beds.
— for teaching me how to pray.
— for coming to all my Little League games and for keeping quiet when other fathers wouldn't.
— for loving my mother with all your heart.
— for cooking me cheeseburgers.
— for building that voice inside me that said "no" when I was tempted to get in a car after I had been drinking.
— for teaching me to hit to the right when I have two strikes.
— for giving me a hug when I badly needed one.
— for picking me up from the train station at night when I was afraid to walk home.
— for smiling often.
— for helping me buy my first car.
— for wearing that ugly paper tie I made you in first grade.

— for teaching me to root for the underdog.
— for praying for me.
— for fighting for our country in the war.
— for teaching me I can never say "please" and "thank you" too often.
— for giving me life even after you lost a son.
— for taking me out for ice cream the night I struck out with the tying runner on third.
— for teaching me to be generous to those less fortunate than me.
— for being a wonderful grandfather.
— for telling me it's okay to cry.
— for being my hero.
— for being my friend.

James Ruka

Who Is Jack Canfield?

Jack Canfield is one of America's leading experts in the development of human potential and personal effectiveness. He is both a dynamic, entertaining speaker and a highly sought-after trainer.

He is the author and narrator of several bestselling audio- and videocassette programs, including *Self-Esteem and Peak Performance, How to Build High Self-Esteem, Self-Esteem in the Classroom* and *Chicken Soup for the Soul—Live*. He is regularly seen on television shows such as *Good Morning America*, 20/20 and *NBC Nightly News*. Jack has co-authored numerous books, including the *Chicken Soup for the Soul* series, *Dare to Win* and *The Aladdin Factor* (all with Mark Victor Hansen), *100 Ways to Build Self-Concept in the Classroom* (with Harold C. Wells) and *Heart at Work* (with Jacqueline Miller).

Jack is a regularly featured speaker for professional associations, school districts, government agencies, churches, hospitals, sales organizations and corporations. His clients have included the American Dental Association, the American Management Association, AT&T, Campbell Soup, Clairol, Domino's Pizza, GE, ITT, Hartford Insurance, Johnson & Johnson, the Million Dollar Roundtable, NCR, New England Telephone, Re/Max, Scott Paper, TRW and Virgin Records. Jack is also on the faculty of Income Builders International, a school for entrepreneurs.

Jack conducts an annual eight-day Training of Trainers program in the areas of self-esteem and peak performance. The program attracts educators, counselors, parenting trainers, corporate trainers, professional speakers, ministers and others interested in developing their speaking and seminar-leading skills.

For further information about Jack's books, tapes and training programs, or to schedule him for a presentation, please contact:

The Canfield Training Group
P.O. Box 30880 • Santa Barbara, CA 93130
Phone: 805-563-2935 • Fax: 805-563-2945
To e-mail or visit our Website: *www.chickensoup.com*

Who Is Mark Victor Hansen?

Mark Victor Hansen is a professional speaker who, in the last twenty years, has made over four thousand presentations to more than two million people in thirty-two countries. His presentations cover sales excellence and strategies; personal empowerment and development regardless of stages of life; and how to triple your income and double your time off.

Mark has spent a lifetime dedicated to his mission of making a profound and positive difference in people's lives. Throughout his career, he has inspired hundreds of thousands of people to create a more powerful and purposeful future for themselves while stimulating the sale of billions of dollars worth of goods and services.

Mark is a prolific writer and has authored *Future Diary, How to Achieve Total Prosperity* and *The Miracle of Tithing*. He is coauthor of the *Chicken Soup for the Soul* series, *Dare to Win* and *The Aladdin Factor* (all with Jack Canfield), *The Master Motivator* (with Joe Batten) and *Out of the Blue* (with Barbara Nichols).

Mark has also produced a complete library of personal empowerment audio- and videocassette programs that have enabled his listeners to recognize and use their innate abilities in their business and personal lives. His message has made him a popular television and radio personality, with appearances on ABC, NBC, CBS, HBO, PBS and CNN. He has also appeared on the cover of numerous magazines, including *Success, Entrepreneur* and *Changes*.

Mark is a big man with a heart and spirit to match—an inspiration to people of all ages who seek to better themselves.

For further information about Mark write:

MVH & Associates
P.O. Box 7665
Newport Beach, CA 92658
Phone: 714-759-9304 or 800-433-2314
Fax: 714-722-6912
Website: *www.chickensoup.com*

Who Is Jeff Aubery?

Jeff Aubery is married to Patty Aubery, coauthor of *Chicken Soup for the Christian Soul* and *Chicken Soup for the Surviving Soul*. Jeff is no stranger to the *Chicken Soup* phenomenon. An entrepreneur in his own right, Jeff founded and owns Tornado Golf Co., an industry-leading OEM golf-bag manufacturing company. Committed to golf as a lifetime passion, Jeff is an active sponsor of junior golf programs and charity golf tournaments all over the world. Jeff coauthored *Chicken Soup for the Golfer's Soul*. An avid golfer, Jeff makes time for a round whenever possible, and has enjoyed playing with some of the greatest names in the sport at many of the world's most famous courses.

The couple and their two sons make their home in Santa Barbara, California. A dynamic and enthusiastic speaker and golfer, Jeff is available for personal appearances and can be reached at:

Tornado Golf, Inc.
4350 Transport Street, Suite 103
Ventura, CA 93003
phone: 800-GOLF-BAG
Website: *www.golfbags.com*

Who Are Mark and Chrissy Donnelly?

Mark and Chrissy Donnelly are a dynamic married couple working closely together as coauthors, marketers and speakers.

They are the coauthors of the #1 *New York Times* bestsellers *Chicken Soup for the Couple's Soul*, *Chicken Soup for the Golfer's Soul* and *Chicken Soup for the Sports Fan's Soul*. They are also at work on several other upcoming books, among them *Chicken Soup for the Baseball Fan's Soul* and *Chicken Soup for the Friend's Soul*, as well as *Chicken Soup for the Romantic Soul*.

As cofounders of the Donnelly Marketing Group, they develop and implement innovative marketing and promotional strategies that help elevate and expand the *Chicken Soup for the Soul* message to millions of people around the world.

Mark grew up in Portland, Oregon, and unbeknownst to him, attended the same high school as Chrissy. He went on to graduate from the University of Arizona, where he was president of his fraternity, Alpha Tau Omega. He served as vice president of marketing for his family's business, Contact Lumber, and after eleven years resigned from day-to-day responsibilities to focus on his current endeavors.

Chrissy, COO of the Donnelly Marketing Group, also grew up in Portland, Oregon, and graduated from Portland State University. As a CPA, she embarked on a six-year career with Price Waterhouse.

Mark and Chrissy enjoy many hobbies together including golf, hiking, skiing, traveling, hip-hop aerobics and spending time with friends. Mark and Chrissy live in Paradise Valley, Arizona, and can be reached at:

Donnelly Marketing Group, LLC
2425 E. Camelback Road, Suite 515
Phoenix, AZ 85016
phone: 602-508-8956 fax: 602-508-8912
e-mail: *soup4soul@home.com*

Contributors

Pamela Underhill Altendorf lives in Weyauwega, Wisconsin, with her husband. She studied writing at the University of Wisconsin-Stevens Point, and her stories have appeared in newspapers and magazines. In addition to writing, Pam enjoys traveling and gardening. She may be reached by e-mail at: *Salt7@wildmail.com.*

Mitch Anthony is a recognized keynote speaker with fifteen years' experience giving over twenty-two hundred speeches around the world. He is the host of the nationally syndicated radio feature, *The Daily Dose,* which is heard on 150 stations worldwide. Mitch is also an award-winning author of numerous columns and magazine articles, and three books including *StorySelling for Financial Advisors.* He has been quoted in *USA Today, Reader's Digest, L.A. Times,* etc., and has appeared on several national radio and TV programs.

Dave Barry has been at the *Miami Herald* since 1983. He won the Pulitzer Prize for commentary in 1988. Barry writes about various major issues relating to the international economy, the future of democracy, the social infrastructure and exploding toilets.

Stefan Bechtel is the author or coauthor of five books, including *The Good Luck Book* and *The Practical Encyclopedia of Sex and Health,* which has over 1 million copies in print. He was a founding editor of *Men's Health* magazine. His work has appeared in *Esquire, The Washington Post* and elsewhere.

Stacey Becker has just started her first year at Brooklyn Law School. Her father still calls ten times a day along with her mother, who is just as amazing as he is. Stacey joined a coed softball league in Brooklyn, and her father regularly attends these games.

Jim (Fieberg) Berlin was a marine, a journalist, and at age twenty-four became the youngest nationally syndicated newspaper columnist in America. He later joined the Phoenix PD, retired as a lieutenant after twenty years on the street, then served a year in Bosnia with the International Police Task Force. He and his wife, Linda, reside in Arizona.

Dee Berry currently pursues her passions for writing, fishing and gardening in Washington state. She would like to thank her dad for teaching her to sit still long enough to catch something. That lesson has served her well in life. She can be reached at *DeeBerryWrites@hotmail.com.*

Jeff Bohne is the proud father of Elizabeth, who works for a television station, and Andrew, a landscape architect. He and his wife, Nancy, live in Amherst, Massachusetts. He is responsible for customer service at Phoenix Investment Partners. Jeff enjoys going to UMass athletic events and working with several local charities.

Michele Campbell lives in a small Missouri town near the Mississippi River. She works in a local manufacturing company, is married with four children, and writes short stories, children's books and novels in her spare time.

Bob Carlisle is an accomplished singer/songwriter who has showcased his poignant, sensitive observations with such hits as "Butterfly Kisses" and "A Father's Love." Beyond his music, Carlisle has published several books, exploring another outlet to express his passionate love for his family. His bestselling titles include *Butterfly Kisses*, *A Father's Love* and *Sons: A Father's Legacy*.

Ron Chapman has been in broadcasting for more decades than he now wishes to count. He's been the cornerstone of adult contemporary station KVIL-FM for so long that anything preceding seems ancient history. He cofounded a radio station institution called the *Charlie & Harrigan Show*, a show which ran for several years on Dallas's KLIF Radio.

In the mid-sixties, he became famous as the host of an after-school dance show on Channel 8 television called "Sump'n Else." This was a "must see" from 1965 through 1968.

He is a two-time Marconi Award-winner who lives by the creed that "The good old days begin tomorrow morning!" He plans to be there to tell North Texas!

Beth Clark, president of Allegro Training and Consulting, inspires people to live every moment passionately; "replace prejudice with love;" and to move from losing their minds to mind-mastery. She is a highly sought-after humorist and transformational speaker who introduces people to their highest potential.

Brent L. Cobb does the dishes and laundry as a stay-at-home father of four, and freelance writer in McCook, Nebraska, where he spent eleven years as a reporter, columnist and editor at the *McCook Daily Gazette*. Fatherhood and family life were frequent subjects in his weekly column, *Off the Cobb*. He recently completed his first untitled nonfiction book about a Depression-era minor league baseball player and is working on his second book. He can be reached at 308-345-1821, or by e-mail at *bcobb@ns.nque.com*.

Richard Cohen has been a *Washington Post* columnist since 1976. His column generally appears on *The Post's* opinion page on Tuesdays and Thursdays. He also writes the "Critic At Large" column in the *Sunday Washington Post Magazine*.

Sean Coxe is a musician and writer who currently teaches English as a Second Language for the Intensive English Institute at Francis Marion University in Florence, South Carolina.

Barbara Crowley's nonfiction articles have appeared in *Once upon a Time* and *Yesterday's Magazette*. "Childhood memories continue to be the constant fuel for my writing." Barbara resides in Nokomis, Florida. Visit her Website at *www.bacrowley.com*.

F. Anthony D'Alessandro earned his B.S. in Education from St. John's University, and his M.S. with a reading specialization from Adelphi University. He was awarded a certificate for completing studies at the Giselle Institute of Child Development. He is certified to teach elementary school, English (grades 7–12), and reading (K–12). He's been employed as a junior varsity cheerleading coach and a high school newspaper advisor, and has served as a reading teacher for elementary grades through high school. He's also taught adult education and lectured at Villanova University. In 1984, he was elected "Educator of the Year" by the Council of School Administrators.

Published widely, his poems and articles have appeared in *Modern Bride, Newsday, The San Francisco Chronicle, Ascent Literary Journal, Endless Vacation, American School Board Journal, The Principal and Teaching K-8.* He recently retired after a twenty-five-year career at the Half Hollow Hills School District, which is among the top five in New York State. D'Alessandro is the father of three grown children. Mary-Kim is a certified teacher and mother who lives in Nashville, Tennessee. Her husband Steve coaches basketball at Vanderbilt University. Peter is an attorney and NBA sports agent. Jon is a teacher and basketball coach. A grandfather, Alle was F. Anthony's first grandchild. Gabriella and Marianna have recently joined her.

Dr. Frank M. Dattilio is on the faculty of psychiatry at both the University of Pennsylvania School of Medicine and Harvard Medical School. He is co-author and editor of ten professional books and more than one hundred articles that have been translated into over one dozen languages. He can be reached at *datt02cip@cs.com.*

Gunter David was a reporter on major city newspapers for twenty-five years before obtaining a master's degree in family therapy. Retired from Johnson & Johnson, where he counseled employees and their families, he has had fourteen stories published in literary journals and anthologies, including *Chicken Soup for the College Soul.*

Stephen Fay is a native of Berkley, California. He received his Bachelor of Arts from the California State University at Chico, and his Master's in Arts from Holy Names College in Oakland, California. He is managing editor of *The Ellsworth American,* a weekly newspaper in Ellsworth, Maine.

Dr. Stanley Frager is a professional, motivational speaker who gives wonderful talks to students, parents and corporations. He conducts tremendous workshops and seminars on stress management, leadership and maximizing personal effectiveness. He is the author of *The Champion Within You.* He can be reached at Frager Associates, 3906 Dupont Square South, Louisville, Kentucky 40207 or by calling 502-893-6654.

Becky Freeman is a bestselling author, national speaker, magazine columnist and hostess of "The Little Bookshop" radio show. Her many inspirational humor books include titles *Worms in My Tea, A View from the Porch Swing, Real Magnolias* and *Chocolate Chili Pepper Love.* Drop by for a visit at *www.beckyfreeman.com!*

Calvin Louis Fudge was born in Little Rock, grew up and was educated in the El Dorado, Arkansas, schools; SAU, Magnolia, Arkansas; Henderson State, Arkadelphia, Arkansas; and U. of Mississippi. He taught English and literature in Magnolia School and published his first novel in 1962. Other novels, a biography, short stories and a collection of short pieces followed. Now retired, he lives on Magnolia Highway in El Dorado.

John G. "Giovanni" Grippando received his B.S. with Honors in Business Administration/Management Specialization from Palm Beach Atlantic College. He speaks five languages and completed cultural studies in Italy. John may be reached via e-mail at *JohnGiovanni@juno.com.* His poem is dedicated with love to Candace and Marisa, the most wonderful wife and daughter one could ever have had.

Susan J. Gordon is the author of *Wedding Days: When and How Great Marriages Began,* about the courtships and marriages of famous couples in history. Currently she is writing a book about family histories. A native New Yorker, she also writes essays and articles for many national magazines and newspapers.

Lenny Grossman lives in Philadelphia with his wonderful wife and two exquisite children. He is an avid reader and movie fanatic. He has kept a record of every movie he has seen: present count 2,322. He aspires to be as good a husband and father as his dad.

Mike Harden began writing "In Essence" for *The Columbus Dispatch* in 1983. A Columbus native and 1973 graduate of the Ohio State University School of Journalism, he has worked as an associate editor for *Ohio Magazine,* contributing editor for *Columbus Monthly* and as a columnist for the *Columbus Citizen-Journal.*

His work has appeared in a variety of publications, including *The New York Times* and *Country Music Star News.* His columns have won first-place awards from United Press International, Associated Press Society of Ohio and the National Society of Newspaper Columnists. His nationally syndicated column goes out to 350 newspapers across the U.S.

He is the author of eight books, one of which, *Fight for Life,* was the subject of an ABC-TV movie.

Allison Harms and her family live in the Pacific Northwest. She finds that the climate inspires reading, writing, furniture arranging and the growing of pumpkins.

Walt Harrington is an award-winning journalist and former staff writer for the *Washington Post Magazine,* and is currently Professor of Journalism at the University of Illinois at Urbana-Champaign. He is the author of *At the Heart of It: Ordinary People, Extraordinary Lives* and *American Profiles: Somebodies and*

Nobodies Who Matter.

Loralee H. Hartje is a native from the Windy City, Chicago, who migrated to quaint Cary, Illinois. She has three wonderfully inspiring children who encourage her to write her own stories and poetry. She has directed several original plays for church, scouts and school groups; most recently, she has been reporting for the local college paper. Lori is in the process of self-publishing a spring story. Her personal theme is simply that God has blessed each of us with a special gift that we should develop in positive ways. She tries to inspire others to follow their dreams and use their individual talents.

Jim Hornbeck, fifty-four, is editor and publisher of *The Daily News,* a small daily newspaper that serves Wahpeton, North Dakota, and Breckenridge, Minnesota. Hornbeck and his wife of thirty-two years, Nancy, live in Fergus Falls, Minnesota. Their children, both grown and married, live in the Kansas City area. Hornbeck began his career in newspapering at age fourteen as a cartoonist for a weekly newspaper in Danville, California. Since those early days, Hornbeck has been a sportswriter, sports editor, feature writer, advertising salesperson, advertising manager and marketing director.

Adelaide Isaac is a senior at Catalina Foothills High School in Tucson, Arizona.

Gerald Winner, Jerry, as he was known, was an artist born in Durango, Colorado. He enjoyed painting, photography, picture framing, stained glass and woodworking. His work is proudly displayed in the homes of his family. Jerry and his devoted wife, Jo, moved from Denver, Colorado, to St. George, Utah in 1990 and fell in love with the desert. He passed away from cancer on May 21, 1999. Jo, whose hobby is writing, submits his story and biography in his memory.

Tina Karratti is a wife and mother of two boys. She lives in Southern California and works for a major pharmaceutical company. Her favorite thing to do is spend time with her kids and have big family gatherings. She's a great cook!

June Sandra Karshen is a freelance writer and educator. She enjoys inspiring young writers and is currently working on a picture book. "A War Story" was written as a birthday present for her father. This selection was submitted in his honor (John Sevenn Karshen 1914–1993). Sandy can be reached at *karshen@nconnect.net.*

Linda Kerby has been a Registered Nurse for thirty years, combining a teaching and writing career with clinical practice. She lives in a wonderful neighborhood in Leawood, Kansas, where the neighbors are especially nice.

Tom Krause is a motivational speaker, teacher, coach and the founder of Positive People Presentations. He speaks in the area of motivation to teenagers, teaching staffs, business organizations and any organization dealing with teen issues. He is the author of *Teaching Hearts—Teaching Greatness:*

Stories from a Coach to Touch Your Heart and Motivate Your Soul, a motivational book for teenagers and adults. He can be reached at *justmetrk@aol.com.*

Rabbi Paysach J. Krohn is a fifth-generation Mohel and has authored one book on Ritual Circumcisions and five books and on Jewish Short Stories, know as "The Maggid Series" all published by Mesorah/Artscroll, Brooklyn, New York. He lectures worldwide and has a tape series of sixty-five lectures. Can be reached at *krohnmohel@aol.com.*

Jay Leno began his career in nightclubs, where he worked three hundred nights a year before hitting it big in 1992 with his own late-night talk show. By that time, Leno had appeared on television, acted in a few films (1978's *American Hot Wax*), and hit pay-dirt with his late-night television appearances (he made a record number of visits to *Late Night with David Letterman*); for several years, he served as Carson's permanent guest host. He vied with Letterman to inherit Johnny Carson's *Tonight* show seat in 1992. His victory was well-publicized and his show beat Letterman's for the Emmy in 1995.

Joan Lewis wanted to share the story "Pass It On" because we must assist those in need. It's not always about what is convenient for ourselves. We should help others, for sometimes you alone will make a vital difference within that person's life. "Pass It On" is dedicated to Colette Coffey.

Richard H. Lomax and his wife Mary live in Nebraska and have three children. Joe and Kathleen are in college and Sean is in high school. Richard supervises the computer department at an electric power plant, plays guitar and sings in the choir at church. He also enjoys reading, traveling and learning—especially history and science.

Ivan Maisel is the *Sports Illustrated* senior writer and a college football analyst for CNN/*Sports Illustrated* and *CNNSI.com.* He also appears on CNN's *College Football Preview* with analysts Trev Alberts and *SI* senior writer Tim Layden. Most recently Maisel covered college football and basketball for *Newsday.* He was a national college writer for the *Dallas Morning News* from 1987 to 1994. He was a football correspondent for ESPN's *SportsCenter* and a columnist for *The Sporting News.* Maisel has received such honors as the Best Enterprise Story from Associated Press Sports Editors in 1997 and Football Writers Association of America in 1993. He was the president of the Football Writers Association of America in 1995. Maisel attended Stanford University, earning a bachelor's degree in American Studies. Maisel lives in Connecticut with his wife and three children.

Robert D. McLane II has lived in Grants Pass, Oregon, all but two years of his life. He has been married to his wife Vicki for sixteen years. They have two beautiful children, Robby and Leslie. Robert is a physical therapist assistant and massage therapist. He is also an avid fisherman and hunter.

W. W. Meade began writing at the age of fourteen. His first short story was published in *Collier's Magazine* when he was twenty-two. He wrote fiction for the *Saturday Evening Post, Gentlemen's Quarterly* and *Good Housekeeping* among others. He then turned to writing nonfiction for magazines such as *Cosmopolitan, Redbook* and the *Reader's Digest*. Later he took a position in the publishing world and became Managing Editor of the *Reader's Digest* Book Club and later of *Cosmopolitan*. His last position in publishing was as President and Editor in Chief of Avon Books, a position he held for ten years. Today, Walter lives in Florida and writes articles for many magazines and periodicals. He can be reached at 4561 NW 67th Terrace, Lauderhill, Florida 33319.

Jan Nations is executive producer of a worldwide radio program. Previous publishers include Multnomah, Starburt, *Chicken Soup for the Single's Soul* and *Teachers in Focus* magazine. She has three grown children (twin boys and one daughter) and five young grandchildren.

Hugh O'Neill has been writing and performing commentary on fatherhood for several years, including work for National Public Radio's *Morning Edition*. He is the author of *Daddy Cool* and *Here's Looking at You, Kids*. He has also written for several magazines as well as for television's *The Cosby Show, Thirtysomething* and *Sisters*. He lives in Princeton, New Jersey.

George Parler is a resident of Many, Louisiana. He is married and the father of three daughters. He is a minister of the gospel, a Christian songwriter and a member of a contemporary Christian music group called the Answered Prayer Band.

Bob Perks is a professional speaker, vocalist and author of *The Flight of a Lifetime!* He is a member of the National Speakers Association and National Writers Association. Visit *www.BobPerks.com* for his free weekly messages "I Believe in You!" or contact him at *Bob@BobPerks.com*.

Linda Rivers has been a motivational public speaker for the past twenty years on issues relating to children. She is a published author, and is currently finishing the first of six books in the Wendy Rivers series, with *A Spirit Never Broken* due out in late 2001 and *Circle "R" Ranch Kids* in 2002.

Victoria Robinson lives in a small Texas town with her husband, Asa. She is a homemaker and has written poetry and short stories all of her life to get the events of her life on paper. She has two children and four grandchildren. Now that her children are grown, she has settled down to do what she loves: writing! Having her work published is a dream come true! You may contact Victoria at 235 Port Road, Angleton, TX 77515, by e-mail at *victoria@computron.net*, or by phone at 409-848-3530.

Dr. Gary Rosberg, along with his wife, Barbara, are America's Family Coaches (*www.afclive.com*). Co-hosts of the national, daily radio program, *America's Family Coaches . . . LIVE!*, team speakers for their own conferences and seminars, and coauthors of the new release, *The 5 Love Needs of Men and Women*, the Rosbergs reach out to families across America with the message of strengthening and maintaining strong, healthy relationships.

James Ruka has had works published in numerous poetry anthologies. His poems can be found in the *International Poetry Hall of Fame* on the World Wide Web. A recent graduate of the *Institute of Children's Literature*, he is currently writing a novel. Recently married, he is working on starting a family and building his career as an author.

Scott Sanders was born in Tennessee, grew up in Ohio, studied in England, then settled down to write and teach in Indiana. He has published eighteen books, including *The Force of Spirit, Hunting for Hope, Secrets of the Universe, Writing from the Center* and *Staying Put.*

Chris Schroder graduated from the University of Virginia and worked for six Southeastern daily newspapers before starting his own in his hometown of Atlanta in 1994. Schroder Publishing employs eighteen great folks who produce positive community newspapers. He's a writer, a speaker and father to Sally and Thomas. E-mail: *schroder@mindspring.com*, Website: *www.chrisschroder.com.*

Bill Shore is the founder and executive director of Share Our Strength, the nation's leading anti-hunger, anti-poverty organization that mobilizes industries and individuals to contribute their talents to fight hunger and poverty. A native of Pittsburgh, Pennsylvania, Shore is forty-five years old. He earned his B.A. at the University of Pennsylvania and his law degree from George Washington University in Washington, D.C.

Terri Sjodin is an entrepreneur, author and speaker. In 1990 at the age of twenty-six, Terri went into business for herself, building Sjodin Communications, a public speaking, sales training and consulting firm from a spare room in her home. Since then, she has earned national recognition for her work and is considered one of the most successful young female professional speakers in the country. Terri has developed a distinguished client list ranging from actors, athletes, corporate and association presidents to large professional sales organizations. She is author of *SALESpeak: Everybody Sells Something* (Summit 1995). Her articles have been published in over fifty national and trade publications. Terri promotes mentor/protégé relationships to both young people and adults through foundations and corporate organizations.

Rosalie Silverman is seventy-one years of age and has been married for forty-nine years. Writing short stories and poetry has been her passion since high school, and she encourages her five grandchildren to experience the joys of creative writing.

Holly Smeltzer is a Christian wife and mother of three. Each day she seeks to walk with the Lord, to whom she is thankful for her many blessings. She looks after her family, a senior friend and her mom, who is her best friend. She has always loved writing stories and reading.

Andy Smith was raised in San Diego, California, and now resides in Nashville, Tennessee. He is a writer of books, plays, columns, articles, songs and commentaries. For more information, please visit his Website at *www.TKRwriteNOW.com.*

Ken Swarner writes the syndicated humor column *Family Man,* which appears weekly in dozens of newspapers in the U.S. and Canada. He lives in the Pacific Northwest with his wife and two children. He can be reached at 253-596-8553, or at *swarnerkm@aol.com.*

Charles Swindoll now serves as president of Dallas Theological Seminary and host of *Insight for Living,* a radio broadcast that is aired daily world-wide. He has authored more than twenty-five bestselling books, includ-ing *The Grace Awakening* and *Laugh Again.* Dr. Swindoll and his wife reside in Dallas, Texas.

Harold L. "Bud" Tenney was born in Reno, Pennsylvania. He is a Christian, married and the father of two sons. He worked as a machinist, earned an A.A. degree in business at Mesa Community College, and an A.A. degree in mor-tuary science at California College of Mortuary Science, Los Angeles, California. Bud owned and operated Carr-Tenney Mortuary from 1980 to 1995. He is now a retired funeral director and is currently working on a degree in naturopathic medicine.

Marty Trammell is married to the world's most inspirational woman and shares with her the privilege of raising three modern-day knights, Justin, Christopher and Joshua. He is a communications professor at Western Baptist College and enjoys working with the fine people at Valley Baptist in Perrydale and Sumpter Community School in Salem, Oregon.

Mark Treyz is a litigation attorney and pro-tem judge in Tacoma, Washington. He is a graduate of Northwest Nazarene College and the University of Puget Sound School of Law. Married to his wife Elva since 1984, he has three children, Taryn, John and Madison. Mark is currently working on his first novel.

Jim Warda, author of *Where Are We Going So Fast? Finding the Sacred in Everyday Moments* (with a foreword by Jack Canfield), also writes for the *Chicago Tribune.* In addition, he delivers workshops on leadership, parenting, mar-riage and finding meaning in the moments. Contact Jim at: 847-642-5108 or *wordwindj@aol.com.*

Erik Weihenmayer is a speaker, writer and adventurer. He has scaled four continental summits plus El Capitan, the famed 3,300-foot rock face in Yosemite, and Polar Circus, a 3,000-foot ice waterfall in the Canadian Rockies. Erik has never let his blindness interfere with his passion for an exciting life. "Someone once told me I needed to realize my limitations, but I've always thought it more fun to try to realize my potential." Erik will attempt Everest in Spring 2001 in an expedition sponsored by the National Federation of the

Blind. Read his autobiography *Touch the Top of the World* and visit his Website *www.highsightspresentations.com.*

Bob Welch is features editor of *The Register-Guard* newspaper in Eugene, Oregon, and author of *A Father for All Seasons* (Harvest House, $14.99). He has been published in *Reader's Digest, Sports Illustrated* and *Focus on the Family.* Bob may be reached at 409 Sunshine Acres Dr., Eugene, OR 97401, or via e-mail at *bwelch1@concentric.net.*

Steven M. Wheat, an Ozarks writer, father, husband and U.S. Marine veteran, has spent the last twenty-four years on the support staff of Southwest Missouri State University, where he now studies creative writing. "The Turtle" is dedicated to the memory of his late father, Leslie Gene Kennon. The author can be contacted at P.O. Box 1001, Branson West, MO 65737.

Hank Whittemore is the author of seven nonfiction books, including *The Super Cops* (made into an MGM movie), *Find the Magician,* and *CNN: The Inside Story.* He's also written many award-winning documentaries for both network and public television, as well as over one hundred cover stories for *Parade Magazine.* He lives in Upper Nyack, New York.

Floyd Wickman is a salesman, speaker, trainer and author and has been called "The Extraordinary Man" by *Success Magazine.* As a salesman, his production placed him in the top one tenth of 1 percent in his industry for seven consecutive years. He was recognized with the "Oscar" of speaking awards, the Council of Peers Award of Excellence by The National Speakers Association. He is founder of Floyd Wickman Courses, one of the nation's largest training companies and creator of the life-changing "Sweathogs" program. This program graduates a student every ten minutes of every work day. Floyd is author of three books, has over 100 published articles and he was given the "Platinum Award" for over one million audiocassettes sold. Floyd and his wife of twenty-nine years are natives of Michigan.

David Wilkins was born in July 1955 and lives in San Jose, California. He has been married twenty-four years to his wife Sue. They have a seventeen-year-old daughter, Sarah, and a twenty-year-old son, Jason. Dave received his B.A. in management from St. Mary's College.

Ernie Witham writes a humor column called "Ernie's World" for the *Montecito Journal* in Montecito, California. His humor has also been published in *The Los Angeles Times, The Santa Barbara News-Press,* various magazines and several anthologies including *Chicken Soup for the Golfer's Soul.*

Permissions

We would like to acknowledge the following publishers and individuals for permission to reprint the following material. (Note: The stories that were in the public domain, or that were written by Jack Canfield, Mark Victor Hansen, Jeff Aubery and Mark or Chrissy Donnelly, are not included in this listing.)

A Moment Can Last Forever. Reprinted by permission of *Christian Herald.* ©1969 *Christian Herald.*

Wake-Up Call. Reprinted by permission of Bob Welch. ©2000 Bob Welch.

Warning: An American Teenager Is Loose in Europe, Babies and Restaurants Are the Chernobyl of Parenting and *That's My Boy.* Reprinted by permission of Dave Barry. ©2000 Dave Barry.

How I Got into the Movies. Reprinted by permission of Gunter David. ©2000 Gunter David.

The Smell of Grass. Reprinted by permission of Adelaide Isaac. ©1999 Adelaide Isaac.

Rapid Rites of Passage. Reprinted by permission of Stefan Bechtel. ©2000 Stefan Bechtel.

Time for "The Talk." Excerpted from *Fathers, Sons and Brothers* by Bret Lott, ©1997. Reprinted by permission of Bret Lott.

Mollie's Moment. Reprinted by permission of Bill Shore. ©1999 Bill Shore.

The Tooth. Reprinted by permission of David R. Wilkins. ©1998 David R. Wilkins.

The Red Chevy. Excerpted from *Father's Love* by Bob Carlisle. ©1999 Reprinted by permission of Word Publishing.

My First Fish Story. Excerpt as submitted, from *Leading with My Chin* by Jay Leno. Copyright ©1996 by Big Dog Productions, Inc. Reprinted by permission of HarperCollins Publishers, Inc.

Finding My Way with Jesse. From *Hunting for Hope* by Scott Russell Sanders. ©1998 by Scott Russell Sanders. Reprinted by permission of Beacon Press, Boston.

He's Your Fish, Son. Excerpted from *Stories for a Man's Heart* by Alice Gray. Multomah Press, ©1999. Reprinted by permission of Marty Trammell.

Father at Sea, Daddy Loves His Car and *Down Suicide Hill.* Excerpted from *A Man Called Daddy.* ©1996 by Hugh O'Neill and published by Rutledge Hill Press, Nashville, Tennessee.

Becoming a Jock. Reprinted by permission of Andy Smith. ©2000 Andy Smith.

Softball People. Reprinted by permission of Stacey Becker. ©2000 Stacey Becker.

Hunters' Bond. Reprinted by permission of Frank M. Dattilio. ©2000 Frank M. Dattilio.

The Family Ski Trip. Reprinted by permission of Ernie Witham. ©1998 Ernie Witham.